Modal Translation

The Relevance of Worlds

Paul Hanmer
Nottingham University

Series in Philosophy

VERNON PRESS

In the Americas:	*In the rest of the world:*
Vernon Press	Vernon Press
1000 N West Street, Suite 1200,	C/Sancti Espiritu 17,
Wilmington, Delaware 19801	Malaga, 29006
United States	Spain

Series in Philosophy

Library of Congress Control Number: 2023936065

ISBN: 978-1-64889-891-4

Also available: 978-1-64889-625-5 [Hardback]; 978-1-64889-708-5 [PDF, E-Book]

Cover design by Vernon Press using image by Gerd Altmann from Pixabay.

For my parents, David and Mary

Table of Contents

Introduction   vii

1 **An ontological commitment to worlds**   1

2 **Ontological commitment and ordinary language**   19

3 **Beyond belief**   35

4 **Theoretical parsimony**   55

5 **Analyticity**   73

6 **Modal agnosticism**   91

7 **The problem of advanced modality**   107

8 **A set theoretic solution**   123

Bibliography   143

Index   153

Introduction

"That which does not kill us
makes us stronger"
Friedrich Nietzsche

I cannot claim that as a six-year-old, I was ever troubled by the uncertainty of Euclid's fifth axiom. My introduction to philosophy was somewhat less cerebral. In 1981, I first encountered the partial aphorism taken from Nietzsche's *GotzenDammerung*. It was part of the opening sequences of the film *Conan the Barbarian*, and it hit me like a thunderbolt. In the following years, I sought out literature on and by Nietzsche. I was often puzzled, however, by the contrast between the conventional wisdom surrounding his work and the work itself. For example, the accusation that he was a proto-Nazis set against his clear admiration for the Jewish community. In a similar vein, many philosophers have been left incredulous by David Lewis' genuine modal realism **(GMR)**. In particular, with respect to Lewis' claim that there is more than one world or universe. John Mackie, for instance, designates **GMR** a form of "Ptolemaic astronomy" (Bennett 2003, p. 167) in a remark intended "derisively" (ibid., p. 167) but which Lewis was happy to accept as an accurate description of his position. "Lewis neatly expounded this matter through a 'Ptolemaic astronomy' – an explanatory model that portrays a system of nested 'spheres' with α, the actual world, at the centre:" (ibid., p. 167: Lewis 1973, pp. 14 ff.).[1] In this regard, the choice is between two incompatible theses: either a single 'world' or universe or a plurality of 'worlds' or universes.

Lewis' counterpart theory translates one language, quantified modal logic **(QML),** into another, first-order predicate logic **(PL)** supplemented by counterpart-theoretic predicates. The standard translation of *de dicto* modal sentences is usually secured by quantification over possible worlds. Counterpart theory extends this practice to include *de re* modal sentences. The standard practice of quantification over possible worlds is expanded by counterpart theory to

---

[1] Saul Kripke is not persuaded by Lewis' spatiotemporal interpretation of a 'possible world'. He does make use of the notion, however. Kripke illustrates his model theoretic interpretation of the phrase by way of an "analogy": suppose we roll a pair of ordinary dice that results in two numbers displayed face upwards. Although there are thirty-six possible combinations only one is realised in respect of which numbers are face-up. The thirty-six possibilities each represent a mini 'possible world' whilst the two numbers that land face-up represent the 'actual world' (Kripke 1980, p. 16).

include de-re-representation. Counterpart theory is composed of four conceptual primitives, eight postulates, and a set of translation principles (Lewis 1968 [1983], pp. 27-31). The exceptional practice of translating ordinary modal discourse into **QML** is abandoned in favour of standard translation into predicate logic with identity, supplemented by counterpart theory. In addition to quantification over possible worlds, counterpart theory quantifies over an 'unrestricted domain' of *possibilia* or worlds and non-worldly individuals. When we discuss what could, might, or ought to happen, we talk about a possible world in which what could, might, or ought to happen, did happen. Counterpart theoretic translation exploits an equivalence between the modal operators of box '□' and diamond '◊' – respectively, necessity and possibility – and the universal and existential quantifiers. It is motivated by well-rehearsed problems associated with intensional languages, e.g., **QML**. Lewis' solution to these problems is located in the systematic translation of **QML** into the extensional language of **PL** (§ 2.2) (ibid., p. 29). The *general* scheme takes the form of a direct definition or biconditional whose *analysandum* [left side] is a sentence ɸ of **QML** and whose *analysans* [right side] is a sentence ɸ $^\beta$ of **PL**. The counterpart theoretic translation of modal discourse can be illustrated by the translation of two de re modal sentences (ibid., p. 31):

A.   Jeremy Corbyn could have been Prime Minister **(ordinary language)**

B.   ∃x ◊ ((Fx & ∀y (Fy → y=x)) & Gx) **(QML)**

C.   ∃x ¬ (Fx & Gx) & ∃y ∃z (Wy & Izy & Czx & Fz)) **(counterpart theoretic)** – it is not the case that the leader of the Labour Party in 2019 or G is the Prime Minister or F, but some counterpart z of x, at a world y, is F.

D.   Boris Johnson is essentially a human being **(ordinary language)**

E.   ∃x □ (Fx & Hx) **(QML)**

F.   ∃x ((Fx & Hx) & (∀y ∀z ((Wy & Izy & Czx) → Hz)) **(counterpart theoretic)** – x is F and H, and every counterpart z of x, in any world y, is H.

As a "descriptivist" (Lewis 1983e [1999], p. 60), Lewis substitutes a proper name for a definite description before incorporating that description into the apparatus of counterpart theory. In the case of A-C, the proper name "Jeremy Corbyn" at A is analysed in descriptivist fashion as, say, "the leader of the Labour Party in 2019". Interpreted in terms of **QML**, B states – in context – that it is possible that the (unique) Prime Minister or F might have been the leader of the Labour Party in 2019 or G. The **QML** translation of A at B has a clear affinity with Bertrand Russell's seminal analysis of so-called 'denoting phrases'. The counterpart theoretic translation of B at C states that the leader of the

Labour Party in 2019 or G is not the Prime Minister or F, although some counterpart of G, in some non-actual world, is F. In statements D-F, the use of the proper name "Boris Johnson" in D is substituted in descriptivist fashion as, say, "the Prime Minister". Interpreted in terms of **QML**, E states – in context – that necessarily the Prime Minister, or F, is a human being, H. The counterpart theoretic translation of E states that the Prime Minister, or F, is a human being or H, and every counterpart of F in every world is a human being.

In order to provide a successful analysis of modality (Lewis 1973, p. 88: 1986a, pp. 3-4), Lewis advocates two distinct theses. The first is a counterpart theoretic interpretation of modal discourse (Lewis 1968 [1983]: 1971 [1983]). The second is **GMR**, a metaphysical thesis relating to the nature of possible worlds and other *possibilia*. Although Lewis advocates for both, care must be taken to distinguish the two. One may be persuaded by the counterpart theoretic interpretation of modal discourse, for example, without thereby incurring a commitment to **GMR**.

Proponents of counterpart theoretic translation claim it as an analytic truth. The claim is justified on the basis of several alleged theoretical benefits secured by counterpart theory (Divers 1997, p. 142: cf. Divers & Melia 2002). These benefits are directly associated with the translation of modal sentences by way of the quantifier-predicate model of **PL.** Theoretical *desiderata* include the simplification and clarity of the logical, semantic, and expressive resources enjoyed by the scheme (§ 1.1). It is a central presumption of my argument that Lewis' modal translation scheme *is* an analytic truth (chapter five). However, I argue that this claim is justified on the grounds that differ from the aforementioned proponents of modal translation. I argue that the counterpart theoretic translation of modal sentences is analytic – in part – on the grounds that the concept *ways things could have been* 'contains' the concept *possible world*. I restrict the scope of my examination of analyticity, therefore, to the notion or concept of a 'possible world'; one of the primitive predicates of modal translation. As such, my account is only a partial defence of the analyticity of the overall translation scheme.

Analyticity aside, the main problem I address is one of the expressive adequacy of counterpart theoretic translation. How does Lewis' modal translation scheme translate extraordinary or advanced modal sentences? Advanced or extraordinary modal sentences represent a challenge to the expressive adequacy of counterpart theoretic translation. Specifically, modal sentences that ought to be true – by **GMR** lights – are translated as false by the scheme. For example, take the modal sentence 'necessarily, there is a plurality of worlds', which is true – by **GMR** lights – but is translated as false by the scheme. It is false because the counterpart theoretic interpretation of modal sentences does not sanction worlds that overlap (Lewis 1986a, p. 2); the analyses of this modal sentence state that at every world, there is a plurality of worlds, i.e., that every world has worlds as parts. The problem of advanced modality is generated by the interpretation of terms as world-restricted (chapter seven). The associated spectre of expressive *in*adequacy looms over the counterpart theoretic interpretation of advanced modal sentences in several domains of discourse, e.g., sentences about set theory, natural properties, and propositions. Absent the preservation of their 'intuitive' truth-value, these sentences confound the logical, semantic, and expressive advantages of standard modal translation. Hence, the theoretical benefits secured by the quantification-predicate model are vulnerable to refutation by way of advanced modal claims. Therefore, genuine realism must preserve the 'intuitive' truth-value of advanced modal sentences, preferably by way of the conceptual tools already available to **GMR**. The primary aim of this dissertation is to preserve the 'intuitive' truth-values of advanced modal sentences using the conceptual resources of **GMR**. In particular, I intend to preserve in translation the use of the primitive predicate 'Ixy' or 'x is in a possible world, y' (Lewis 1968 [1983], p. 27). My solution makes explicit the continued use of the predicate 'at a world, w'. Hence, the postulation of a plurality of worlds continues to be pivotal in solving the problem of advanced modal claims. I distinguish my thesis from John Divers' redundancy theory, recommended by him as the solution most conducive to the prior commitments of genuine realism.

Lewis notes that he drew inspiration for counterpart theory after reading a short story by L. Sprague de Camp (ibid., p. 28 fn. 3). Coincidentally, L. Sprague de Camp was the 'technical advisor' on the film *Conan the Barbarian*. This monograph is based on a Ph.D. thesis at the University of Nottingham.

Chapter One: An ontological commitment to a type of entity K, i.e., possible world, is central to Lewis' modal translation scheme. The scheme adopts and expands on our normal practice of translation into **PL** supplemented by a counterpart theoretic interpretation of de re modal sentences. In addition to the standard quantifiers of **PL**, four new primitive predicates are introduced to the translation scheme, e.g., 'x is in possible world, y'. I argue that the primitive predicate 'x is in possible world, y' is an essential component of the genuine realist interpretation of modal sentences. To this end, a solution to the problem of advanced modal sentences is provided by admitting sets as an ontological commitment of 'total theory'. In this chapter, I identify the quantifier criterion of ontological commitment endorsed by Lewis. Possible worlds and sets are amongst the types of entities to which genuine realism is ontologically committed. However, the quantifier criterion is usually understood to be reserved for the *explicit* ontological commitments of a theory. Although a conceptual primitive of **GMR**, sets are not a component of the original translation scheme (1968). Hence, I raise the possibility of *implicit* ontological commitments of a theory to a type of entity K. Surprisingly, I find that Quine endorses the notion of a theory's implicit ontological commitments. However, even if an implicit commitment to a type of entity is endorsed, Lewis' main concern in regard to sets remains unresolved. Lewis' concern about sets – as a distinct type of entity – is captured by the 'singularist dogma' (Lewis 1991). Does a collection of four apples imply the existence of a distinct type of entity, the *set* of four apples? I conclude the chapter with a somewhat cursory examination of the problem of plural predication as it applies to my proposed set theoretic solution to the problem of advanced modality.

Chapter Two: Quine aims to regiment the idioms of ordinary language into canonical notation, preferably **PL**. His preference is based on a desire for referential transparency. Unlike Quine, Lewis argues that ordinary language can reveal the *serious* ontological commitments of a theory: given the proper context, the quantifier and predicate expressions of ordinary language can be put to serious ontic use. I identify the criteria whereby the paraphrase of ordinary language may reveal the serious ontological commitments of a theory (Lewis & Lewis 1970 [1983]). I test the supposition that the serious ontological commitments of a theory may be expressed in ordinary language. The phrase of ordinary language I use to test this supposition is the 'ways things could have been' [but are not]. I conclude that the use of this ordinary language phrase may entail a serious ontological commitment to a distinct type of entity, possible world(s).

Chapter Three: Lewis accepts common sense judgements both as a *desideratum* of philosophical theory and a criterion of a genuine paraphrase. For Lewis, the desideratum of a common sense judgement is at loggerheads with the oft-cited criticism of incredulity. What is the source of the incredulity oft provoked by **GMR**? I utilise the notion of a 'Moorean fact' in order to identify the source of the incredulous stare. The putative 'Moorean fact' that I utilise pertains to our original dilemma – posed above – that there is only one world or universe. The incredulity provoked by the denial of this 'fact' has been used to justify the dismissal of **GMR** as a plausible philosophical theory. Plausibility, however, can take several forms. If incredulity is to be a decisive objection to a philosophical theory, then a 'strong' form of theoretical conservatism must be in play. Strong conservatism states that no philosophical theory could dislodge the certainty of a Moorean fact. On the other hand, if incredulity is understood as a defeasible objection, then a 'weak' form of theoretical conservatism is in play. Weak conservatism states that there may be a reason to reject the certainty of a Moorean 'fact'. They may include a preponderance of theoretical benefits other than an accord with common sense judgement. I conclude that Lewis advocates a weak theoretical conservatism that grants the incredulous stare a defeasible role in theory choice. The price attached to weak conservatism is a failure to satisfy the third criterion of a genuine paraphrase. Namely, the paraphrase of 'ways things could have been' by 'possible world' would *not* be endorsed by a community of ordinary language users.

Chapter Four: As a theoretical virtue, Lewis argues that methodological parsimony should be evaluated on the basis of the number of *different* types of entity postulated rather than the *number* of entities of each type. Hence, an ontological commitment to a single type of entity should be preferred over the postulation of multiple types of entity – the homogeneity thesis. He acknowledges the theoretical virtue of qualitative, not quantitative parsimony (Lewis 1973). I examine the allegation that Lewis' dismissal of quantitative parsimony is too quick. I contrast an ontological commitment to a single type of entity – possible worlds – with a case study from the history of science. I argue that quantitative parsimony ought to play a derivative role with respect to theory choice. In conclusion, that qualitative parsimony favours **GMR,** whilst quantitative parsimony does not count against it. I then turn to examine an antecedent question. How should the ontological commitments of rival theories be calculated? If we accept that the quantification-predicate model reflects the 'structure' of reality, it is incumbent upon us to provide a philosophical account of the notion of a property. Lewis' account of a 'natural property' fulfills this obligation by identifying the joints at which nature 'ought to be carved'.

Chapter Five: A traditional demand imposed on philosophical analysis is that of analytic truth. I defend the view that the counterpart theoretic translation scheme is an analytic truth. That is to say, a translation that is true by virtue of the meaning of its constituent terms. To this end, I distinguish the semantic and metaphysical aspects of the translation scheme, e.g., Stalnaker accepts that 'actual' is an indexical term – the semantic aspect – but rejects the plurality of concrete worlds – the metaphysical aspect (Stalnaker 1996 [2003], p. 40: 1976/1984 [2003]). This distinction leads to a defence of the 'insubstantiality thesis': that the truth of an analytic sentence *is* exclusively determined by virtue of the meaning of its terms. I restrict my defence of analyticity to just one element of the translation scheme; the predicate expression 'possible world' is a genuine paraphrase of 'ways things could have been'. One of the implications of the insubstantiality thesis is that no restrictions are imposed on the correct interpretation of the term 'possible world'. A 'possible world' could be interpreted as a discrete spatiotemporal continuity, a set of maximally consistent propositions, a collection of unactualised properties, etc. Williamson (2007) rejects the insubstantiality thesis. His critique partly rests on its perceived failure to distinguish semantic from meta-semantic facts. How does Lewis' paraphrasing by stipulation – a meta-semantic fact – establish an analytic truth – a semantic fact? I re-assert the insubstantiality thesis and attempt to rebut Williamson's objection. My rebuttal takes the form of a 'bridge' constructed to unite the meta-semantic and semantic aspects of language. I argue that the expressions 'ways things could have been' and 'possible world' should be understood as stipulated synonyms. As components of the argument from paraphrase these expressions help secure the analyticity demanded of traditional philosophical analysis.

Chapter Six: John Divers advocates a form of anti-realism with respect to the analysis of modal sentences (Divers 2004: 2006). The type of anti-realism he endorses is that of worldly agnosticism. The worldly agnostic can accrue the theoretical benefits associated with the quantificational-predicate model *and* withhold assent to an ontological commitment to a plurality of worlds (Divers 2004, p. 683). The threat posed by worldly agnosticism to my central thesis is clear. The first step in Divers' endeavour is to demolish the realists' conception of possible worlds; conceived either as discrete, spatiotemporal entities or as abstract sets of complete and consistent propositions. He argues that the causal isolation associated with each world type entails that modal truth is beyond our epistemological and semantic grasp. Modal truth is not beyond our epistemological and semantic grasp; ergo realism must be defective. In place of modal realism, Divers argues that we should adopt a moderate agnosticism with respect to possible but non-actual worlds (ibid., p. 669). However, he is willing to acknowledge a flaw in the agnostic's argument. The moderate agnostic is vulnerable to the charge of an assertibility-belief gap (ibid., p. 675). That is, the modal realist can justify a belief in a de re possibility that the worldly agnostic cannot. Furthermore, the modal realist can assert that the relevant modal belief is both rational *and* indispensable. In reply, Divers develops three strategies designed to show that the relevant modal belief is, in fact, rationally dispensable (ibid., p. 678). I argue that each strategy falls short of its intended target.

Chapter Seven: The problem of advanced modal claims is one that threatens the expressive adequacy of standard modal translation (1968). Some modal claims fail to retain their pre-theoretical truth-value post-translation. Divers' proposed solution to this problem is based on the redundancy in the translation of the predicate expression 'x is in possible world, y' and, by implication, 'y is a possible world' (Divers 1999: 2002, pp. 48-49). He argues that genuine realism ought to adopt a non-standard translation of advanced modal claims. The debate surrounding advanced modality is ongoing (see Jago 2016). Noonan, for example, challenges the coherence of the standard model based on a derivation of consequences that are unpalatable to genuine realism (Noonan 2014: cf. Divers 2014). These consequences are due to the traditional demands of genuine philosophical analysis, e.g., strict adequacy. One consequence of strict adequacy is that the standard analysis of modal sentences entails the necessary de re existence of, say, talking donkeys! (Noonan 2014, Section 2 p. 3) Noonan's challenge is not restricted to the analysis of advanced modal claims. It is partly based on work in this field by Josh Parsons (Parsons 2011). Parsons argues that genuine realism is committed to a number of theses which are collectively inconsistent (Parsons 2011, p. 3). Hence, Divers' attempt to distinguish advanced modal claims as candidates for non-standard translation is misplaced (ibid., p. 10). It is a distinction without a difference. To interpret *any* modal sentence – either standard or advanced – through genuine realism is in vain. In reply, I argue that the alleged inconsistency, identified by Parsons, can be resolved and that the problem posed by advanced modal claims remains genuine.

Chapter Eight: I offer a solution to the problem of advanced modal claims compatible with the primitive conceptual resources of **GMR**. I retain the predicate expressions of standard modal translation (1968), esp. 'x is in possible world, y' and 'y is a possible world'. Importantly, I retain the relevance of worlds as a component of the analysans of modal translation [right side, biconditional]. Hence, my proposed solution retains the primitive conceptual apparatus of **GMR** and should be preferred over Divers' redundancy theory. I examine a number of potential objections and replies to my solution. Does the membership relation of set theory rest on a 'magical relation' against which Lewis has elsewhere inveighed? Are sets dispensable – do they impose an unnecessary ontological commitment on a theory? Do the antinomies of set theory generate a reason to dispense with sets altogether? I conclude that although no 'knockdown argument' in favour of my proposed solution is available, it should nonetheless be preferred on the grounds of reflective equilibrium.

1

An ontological commitment to worlds

1.1 Introduction

Lewis (1968) presents a modal translation scheme intended to rescue formal discourse from an apparent incongruity. With the appropriate adjustments in place, the normal practice of conducting formal discourse in the language of extensional logic need not be abandoned. This theoretical desideratum is subsequently withdrawn (Lewis 1974 [1983]: 1983b [1983], p. 46). The exception to our normal practice is modality. In the case of modality, a non-extensional quantified modal logic (QML) is adopted: "Why this departure from our custom? Is it an historical accident, or was it forced on us somehow by the very nature of the topic of modality?" (Lewis 1968 [1983], p. 26). Lewis argues that we are not compelled to adopt QML as an unavoidable consequence of modal discourse. In the alternative, he invites us to 'translate' modal sentences of QML into sentences of predicate logic (PL) supplemented by counterpart theory with a suitable domain of quantification: "The domain of quantification is to contain every possible world and everything in every world." (ibid., p. 27). Lewis' innovation represents an extension of the strategy of translating modal discourse by way of quantification over possible worlds. Thus, normal practice is preserved, and the 'incongruity' dissolved.

The modal operators are substituted without loss. In their place is the syntax of first-order logic – truth-functional operators, quantifiers, variables, and identity – together with four primitive predicates. Each predicate is to be attributed its ordinary language meaning. The predicates are supplemented by eight postulates – P1 to P8 – that comprise counterpart theory (ibid., pp. 26-27).[1] The predicate 'Wx' designates the propositional function "x is a possible

---

[1] 'World' is an ambiguous term. In the Lewisian sense this predicate designates a universe; a discrete spatiotemporal unity. In addition to the primitive predicate 'Wx' introduces 'Ixy' for the propositional function *x is in possible world y*, 'Ax' for the propositional function *x is actual*, and 'Cxy' for the propositional function *x is a counterpart of y*. The primitives are to be understood, in part, based on the following eight postulates: P1 Nothing is in anything except a world; P2 Nothing is in two worlds; P3 Whatever is a counterpart is in a world; P4 Whatever has a counterpart is in a world; P5 Nothing is a counterpart of anything else in its world; P6 Anything in a world is a counterpart of itself; P7 Some world contains all and only actual things; P8 Something is actual (Lewis 1968 [1983], p. 27)

world" (ibid., p. 27). As an element of the modal translation scheme, this predicate expression incurs an ontological commitment to a type of entity; possible world(s). Lewis willingly accepts *entia non grata* in the form of unactualised possibilia – including worlds other than the actual world – which form the domain of quantification. For example, Hubert Humphrey is a world-bound individual who lost the 1968 U.S. Presidential Election. It appears reasonable to suppose that Humphrey might have won. This does not entail that Humphrey – himself – is 'in' another world where he was victorious. Rather, Humphrey has a counterpart 'in' a non-actual world who won *that* world's counterpart of the 1968 U.S. Presidential Election (ibid., pp. 27-28: cf. Quine 1960 [2013], Section 50).

GMR offers one type of quantificational analysis of modality. As a philosophical technique, the quantification-predicate model originated partly in Russell's "On Denoting". The foundation of Russell's analysis is the *variable* (Russell 1905 [2001], p. 212). In Russellian terms, 'Wx' is a proposition, or more accurately a propositional function, in which the variable 'x' is both a constituent and wholly undetermined (ibid., p. 213 fn. 2). Lewis' accrues several theoretical advantages as a consequence of interpreting modal discourse in quantificational terms (Divers 1997, pp. 141-42). Firstly, the substitution of modal expressions by their 'worldly' equivalents facilitates modal logic by proxy in the form of first-order logic – the **logical** resources required to tackle modality are simplified, e.g., as logical primitives, modal operators require special axioms and rules of inference. Secondly, when added to the reservoir of logical primitives, modal operators needlessly enmeshed us in intensional **semantics**. A viable alternative to modal operator language is available in the form of *direct* semantics – with a suitably rich model – of a 'worldly' extensional language. Thirdly, there are a number of related – but usually conflated – **expressive** advantages: (i) if restricted to the use of sentential modal operators and 'actualist' quantifiers, then our ability to articulate modal concepts may be infringed. This infringement is ameliorated by the inclusion of quantification over a domain of worlds and their inhabitants. (ii) We acquire the ability to represent modal content in a straightforward and understandable way by equivalently 'worldly' expressions – iterated modality is replaced by multiple quantificational generalities and accessibility relations. (iii) Using a 'worldly' language allows a significant gain in expressive power over standard modal operator languages – the latter negatively entails an expansion to the number of primitive logical resources and restricts the range of expression. In order to secure these theoretical benefits, I defend the World Relevance Principle **(WRP)**:

> **WRP**: The analysis of de dicto modal sentences ought to be based on the assumption that modal operators *both* 'unite' worlds under quantification

and restrict the domains of the quantifiers that fall within their scope (Lewis 1968 [1983] p. 40: 1986a, pp. 5-13).

This chapter will examine Quine's quantifier criterion **(QC)** of ontological commitment. As a source of the quantification-predicate model of philosophical analysis, I present a standard interpretation of Russell's "On Denoting" (Section 1.2). Inspired by Russell, Quine applies the quantification-predicate model to the notion of ontological commitment (Quine 1948 [1980], p. 5: 1960 [2013], Section 37-38) (Section 1.3). I propose a solution to the problem of advanced modality that requires an ontological commitment of theory to sets. To this end, I investigate the plausibility of identifying the *implicit* ontological commitments of a theory (Section 1.4). Lewis expresses reservations regarding an 'implicit' ontological commitment to *sets*. His reservations are articulated by the 'singularist dogma' as a consequence of singular quantification. I address Lewis' concern and offer a tentative solution by way of reply (Section 1.5). I conclude the chapter with a brief investigation regarding the likelihood of identifying the serious ontological commitments of a theory expressed in the idioms of ordinary language (Section 1.6). For the sake of brevity, I will disregard several important questions. What are the subtle distinctions of interpretation regarding the **QC** itself? How appropriate is the **QC** to the enterprise of identifying a theory's ontological commitments?

1.2 Russell: quantification, predication, and existence

The notion of a functional expression is adapted from the concept of a mathematical function. The value of a variable 'y' in the functional expression 'y = 3x' is said to be a function of 'x'. Different numerals can be 'inserted' in place of 'x' to generate different values for 'y'. The variable 'x' may 'stand in' for different numbers or the *arguments* of the function. Hence, the argument two yields the value six (6 = 3 x 2), the argument three yields the value nine (9 = 3 x 3), and so on. A function can also be represented as a set of ordered pairs; where the first number represents the *argument* of the function and the second represents the *value* generated by the function for that argument, e.g., the functional expression 'y = 3x' can be represented by the set of ordered pairs: {<1,3>, <2,6>, <3,9>...}. The set of ordered pairs is said to be the *extension* of the function. In addition, mathematical functions may have more than one argument place, e.g., two argument places 'z = 3x : 6y' that can be represented by a set of ordered triples, where the first number represents the argument 'x', the second number represents the argument 'y' and the third number, the value 'z', generated by the function for those arguments. The word 'inserted' is used to indicate the 'gap' in the functional expression to be 'filled' by numerals used as arguments, e.g., 'y = 3( )'. The brackets – or variable – of a functional expression 'hold' a place for an argument of the appropriate kind; an argument in the form of an expression that will generate a value. For Russell, this feature indicates that functional expressions are "wholly undetermined" (Russell 1905 [2001], p. 213).

Thus far, functions have taken numbers as arguments and generated numbers as values. Frege's innovation was to apply the functional model of mathematics to the semantics of predicates, connectives, and quantifiers (Frege 1879 [1980]: 1891 [1980]: 1892b [1980])).[2] In a series of publications, Russell employs Frege's ideas to resolve a number of philosophical puzzles. For example, he utilises the quantification-predicate model in order to argue that "a phrase may be denoting, and yet not denote anything; e.g., 'the present King of France'."[3] (Russell 1905 [2001], p. 212: 1919 [1996]) In "On Denoting," Russell applies his theory of descriptions to four puzzles, one of which is the problem of apparent reference to non-existents (Russell 1905 [2001], p. 215).[4] Russell offers a *contextual definition* of the word 'the' as that word is standardly used as part of a singular definite description, i.e., 'the [unique] so-and-so'.

Consider sentence (A):

A.   The present King of France is bald

A number of sentences appear to be individually true of (A) and yet collectively inconsistent (Lycan 2000, pp. 13-14):

A1: (A) is meaningful, it is not nonsense

A2: (A) has the grammatical form of a subject-predicate sentence

A3: A meaningful subject-predicate sentence can *only* be meaningful in virtue of picking out a thing and ascribing a property to that thing

A4: (A)'s subject term does not pick out a thing that exists, i.e., the present King of France

A5: If A1, A2, and A3 are true and given the truth of A4, then either (A) is not meaningful – is nonsense – or (A) picks out a thing that does *not* exist, *but*

A6: There is no such thing as a 'non-existent thing'

---

[2] Frege distinguished 'function' from 'functional expression'. A 'functional expression' is a linguistic item whilst 'functions' are extra-linguistic abstract entities (Frege 1891 [1980]: Miller 1998, p. 306 fn. 12)

[3] I do not wish to imply that Russell and Frege's philosophy of language align (Uzquiano 2017, Section 4.1): Russell, for example, rejected Fregean 'sense' on the grounds that it is incoherent (Russell 1905 [2001], p. 214) and superfluous (Russell 1905 [2001], pp. 214-15)

[4] They are (a) the apparent reference to non-existents, (b) the problem of negative existentials, (c) Frege's puzzle about identity and (d) the problem of substitutivity. Russell argues that each can be resolved without the need to posit a Fregean 'sense'.

The consistency problem appears to be rooted in the subject or 'denoting phrase' of (A), i.e., 'the present King of France'. The meaningful use of a 'denoting phrase' seems to require a denotation, and yet (A) appears to be meaningful despite the absence of a denotation, i.e., the present King of France (Russell 1905 [2001], p. 214). In order to tackle this incongruity, Russell employs the philosophical technique of paraphrase; the subject or 'denoting phrase' of (A) is analysed into two distinct components. First, the word 'the' of the singular definite description is interpreted as an abbreviation of an existentially quantified sentence (ibid., p. 218). Second, the predicate 'present King of France' of the singular definite description is interpreted as introducing the concept of a predicate expression. The *meaning* of the predicate expression plays a critical role in identifying the denotation of the 'denoting phrase'. That is, in order to identify the denotation of the 'denoting phrase' we must first understand the meaning of the predicate 'present King of France'. Only when the meaning of the predicate expression is understood are we able to select the denotation to which the predicate expression is truly ascribed: "Thus we must either provide a denotation [referent] in cases in which it is at first sight absent, or we must abandon the view that the denotation is what is concerned in propositions which contain denoting phrases." (ibid., p. 215). In order to unlock the inconsistency, Russell accepts the second horn of the dilemma by denying A3. In this case, the denoting phrase is interpreted as a propositional function. The true *logical* structure of (A), which 'contains' a grammatical singular definite description as a denoting phrase, is thereby revealed. Russell distinguishes the grammatical and logical structure of the sentence (A). The singular definite description is a grammatical but not a *logical* constituent of a sentence (A) (ibid., pp. 213-14). The correct *logical* analysis of the denoting phrase 'the present King of France' is not as a grammatical subject of a subject-predicate sentence. Instead, 'the present King of France' is analysed – by way of paraphrase – as the propositional function *x is the present King of France*. The logical structure of the *whole* sentence is analysed as a conjunction of three propositions involving quantification:

i. There is at least one present King of France

ii. There is no more than one present King of France

iii. Anything that is a present King of France is bald

By rule, in order for the whole sentence to be true, each conjunct must be true. Clearly, (i) is false, so the conjunction *must* be false. Russell paraphrases the singular definite description in order to dissolve the apparent demand for a denotation implied by the phrase 'the present King of France is bald'.

iv. $\exists x \, (Fx \, \& \, (\forall y \, (Fy \rightarrow y = x) \, \& \, Gx))$

In place of a subject-predicate sentence, 'Fa', that *must* denote to be meaningful, is an existentially quantified proposition whose meaning is unaffected by the lack of a denotation: "that [incomplete] denoting phrases never have any meaning in themselves, but that every proposition in whose verbal expression they occur has meaning." (ibid., p. 213: Russell 1919 [1996], pp. 173 ff.). Therefore, 'the present King of France' is not a singular term, but a grammatical abbreviation that is part of a proposition with a quantification-predicate logical structure, illustrated by (i-iii).

This is the standard interpretation of Russell's theory of descriptions, of which the quantification-predicate model is a part. It is the interpretation to which W. V. O. Quine subscribes (Quine 1960 [2013], Section 37-38). It is also an interpretation disputed in the literature (cf. Hylton 1990: Griffin 1996: Noonan 1996).[5] Did Russell account for the meaningful use of a denoting phrase – absent a denotation – *before* 1905? The disputed exegesis of Russell's motivation need not detain us, however. At this juncture, I am only interested in Russell's *first* employment of **PL** or modern quantification theory. In 1905 Russell departed from the "fruitless complexes of [his] early theory of quantification." (Griffin 1996, p. 46) For my purposes, the novelty of "On Denoting" lies in using the quantification-predication model of **PL**. The source identified, I now examine how the model applies to Quine's quantifier criterion of ontological commitment.

1.3 The quantifier criterion

Identifying the ontological commitments of a theory to a type of entity K is a task of meta-ontology.[6] In order to resolve the philosophical puzzles of ontology, prior systematic identification of a theory's ontological commitments is required: "We look to bound variables in connection with ontology not in order to know what there is, but in order to know what a given remark or doctrine, ours or someone else's, *says* there is; and this much is quite properly

---

[5] In *Principles of Mathematics* (1903) Russell invokes the notion of a *denoting concept* to account – in part – for meaningful instances of denoting failure such as 'the present King of France'. The traditional interpretation of *Principles* is that although *terms* may not exist they 'persist' in some form, perhaps in Russell's realm of *being*. Arguably, this interpretation is superfluous as Russell states that not all *denoting concepts* denote: "[A] concept may denote although it does not denote anything [...] These propositions appear to be true, and it would seem that they are not concerned with the denoting concepts, but with what these concepts denote; yet that is impossible, for the concepts in question do not denote anything ..." (Russell 1903 [2010], Section 73 p. 74).

[6] See Peter van Inwagen (1998 [2001], esp. p. 13).

a problem involving language." (Quine 1948 [1980], pp. 15-16). Identifying a criterion of ontological commitment – however that notion is unpacked – is essential to the philosophical rigour of ontological discourse (Uzquiano 2017, Section 4.2). How is the criterion of ontological commitment to be unpacked?

Firstly, the criterion ought to be referential: "a theory is committed to those and only those entities to which the bound variables of the theory must be capable of *referring* in order that the affirmations made in theory be true." (Quine 1948 [1980], pp. 13-14 my emphasis) The criterion ought to be descriptive rather than prescriptive. That is, although Quine's general method of ontology *is* prescriptive, his meta-ontology is not. Ontology is the endeavour to regiment competing theories in the language of canonical notation, preferably **PL** (Quine 1998c [1998]). We determine and then endorse the 'best' theory on epistemic grounds, e.g., simplicity or fruitfulness. The ontological commitments of a theory are not a theoretical virtue, but a means to assess potential virtues, e.g., parsimony. We should endorse the 'best' theory available; understood as the theory that is ontologically committed to those types of entity K that are the values of the bound variables that constitute its referential truth.

The distinction is an important one. To conflate meta- and genuine ontology is to leave the identification of a theory's ontological commitments open to the charge of circularity. The ontological commitments that we ought to endorse depend on which theory is 'best', but the 'best' theory is determined – in part – by the theoretical desideratum of simplicity. Essentially, the 'best' theory is the one with the fewest – *ceteris paribus* – ontological commitments *but* the ontological commitments that we should endorse are those of the 'best' theory! This potential problem is rebutted by the distinction: the criterion of ontological commitment is a criterion of meta-ontology. It facilitates theory choice but does not determine which theory ought to be chosen. The theory that we ought to endorse is dependent – in part – on parsimony, but we cannot know which theory to select until we know the types of entity to which it *is*, in fact, committed. If a quantified-predicate expression, say, '∃x Photon(x)' is a component of a particular theory, then the bound variable 'x' must range over photons within the domain of discourse in order for the theory to be true. In this case, the theory is ontologically committed to a type of entity, the photon. With these points duly noted, I offer a definition of the quantifier criterion of ontological commitment:

The Quantifier Criterion (QC):

A sentence of **PL** carries an ontological commitment to a type of entity K just in case Ks must be counted amongst the values of the variables in order for the sentence to be true (Quine 1948 [1980], pp. 12-13).[7]

Quine's **QC** of ontological commitment represents a relation between a theory and a postulated type of entity K. A theory ought to be expressed in canonical notation and interpreted by way of Tarskian semantics. Each predicate of a theory, for instance, should be assigned a class or set as an interpretation. A monadic predicate is interpreted by way of set membership, the set whose members consist of objects in the domain of discourse that occupy the argument place of an incomplete symbol that, combined with a predicate expression, yield a true sentence, e.g., 'Fa' is true if, and only if, the object referred to by 'a' belongs to the extension of 'F'. A polyadic predicate, on the other hand, should be interpreted by way of the set membership of ordered n-tuples; 'Fab' is true if, and only if, the objects designated by 'a' and 'b' in the domain of discourse form an ordered pair as members of a set {(a,b)}. Quantifiers are assigned an objectual rather than substitutional interpretation. An objectual interpretation of an existential quantified expression states that '∃x φx' is true if, and only if, the open formula 'φx' is satisfied by some object in the domain of discourse (Hylton 2010, p. 256). Alternative domains of discourse facilitate our ontological deliberations: the referential truth of interpreted theories can be evaluated based on how their respective bound variables range over the objects of *different* domains of discourse. A philosopher may avoid an unwanted ontological commitment to a dubious kind of entity K by way of a challenge to the proposed regimented paraphrase of canonical notation in order to demonstrate that no such commitment to Ks is entailed (Quine 1948 [1980], p. 13: 1953a [1980], pp. 103-07).

The **QC** is now accepted as philosophical orthodoxy with respect to identifying the ontological commitments of a theory (Bricker 2016, Section 1.1). Quine's referential apparatus is an expansion of the logical analysis of a 'denoting phrase' constructed by Russell.[8] In addition to singular definite

---

[7] This proposed definition of the QC includes a modal 'must' that is incompatible with an extensional or 'referential' account of ontological commitment (Quine 1953b [1980], pp. 139-59). Although repugnant to Quine, GMR offers a solution: an unrestricted domain of possibilia whose inhabitants, when assigned as the value of a bound variable, yield true theoretical sentences – in this respect, '∃x Unicorn(x)' is no less extensional than '∃x Horse(x)' (see Bricker 2016, Section 1.3).

[8] Although Quine's philosophical *technique* is Russellian, his motivation and application of the technique is not. Quine (and Lewis), for example, aim to eliminate all singular

descriptions, Quine includes pronouns as grist to the referential mill. "On Denoting" includes a philosophical analysis of proper names based on the supposition that each proper name abbreviates a singular definite description. Once the semantic content [9] of a name is identified as a singular definite description, we need only apply Russell's analysis and dissolve the apparent need for a denotation as an essential component of meaning. How should Russell's analysis proceed if no equivalent singular definite description presents itself? Quine's solution is to introduce or 'invent' primitive predicates, each uniquely true of the object or person named. The 'invented' predicate may refer to an attribute of the object or person named, e.g., the proper name 'Pegasus' can be analysed by way of the predicate 'is-Pegasus' or 'pegasizes' (Quine 1948 [1980], p. 8).

Hence, the analysis of:

v.   Pegasus has wings

proceeds by way of an existentially quantified sentence (as at i-iii above):

vi.   There is one and only one thing that pegasizes and it has wings

Quine's serious ontic discourse would presumably entail a denial of the existence of a unique winged horse.[10] The first conjunct is false, and so the truth value of the sentence (vi.) is false (cf. Cartwright 1960 [1987]: Kripke 2013). Theoretical discourse is regimented, and "we move closer to a stage at which all of our ontological commitments are carried by constructions which invariably express the ontological assumptions of those who employ them in serious assertions." (Hookway 1988, p. 23) For Quine, the analysans [right side,

---

terms whilst Russell accepts a category of ineliminable singular terms or logically proper names (Quine 1960 [2013], Section 38: Hylton 2010, pp. 383-84 fn. 2).

[9] Definition: The semantic value of an expression is that feature of it that determines whether sentences in which it occurs are true or false (Miller 1998, p. 10).

[10] Quine's reluctance to include de re modality amongst the topics of serious discourse parallels his concern about true negative existential statements. "I suspect that the main motive for this expansion [possible entities] is simply the old notion that Pegasus, for example, must be because otherwise it would be nonsense to say even that he is not." (Quine 1948 [1980], p. 4) It is at least questionable, however, whether Quine's injunction to reserve the paraphrase of ordinary language for 'serious' commitments applies in this case (Quine 1953a [1980], p. 103). Kripke's ontological commitment to fictional characters interpreted by way of the quantifier-predicate model is a serious one. The quantifier in question is expressed in the idiom of ordinary language, not PL (Kripke 2013, pp. 69-70).

biconditional] ought to be expressed in canonical notation, preferably in the language of **PL**.[11]

How should sentences of ordinary language be paraphrased into sentences of **PL**? Paraphrase should proceed on the grounds of pragmatism, not synonymy.

> We do not claim synonymy. We do not claim to make clear and explicit what the users of the unclear expressions had unconsciously in mind all along […] We fix on the particular functions of the unclear expressions that make it worth troubling about, and then devise a substitute, clear and couched in terms to our liking, that fills those functions. Beyond those conditions of partial agreement, dictated by our interests and purposes, any traits of the explicans come under the head of 'don't cares' (§ 38). (Quine 1960 [2013], Section 53 p. 238)

Quine favours a Tarskian interpretation of the quantifiers. A Tarskian interpretation, however, may serve to endanger the quantifiers of PL. That is, they may fail to meet a sufficiency condition for the accurate determination of the types of entity to which the theory is committed. The **QC** may commit a theory to a type of entity that it ought *not* to be committed and so over-generate a theory's ontological commitments. If the ontological commitments of a theory are skewed in this way, then philosophical controversy is generated rather than resolved. If quantifiers are open to several interpretations – Tarskian and non-Tarskian – then how can the **QC** accurately determine a theory's ontological commitments? Do different interpretations of the quantifier result in different ontological commitments? Take by way of example, the problem of the empty domain of discourse. Standard Tarskian semantics excludes the empty domain; valid well-formed formulae are those that yield true formulae under all interpretations of their non-logical symbols and overall *non-empty* domains. As a result, universal quantified sentences carry existential implications: that is, '∃x φx' may be logically deduced from '∀x φx'. Recall **PL** neither recognises the empty domain nor mandates which *type* of entity ought to be included in the domain of discourse.[12] In general, any predicate letter could be assigned to 'φx', generating an ontological commitment to that type of entity.

---

[11] The use of the word 'preferably' is required at this juncture. A theory expressed in ordinary language may be assessed as ontologically committed to a type of entity K but the best method of ascertaining a theory's ontological commitments is by regimentation into the canonical notation of PL: "I hail the relative pronoun as the crucial referential particle in ordinary language, and the variable as its mathematical version." (Quine 1998c [1998], p. 533)

[12] Wilfrid Hodges, for example, notes "First-order logic is very robust about questions like these: it doesn't give a damn. If you think that there are fictional people and that they

This existential implication can be avoided by modifying the standard Tarskian interpretation of the universal quantifier. There are interpretations in which the universal quantifier '∀x φx' is true without incurring a 'dubious' ontological commitment to a type of entity associated with the predicate-place 'φx' because there is nothing 'in' the specified domain. For example, a domain of discourse may relate to fictional characters, mythological creatures, or non-actual possibilia. Adjusted in this way, the revised interpretation of the quantifiers reserves all genuine cases of ontological commitment to the scope of the existential quantifier alone. *Inclusive logic*, as the nomenclature suggests, includes the empty domain and so avoids the difficulty of the aforementioned existential entailment (cf. Quine 1953a [1980]). This non-standard interpretation of quantification over the empty-domain of discourse assigns the truth-conditions 'true' to all universal and 'false' to all existential quantifiers. The standard Tarskian interpretation of **PL** fails to recognise the empty-domain of discourse and thus risks over-generating the ontological commitments of a theory to a type of entity K, e.g., fictional characters. Theoretical virtues such as 'rigour' and 'clarity', which motivated the regimented paraphrase of sentences into canonical notation, appear to depend on one's interpretation of the quantifiers and prior existential presuppositions!

The **QC** also distinguishes between a theory's ontological and ideological commitments (Quine 1951b: 1983). The ontological commitments of a theory number those types of entity that a theory *says* exists in order for the theory to be true. The object must inhabit the relevant domain of discourse in order to be the value of a bound variable and ensure the theory's referential truth. The ideological commitments of a theory, on the other hand, are generally those concepts – logical or not – that are expressible by the theory. These two forms of commitment are not equivalent. A theory may be committed to a type of entity K, even though the *concept* of being a K exceeds the conceptual resources of the theory. That is, the relevant concept cannot be expressed in the vocabulary of the theory. Alternatively, a theory may draw upon the conceptual resources of, say, relational terms in order to provide structure to the entities postulated without thereby adding a distinct type of entity to the list of its ontological commitments. I will adopt Quine's approach to this aspect of ontological commitment. I identify the ontological commitments of a theory solely on the basis of the types of entity K postulated and disregard the ideological or predicative aspect of ontological commitment (cf. Sider 2011).

---

have or fail to have this property or that, and can meaningfully be said to be the same individuals or not the same individuals as one another, then fine, put them in your universes." (Hodges 2001, p. 22)

Not all accounts of ontological commitment are based on the **QC,** and not all interpretations of the **QC** are equivalent (see Bricker 2016). Lewis' commitment to a plenitude of possible worlds is explicit and should be understood literally. I defend a thesis in regard to advanced modality that requires a further ontological commitment to sets (chapter eight). Although Lewis does accept set theory, sets need *not* number amongst a theory's *explicit* ontological commitments. Hence, in order to establish an implicit commitment to a type of entity K – in this case, sets – I must establish that the **QC** may admit the *latent* ontological commitments of a theory. It is to this task that I now turn.

1.4 Implicit ontological commitment

Thus far, I have limited the discussion to the explicit ontological commitments of a theory based on the **QC**. A denoting phrase such as '∃(x) Brother(x)' is committed to brothers and nothing else. It is true if, and only if, there is a person or object 'in' the domain of discourse that satisfies the value of the bound variable 'x'. One problem with this restriction to explicit ontological commitment is that we may under-generate the types of entity to which a theory *ought* to be committed. If we fail to meet a necessary condition of an ontological commitment then we under-generate the number of entities to which a theory ought to be committed. For example, we may under-generate the ontological commitments of a theory if we fail to identify all the extrinsic properties of an object (Lewis 1983c [1999], p. 111). The truth of '∃(x) Brother(x)', for instance, appears to imply an additional ontological commitment to a different type of entity *not* identified by the bound variable 'x' of the predicate 'Brother'. This existentially quantified sentence appears to be ontologically committed – by dint of an analytic truth – to a distinct type of entity identified by the very same bound variable 'x,' i.e., 'Sibling'. Clearly, this latter type of entity is *not* co-extensive with 'Brother' since the predicate 'Sibling' is also applicable to 'Sister'. I am my sister's brother and sibling, she is my sibling but not my brother. By the **QC,** '∃(x) Brother(x)' fails to refer to a distinct type of entity in the domain of discourse. The bound variable 'x' of the predicate '∃(x) Brother (x)' implies, by way of an extrinsic property, '∃(y) Sibling(y) & (x ≠ y)' (Rayo 2007, pp. 431-32).

Two lines of defence to this objection are available to one who wishes to reserve the identification of a theory's ontological commitments to those that are explicit. First, she may restrict the number of primitive predicates to those that relate only to *intrinsic* properties. However, this manoeuvre simply postpones the controversy to one of identifying which predicates are intrinsic and which are not. Second, she might cleave to the explicit account of ontological commitment and deny that '∃(x) Brother(x)' does entail '∃(y) Sibling(y)'. For example, dependent on which criterion of ontological commitment is adopted, the predicate '∃(x) Parent(x)' need *not* ontologically commit a theory to a distinct predicate 'ョ(y) Child(y)' by way of a relation to an extrinsic property. The conceptual link between brother-sibling relates to an extrinsic property. If I am your brother, then I must be your sibling. The conceptual link between parent-child is not an extrinsic property in the same way. If I am your parent, then I cannot be your child.[13] Once again, however, this manoeuvre simply postpones the controversy in respect of which extrinsic property entailments of a predicate expression are genuine (Bricker 2016, Section 1.7.4).

Thus far, the implicit ontological commitments of a theory have emerged due to extrinsic links between different properties. These concerns, however, are not limited to the extrinsic properties of a type of entity K. Later I argue that the problem of advanced modality admits of a set-theoretic solution (chapter eight). In order to facilitate this solution, I am required to establish an ontology of sets. My proposed solution might draw encouragement from the standard Tarskian semantics employed by Quine. By Tarskian semantics, every predicate of **PL** is assigned a set as a semantic value; sets must exist as a presupposition of the quantifier criterion. I may suppose that the monadic predicate 'ョ(x) Horse(x)' incurs an implied ontological commitment to the set of horses, for example. This presupposition would be a mistake. Tarskian semantic theory deploys sets in order to *specify* the truth conditions of 'ョ(x) Horse(x),' but it does not impose a type of entity upon the universe in order to satisfy those truth conditions, i.e., that the universe must 'contain' the *set* of all horses. By parity of reason, there is no presupposition that Tarskian semantic theory demands that the universe include horses in order to specify the truth conditions of the same predicate viz. 'ョ(x) Unicorns(x)'. The explicit ontological commitments of 'total theory' appear not to include the apparatus of set theory, at least not precipitately (Quine 1953a [1980], pp. 114-17).

Tarskian semantics aside, an ontological commitment to sets is problematic on the grounds of metaphysical necessity. Metaphysical necessity can appear to link two distinct types of entity, e.g., a set and its membership. If we ignore pure sets for a moment and stipulate that a set cannot exist absent its actual or this-worldly members, then a commitment to the *actual* existence of 'a' incurs a further commitment to the singleton or the unit set 'ョ(x) x = {a}': "There will be many sets that even exist from the standpoint of all worlds, for instance, the numbers. Others may not; for instance, the unit set of a possible individual might only exist from the standpoint of the world that the individual is in." (Lewis 1983b [1983], p. 40) I will argue that this comment is a mistake – a set is

---

[13] Clearly, this example depends upon a domain of discourse restricted to two individuals. A third individual would be required to render 'ョ(y) Child(y)' true of 'x'. This strikes me as a biological rather than conceptual truth, however.

always an abstract object accessible from every world, even if its members are not. A unitary set is no exception. I argue, therefore, that sets ought to be counted amongst (at least) the *implied* ontological commitments of 'total theory' (chapter eight). For Lewis, 'total theory' has two components: the first is **GMR** – there is a plurality of worlds, each understood as discrete spatiotemporal regions populated by concrete individuals; the second is iterated set-theory (ibid., p. 40). In order to persuade those not convinced of this latter explicit commitment, I argue that sets ought to be counted amongst the *implied* ontological commitments of a theory. I now garner support for this argument viz. that sets ought to count among the *implied* commitments of a theory from a surprising source.

Quine is often misconstrued as a 'nominalist' although he rejects nominalism as "incoherent" (Quine 1986b [1998], p. 26). I tentatively suggest that he is willing to attribute *implicit* ontological commitments to a theory. Indeed, there are indications in his published writing to support this contention, e.g., '*there are* perfect numbers above 100' and '*there are* white rhinoceros'. "Saying these things, we also say by *implication* that there are physical objects and abstract entities; for all the [white rhinos] are physicals objects and all the [perfect numbers above 100] are abstract entities." (Quine 1951c [1976], p. 205 my emphasis) An exegesis of Quine's publications is beyond the scope of the present work, but the seeds of doubt are sown. The claim that Quine recognises *only* the explicit ontological commitments of a theory must account for his explicit denial of that assertion. What motivates Quine to include the implicit ontological commitments of a theory? Are the implied ontological commitments merely ideological or truly objectival?

I defer these interesting questions for another day. There are pragmatic reasons to ascribe implicit ontological commitments to 'total theory'. As noted, in respect of extrinsic properties, an analytic truth may link two predicates used to describe the same person or object, e.g., 'x is a brother' and 'x is a sibling'. In respect to the apparatus of set theory, we may wish to ascribe the necessity of set-membership to contingent objects and thereby grant epistemic-semantic access to them from every possible world. I cite Quine as an advocate of the implicit ontological commitments of 'total theory'. However, a problem raised by my citation is that Lewis explicitly rejects the thesis as a pernicious dogma: an ontological commitment to one type of entity – a set – based on a commitment to a distinct type of entity – the member of a set. I will anticipate the arguments of later chapters in order to discuss Lewis' explicit rejection of the "singularist dogma" (Lewis 1991, pp. 62-71). The anticipation is unfortunate but necessary given the context of our discussion viz., the implicit ontological commitments of a theory to a type of entity, sets.

1.5 The 'singularist dogma'

In later chapters, I argue that the problem of advanced modality admits of a set theoretical solution. In order to facilitate this solution, I am required to establish an ontology of sets. Lewis acknowledges that the **QC** *may* identify the implicit ontological commitments of a theory (Lewis 1986a, pp. 5-6). It is rather less likely, however, that he would number sets amongst a theory's *implicit* ontological commitments. As previously noted, orthodox Tarskian semantics assigns a set as a semantic value to every predicate of **PL**. That is, the extension of each predicate is understood as a single quantification over a *collection* of objects rather than an apparent plural quantification over a collection of *objects* (Lewis 1991, p. 65). The predicates of **PL** are interpreted as a singular quantification over an object; a set, or class-like entity. The distinction is not inconsequential:

> Plural quantification is irreducibly plural. It is not ordinary singular quantification over special plural things – not even when there are special plural things, namely classes, to be had. Rather, it is a special way to quantify whatever things there may be to quantify over. Plural quantification, like singular, carries ontological commitment only to whatever may be quantified over. It is devoid of set theory, and it is ontologically innocent. (Lewis 1991, pp. 68-69)

Does an ontological commitment to a collection of talking donkeys, say, imply an ontological commitment to the *set* of talking donkeys? I am compelled to say 'yes' – Lewis says 'no'. My reply is one to which I must cleave in order to propose a set theoretic solution to the problem of advanced modality. Although not interpreted as such by standard Tarskian semantics, the predicates of *plural* quantification are familiar features of ordinary language. That is, some predicates of ordinary language are true of some things without being true of any one of them individually, e.g., 'they are teammates', 'they lifted the piano', 'they were born in different countries' or 'they weigh over 500lbs'. In the case of plural predication, there is no requirement to postulate a set in order to interpret a sentence of the object language with a predicate as a constituent. "We can say without apparent contradiction – and indeed truly – that there are some things such that for no predicate are they all and only the satisfiers of that predicate." (ibid., pp. 64-65) Indeed, if a predicate cannot be true of each individual member of a set, then the relation of set-membership becomes problematic (§ 8.3.1): "There are some things such that for no set are they all and only its members; and some things such that for no proper class are they all and only its members; and some things such that for no property are they all and only its instances." (ibid., p. 65)

Consider, by way of example, the predicate expression "they lifted the piano" (McKay 2006, p. 5). By standard semantics of **PL**, this predicate is interpreted as a single quantification – say, as the set whose members collectively lifted the piano. Thus interpreted, the predicate is false for each member of the set – since no individual could lift the piano alone – but true *of* the members of the set, collectively. *If* the predicate of the object language is false for each member of the set, then how can an individual member of the set acquire set-membership? Each member of the set is a member of the set of which the predicate of the object language is true, collectively. Yet each fails to be a 'member' of the set, as the relevant predicate is false *of* it, individually. "[Hence] to translate [a] seemingly true plural quantification into a contradictory singular quantification is to impute error – grave and hidden error." (Lewis 1991, p. 65)

The fault in part is one of *distribution*: a predicate 'F' is distributive if, and only if, by virtue of the meaning of 'F', whenever some things are F, each one of them is F (ibid., pp. 63-65: McKay 2006, p. 5 fn. 2).[14] Standard **PL** interprets every predicate as distributive. In the case of plural predication, *not* all predicates are distributive. What is the non-standard explanation of plural predication? In his helpful exegesis of Lewis, John Burgess offers a distinction between those who are beguiled by the 'singularist dogma' and those who are not. The 'dogma' is a consequence of the completeness assumption of Boolean algebra that can be expressed in the terminology of second-order logic: "For any class of things, there is a fusion thereof." (Burgess 2015, p. 464) In the alternative, a theoretical ability to deploy plural quantification enables Lewis to exploit the interpretive resources of 'monadic third-order logic'. In the terminology of Hazen (Hazen 1997): "reading the formalism of that logic, a first-order variable *x* is said to range over *individuals*, a second-order variable *X* is said to range over *species*, and a third-order variable **X** is said to range over *genera*." (Burgess 2015, p. 464) The distinction allows the expressive resources of Tarskian semantics to be interpreted in a non-standard way that avoids a commitment to unnecessary ontological inflation.

Reply: The problem posed by the 'singularist dogma' can be dissolved through the apparatus of plural predication. Might there be an alternative way to dissolve the problem which maintains a commitment to standard Tarskian semantics? Ideally, any proposed alternative solution would be conducive to Lewis' metaphysics. I propose that the damage inflicted by the 'singularist

---

[14] The problem of distribution can be overcome by the admittance of "fuzzy sets" (Putnam 1975a [1996], pp. 4, 44-45). In addition to the problem of distribution, McKay identifies the problematic cumulative nature of the standard PL interpretation of predicates. Cumulative in the following sense: "A monadic predicate F is cumulative iff the meaning of the predicate requires that whenever some things *X* are F and some things *Y* are F, then *X* and *Y* together are F." (McKay 2006, p. 7)

dogma' can be mitigated by way of Lewisian mereology: "The simple principle of absolutely unrestricted composition should be accepted as true." (Lewis 1986a, p. 212) Reconsider the predicate 'they lifted the piano'. At first blush and seduced by the singularist dogma, the predicate is interpreted in the standard Tarskian manner as a set whose membership collectively lifted the piano. Suppose that this set has four members: Anne, Bob, Charles, and Duncan. The aforementioned problem of non-distribution now emerges that leaves the predicate of the object language true of the collective membership of the set but false of each member. I propose a solution to the problem based on the Lewisian notion of an 'unrestricted mereological sum': I distinguish between two distinct sets; a set of four members and a second set of one member. Set A consists of four members; Anne, Bob, Charles, and Duncan. Set B consists of a distinct entity; an entity composed of the piano-lifting group and their parts – say, as they hold hands (cf. van Inwagen 1990, pp. 33-37). The semantic value of the relevant predicate is re-interpreted by way of this second set, whose only member is the mereological sum of the people who lifted the piano and their parts. This distributive predicate of the object language is true of this single member of set B; one entity composed of four people or parts, and their respective parts. The need to interpret predicates of the object language in a non-standard plural manner can be avoided and replaced with an alternative interpretation based on the notion of an 'unrestricted mereological sum'.

Lewis argues that we ought to dispense with the primitive notion 'is a member of' and replace it with a new primitive notion of a "singleton" (Lewis 1991, p. 61). Further, as a true reflection of ordinary language, the interpretation of appropriate predicates as plural is ontologically innocent (ibid., p. 68). In the alternative, I cleave to standard Tarskian semantics that interpret 'plural' predicates based on set theory and Lewisian 'unrestricted mereological sums'.

1.6 Conclusion

The stage is set. The development of Quine's criterion of ontological commitment has been traced through Russell's theory of descriptions and his employment of modern **PL**. Hopefully, in what is not too bold a claim, I argue that Quine does acknowledge the possibility of the implicit ontological commitments of a theory to a type of entity K. Implicit ontological commitments are to be acknowledged amongst all the ontological commitments of a theory (Lewis 1986a, pp. 5-6). The endorsement of the implicit ontologically commitments of 'total theory' to sets raises the problem of plural predication. I countered the problem by employing Lewis' notion of an 'unrestricted mereological sum'. I now turn to another contentious issue: what are the ontological commitments of a theory when they are expressed in the idioms of ordinary language? Do the idioms of ordinary language carry any serious meta-ontological weight?

2

Ontological commitment
and ordinary language

2.1 Introduction

S1: I believe that there are possible worlds other than the one we happen to inhabit. If an argument is wanted, it is this. It is uncontroversially true that things might be otherwise than they are. I believe, and so do you, that things could have been different in countless ways. But what does this mean? Ordinary language permits the paraphrase: there are many ways things could have been beside the way they actually are. On the face of it, this sentence is an existential quantification. It says that there exist many entities of a certain description, to wit 'ways things could have been'. I believe things could have been different in countless ways; I believe permissible paraphrases of what I believe; taking the paraphrase at its face value, I, therefore, believe in the existence of entities that might be called 'ways things could have been'. I prefer to call them 'possible worlds'. (Lewis 1973, p. 84)

Chapter One explored the notion of ontological commitment in general. The intensional language of quantified modal logic (**QML**) is 'translated' into the extensional language of predicate logic (**PL**).[1] In consequence, genuine modal realism (**GMR**) incurs a theoretical cost in the form of a substantive thesis; the existence of a plurality of possible worlds. This chapter examines how the quantifier criterion (**QC**) of ontological commitment can be applied not to predicate logic but to ordinary language.[2] The shift to ordinary language is

---

[1] Quine does countenance alternatives to PL as the 'preferred' language of canonical notation on pragmatic grounds (Quine 1998c [1998], pp. 533 ff.). As a consequence, PL is a sufficient but not a necessary condition required to "limn the true and ultimate structure of reality." (Quine 1960 [2013], Section 45, pp. 198 ff.)

[2] H.J. Glock argues that Gilbert Ryle identified an ambiguity in the use of the term 'ordinary language': the term may refer either to the standard use – contrasted with the irregular use of the term in a specific subject – or the everyday use – contrasted with the use of the term by an expert (Glock (2008) *What Is Analytic Philosophy?* Cambridge University Press, p. 14). Actually, Ryle does not identify an ambiguity in the use of the term 'ordinary language'. Instead, he sharpens a distinction too often ignored in modern day philosophical argument (circa. 1953): a distinction between two separate phrases, 'the use of ordinary language' and 'the ordinary use of the expression' '…'. In the former

problematic for Quine because he denies that the serious ontological commitments of a theory can be *directly* identified from ordinary language. The idioms of ordinary language are often referentially opaque. Hence, in order to identify the genuine ontological commitments of a theory, Quine argues that the sentences of ordinary language must first be explicated by paraphrase – preferably – into canonical notation of **PL**. Lewis recognises no such methodological constraint. Persuaded by the **QC** of ontological commitment, the shared beliefs expressed by **S1** identify a type of entity that he refers to as 'possible worlds'; a paraphrase of the ordinary language expression 'ways things could have been'. Lewis diverges from Quine so as to avail himself of the *serious* ontological commitments of a theory couched in terms of ordinary language. He designates this approach "allism" (Lewis 1990 [1999]: Bricker 2016 Section 4.1).[3]

I endorse the use of the **QC** of ontological commitment expressed in the idioms of ordinary language (Section 2.2). I identify Lewis' criteria, the satisfaction of which constitutes a genuine paraphrase relation. A formal translation into the canonical notation of **PL**, presumed to identify the *serious* ontological commitments of a theory, is not amongst them (Section 2.3). I examine a common presumption of the paraphrase technique; that it ought to result in the *explication* of concepts and thereby avoid the morass generated by intensional language (Section 2.4). I then explore the use of the apparently indexical phrase, the 'ways things could have been'. I utilise this phrase as a litmus test to identify how serious the ontological commitments of ordinary language really are. Are the 'ways things could have been' and 'possible world' indexical terms? If they are, could they be used in a language stripped of modal

---

or standard case, "the edges of 'ordinary' are blurred, but usually we are in no doubt whether a diction does or does not belong to ordinary parlance." (Ryle 1953 [2009], p. 315) In the latter or everyday use of the term the question of standard use is irrelevant. "If a term is a highly technical term, or a non-technical term, there remains the distinction between its [standard] stock use and non-stock uses of it." (ibid., p. 315)

[3] A Lewisian 'allist' may over-generate the types of entity to which a theory ought to be committed. The distinction of substitutional and objectual quantification might be lost, for example. Objectual quantification (Tarski) states that an existential quantified sentence '∃x φx' is true iff the open formulae 'φx' is satisfied by some object in the domain of discourse. Substitutional quantification states that '∃x φx' is true iff 'φt' is true, for some singular term 't' of the language. Hence, the QC over-generates if the language includes empty singular terms e.g. 'Sherlock Holmes'. For Quine, all quantifiers should be interpreted objectually (Quine 1969 [1969], p. 106: 1974, p. 139: van Inwagen 1981 [2001]: cf. Gottlieb 1980: Marcus 1993).

notions? (Section 2.5). I conclude with remarks that relate to the third criterion of a genuine paraphrase (Section 2.6).

2.2 The quantifier criterion of ordinary language

The modal idioms of ordinary language exceed the expressive resources of standard **QML**.[4] The sentences discussed in chapter one [left side, biconditional] that utilise the modal operators of box '□' and diamond '◊' do not match the expressive resources of ordinary language (Lewis 1986a, pp. 13 ff.). Do counterpart theoretic sentences [right side, biconditional] fail to match the expressive resources of ordinary language? How does Lewis account for the apparent ontological implications of the **QC** as expressed in the idioms of **S1**? Which segments of ordinary language – to borrow a phrase from Quine – are 'ontologically serious'? In English, the existential quantifier is expressed in a number of phrases, including 'there is/are', 'some', 'few', 'all', 'most', etc. Quine's main objection to the claim that such expressions imply a *direct* ontological commitment to a type of entity is that ordinary language is referentially opaque (Quine 1998c [1998]). It falls to philosophers, therefore, to clarify which of the ontological commitments of ordinary language are genuine when an 'existential quantifier' of ordinary language is used. This task is best achieved by the regimented paraphrase of ordinary language into the canonical notation of **PL**; in which the serious ontological commitments of a theory to a type of entity K are made perspicuous. Critically, an interlocutor may then reject the paraphrase in order to deny the ontological commitments ascribed therein:

> Ordinary language is only loosely referential, and any ontological accounting makes sense only relative to an appropriate regimentation of language. The regimentation is not a matter of eliciting some latent but determinate ontological content of ordinary language. It is a matter rather of freely creating an ontology-orientated language that can supplant ordinary language in serving some particular purposes that one has in mind. (Quine 1977 [1977], p. 168: 1981a [1981], p. 9)

A general concern in regard to a sufficiency condition of the **QC** of ontological commitment expressed by way of **PL** has been identified (§ 1.3). Recall one theoretical desideratum of **PL** is that it is an extensional language. The idioms of ordinary language, on the other hand, are frequently couched in intensional terms. Those fragments of ordinary language interpreted as logical operators 'it is possible that', 'it is believed that' or 'it ought to be the case that' may conceal the ontological commitments to which a theory *should* adhere. The **QC** will not

---

[4] See Lewis 1986a, pp. 8-14 esp. pp. 12-13: the expressive resources of QML may be either 'redundant' or 'inadequate' (Divers 2002, p. 309 fn. 26).

be a necessary condition of ontological commitment if it under-generates cases, for example (§ 1.4). In such circumstances, we fail to identify the ontological commitments of a theory, e.g., because the quantifiers are disguised. Furthermore, the **QC** will not be a sufficient condition of ontological commitment if it over-generates (§ 1.3). If it entails that a theory is ontologically committed to a type of entity to which it should *not* be committed. Again, we erroneously assign to a theory an ontological commitment to a type of entity K, e.g., because the quantifiers are disguised. Disguised quantifiers may quantify over a domain of discourse and entail a plethora of controversial entities *not* obviously entailed by the standard use of ordinary or intensional language. Indeed, this is frequently taken as a fundamental error of **GMR**.

In order to accurately identify the ontological commitments of **GMR**, the regimented paraphrase of **S1** must manifest the latent existential quantifiers expressed by ordinary language. However, a shared belief that 'things could have been different in countless ways' hardly seems to entail a shared belief in a plurality of concrete possible worlds where each possibility is instantiated! In a departure from Quine's pragmatism, Lewis does appear to embark on 'eliciting some latent but determinate ontological content' from ordinary language. If this latency is erroneous, then Lewis is engaged in an "ontological inflation" (Daly 2010, p. 96). Lewis appears to be ambivalent toward Quine's methodology: either he *is* embarked on an exploration of the latent ontological commitments of our shared modal beliefs contra-Quine, or he is *not* embarked on such an endeavour but simply invents an ontology to suit his theoretical purposes pro-Quine. By accepting the **QC**, Lewis' analysis of modal sentences apparently fails to satisfy a sufficiency condition of ontological commitment; it over-generates the types of entity to which a theory ought to be committed.

The application of the **QC** to the modal idioms of ordinary language requires a defence against the charge of ontological inflation. A defence against this charge can be offered on the basis of an orthodox interpretation of Quine's **QC**. To this end, I cite in full the passage in which the *meaning* of the existential quantifier '∃' of **PL** is given. Quine argues:

> The given satisfaction conditions for negation, conjunction, and quantification presuppose an understanding of the very signs they would explain or of others to the same effect. A negation is explained as satisfied by a sequence when the constituent sentence is *not* satisfied by it; a conjunction is satisfied by a sequence when the one constituent sentence *and* the other are satisfied by it; and an existential quantification is satisfied by a sequence when the constituent sentence is satisfied by *some* suitably similar sequence. If we are prepared to avail ourselves thus of 'not', 'and', and 'some' in the course of explaining negation, conjunction, and existential quantification, why not proceed more

directly and just offer those words as direct translations? (Quine 1986a, p. 40 my underlining)

Contrary to Tarski, Quine argues that the meaning of the symbols of **PL** is derived from ordinary language. I suggest, therefore, that Quine is amenable to *direct* paraphrase from one set of ordinary language sentences to another set of ordinary language sentences – at least in principle, if not in practice. Clearly, the theoretical cost incurred by the use of this principle would be high; a loss of clarity usually ascribed to canonical notation.

However, although Quine does appear to argue that the symbols of **PL** derive their meaning from ordinary language, there are well-rehearsed reasons to suppose he would reject the notion of the 'synonymy' of terms (Quine 1951a [1980], p. 23: 1960 [2013], Section 53 p. 238: 1998a [1998], p. 73). Lewis has no such qualms. He argues that – dependent on context – the synonymy of terms is a legitimate relation that might be deployed in support of an argument. These terms include existential quantification: "The several idioms of what we call 'existential' quantification are entirely synonymous and interchangeable. It does not matter whether you say 'Some things are donkeys' [...] or 'Donkeys exist' – you mean exactly the same thing whichever way you say it." (Lewis 1990 [1999], p. 154: 1970 [1983], pp. 207-20) The use of synonyms for existential quantification is not restricted to the 'dry goods' of physical objects. They apply with equal legitimacy to more 'controversial' types of entity: "it does not matter whether you say 'Some famous fictional detective uses cocaine', 'There is a famous fictional detective who uses cocaine', or 'A famous cocaine-using fictional detective exists' – whether true or whether false, all three statements stand or fall together." (Lewis 1990 [1999], pp. 154-55)

Lewis argues that dependent on the context of discourse, the idioms of ordinary language can be 'ontologically serious'. These idioms include synonyms of formal existential quantification. All such expressions are legitimate and can be taken seriously, dependent on the context of their utterance (ibid., p. 155). Admitting some reservations, I conclude that Quine rejects the 'allist' approach to the ordinary language expressions of the **QC**. In order to identify the pragmatic ontological commitments of a theory, Quine argues that the regimented paraphrase of ordinary language should proceed – preferably – by way of **PL**. With the distinction noted, I turn to examine the method of paraphrase employed by both Quine and Lewis. If the 'argument from paraphrase' of **S1** is to be accepted as a legitimate philosophical technique, then Lewis is obliged to explain the nature of the paraphrase relationship. Is the relationship indeed one of synonymy?

2.3 The method of paraphrase

If the method of paraphrase is a genuine philosophical technique, then we are due an explanation of the relationship between the paraphrased terms (cf. Alston 1958: Sider 1999). Are the terms related by factual truth, logical truth, synonymy, or on pragmatic grounds? (Daly 2010, pp. 89 ff.) Modal translation proceeds on the quantificational-predicate model of analysis. Lewis accepts the context-sensitive synonymy of quantificational terms. How are the predicate expressions 'ways things could have been' and 'possible world' related?[5] The aim of the present section is to identify the general criteria the satisfaction of which generate a Lewisian paraphrase. What is Lewis' method of paraphrase? Is the Lewisian method based on the synonymy of terms? Lewis' motivation is to secure the theoretical desideratum of a reductive analysis. To reduce the intensional language of **QML** to the extensional language of **PL** (§ 1.1). However, **S1** represents an explication of modal discourse couched in the terms of ordinary language, e.g., different ways to express the existential quantifier. Together with existential quantification, the paraphrase of the predicate expression 'ways things could have been' commits **GMR** to a plurality of non-actual worlds. That is, a commitment is incurred but only to those modal sentences that are taken to be *true*. For example, 'there is a world at which there is a talking donkey' commits the genuine realist to the existence of a non-actual world if it is accepted as true. For Quine, an analytic statement is one that is stipulated as a matter of convention by a community of investigators in accord with their *purposes*. "But no synonymy relation is presupposed here; what matters is just that the paraphrase be acceptable to all parties for purposes of the continuing investigation." (Quine 1998b [1998], p. 95) Quine employs the **QC** as a means of identifying the ontological commitments of a particular theory to a type of entity K. If the regimented paraphrase of a portion of ordinary language is not committed to Ks, then the theory can be acquitted of that particular ontological commitment. In order to assess a theory's parsimony, we must first identify the types of entity to which a theory is ontologically committed (§ 1.3).

What are the criteria of a legitimate paraphrase? In "Holes" (1970), David and Stephanie Lewis present an imagined dialogue between a realist Bargle and Argle, a nominalist. The paper can be used to illustrate Lewis' method of paraphrase in action. The dialogue concerns an unwelcome ontological

---

[5] The adjective term 'possible' in the phrase 'possible world' may be *alienans*. If a substantive term need not or cannot apply on its own – an expectant father need not be a father and a counterfeit £10 note cannot be a genuine £10 note – then the adjective – 'expectant' and 'counterfeit' – is said to be alienans. Hence, as a 'possible world' need not be a world the adjective 'possible' may also be alienans in this case (see Chapter four).

commitment to a type of abstract object, holes. As expressed in the idioms of ordinary language, Bargle alleges that Argle's putatively 'nominalist' theory implies an ontological commitment to holes. Argle accepts that the relevant expressions of ordinary language *appear* to commit nominalism to abstract or immaterial objects, e.g., 'there are holes in this piece of cheese'. However, this apparent commitment to 'immaterial' holes can be avoided by way of a paraphrase of the relevant terms. The philosophical technique of paraphrase may obviate an ontological commitment not just to the holes in this piece of cheese but to holes in general. The method of paraphrase should (a) preserve the truth or falsity of hole-referring statements, (b) preserve the validity of any argument that employs statements about holes, and (c) be endorsed by a community of ordinary language-users (Lewis & Lewis 1970 [1983], pp. 3-9; Bricker 2016, Section 4.2). Any failure to specify the conditions of a genuine paraphrase would defer the original problem of identifying the ontological commitments of a theory.

How do Lewis' criteria (a-c) apply in the case of an alleged ontological commitment to 'holes'? Argle initially attempts to avoid said commitment by invoking the use of a new primitive predicate, "perforated" (Lewis & Lewis 1970 [1983], p. 4). For example, a sentence such as 'there are holes in this piece of cheese' can be paraphrased as 'this cheese is perforated'. The proposal allows Argle to 'speak with the vulgar' without incurring the burden of an ontological commitment to a type of entity, holes. One problem raised by the introduction of a new predicate relates to the satisfaction conditions of a paraphrase were 'holes' can be counted (ibid., p. 4). In reply, Argle adjusts the predicate 'perforated' to 'n-perforated' for each individual n: "[what] I mean by that is that either both pieces are singly-perforated, or both are doubly-perforated, or both are triply-perforated and so on." (ibid., p. 4) Unfortunately, Argle's freshly adjusted n-place predicate invites further complications. Firstly, the paraphrase sentence – analysans – now depends on an infinite number of *primitive* n-place predicates, in clear violation of restrictions imposed by the use of *regimented* **PL**. Rather than engage in arbitrary 'language chopping,' primitive predicates ought to identify the joints at which 'nature is carved' (§ 4.6). Secondly, the adjustment to an n-place predicate fails to explain statements of comparison, e.g., "how will you say that there are as many holes in my cheese as crackers on my plate?" (ibid., p. 4)

A promising strategy for nominalism is one of ontological reduction. A reduction in the number of ontological commitments of a theory is best achieved by retaining the quantificational and referential apparatus of discourse *whilst* restricting the underlying domain to 'uncontroversial' types of entity. A disputed type of entity – 'holes' – is reduced by regimented paraphrase from 'controversial' immaterial objects to 'uncontroversial' material objects. The ordinary language sentence 'there are holes in this piece of cheese' remains subject to the **QC**, but the assessed ontological commitments relate to material 'hole-linings' and not immaterial 'holes': "The lining of a hole, you agree, is a material object. For every hole there is a hole-lining; for every hole-lining there is a hole. I say the hole-lining *is* the hole." (ibid., p. 5)[6] Although the general strategy of reduction is indicative of Quine's motivation, it is subsidiary to the **QC**. Normally the ontological commitments of a theory are identified as a precursor to the evaluation of a theory's ontological *cost*. The intention is to *avoid* an apparent ontological commitment to a controversial type of entity. In the case of **S1**, however, although the **QC** is used to ensure a theoretical reduction, it nonetheless embraces rather than avoids an ontological commitment to a controversial type of entity. As a reductive strategy in the spirit of Quine, **S1** is deeply problematic. Not only is it at odds with the motivation behind the **QC**, but it ascribes an implicit ontological commitment to 'total theory'. Generally, the ontological commitments of a theory are made explicit by canonical notation (§ 1.4). The **S1** reduction of modal discourse, however, reduces 'ways things could have been' to a paraphrase 'possible world'. A modal expression of ordinary language is reduced to a philosophical term of art with an ontological commitment to a type of entity that is not obviously implied by the original expression. Furthermore, a reduction ought to be one that eliminates rather than invites controversy. Again, in the case of **S1**, the shoe is on the other foot: by accepting the quantification-predicate model, a type of uncontroversial phrase/entity or 'ways things could have been' is reduced to a controversial type of phrase/entity or 'possible world'. That is, 'controversial' in the sense of the genuine realist interpretation of the phrase 'possible world'. The controversy comes when the interpretation of 'possible world' is broached: the move from modal language to world-speak, e.g., taking modality to be reduced to a quantification over something.

I identify the criteria (a-c), the satisfaction of which secures a genuine paraphrase. Lewis accepts, dependent on the context of utterance, the synonymy relation. It appears that synonymy is a prime candidate for the genuine paraphrase of 'ways things could have been' by 'possible world'. Lewis also states that personal preference guides his choice of paraphrase, perhaps

---

[6] Although problems with the reductive strategy persist e.g. the identity conditions of 'holes' and 'hole-linings' do not coincide (Lewis & Lewis 1970 [1983], p. 8) there are several prominent examples of the strategy in play: Davidson (1967 [1980]) argues that action sentences are ontologically committed to events. Adverbs, such as 'slowly', describe an event(s) over which the action sentence(s) in which they are embedded tacitly quantify. Hence, a sentence such as 'John walked slowly' justifies the inference that 'John walked'.

on the grounds of "brevity or familiarity of expression." (Quine 1960 [2013], Section 40 p. 175) I conclude that as a philosophical term of art, 'possible world' can be utilised for the sake of brevity as a genuine paraphrase. Does my conclusion breach the third of Lewis' criteria? I defer the examination of this potential breach to subsequent chapters (esp. three and five). In the meantime, I return to the issue of a genuine paraphrase. If the relevant terms are *not* synonyms, then in what does the paraphrase relation consist?

2.4 Explication

In order to address this question, I turn to an exposition of the philosophical method of explication. Quine's method of explication originated in the work of Rudolf Carnap. Although sympathetic to Carnap's scientific worldview, antipathy toward the analytic/synthetic distinction led Quine to propose a distinctive account of explication.[7]

> Explication is elimination but not all elimination is explication. Showing how the useful purposes of some perplexing expression can be accomplished through new channels would seem to count as explication just in case the new channels parallel the old ones sufficiently for there to be a striking if partial parallelism of function between the old troublesome form of expression and some form of expression figuring in the new method. (Quine 1960 [2013], Section 53 p. 241)

Quine illustrates the method of explication with the problem of defining an ordered pair (Quine 1960 [2013], Section 53, p. 236). I introduced the notion of an ordered pair earlier in relation to the set representation of functional expressions; in the form of a set whose members are an argument-value pair (§ 1.2). In standard set theory, the set {a, b} is identical to the set {b, a} since the order in which set-membership is represented is immaterial in regard to the identity of the set. However, there are circumstances that require the notion of an ordered pair. Unless 'a' and 'b' are identical the ordered pairs <a, b> and <b, a> are distinct (ibid., Section 53 p. 237: Hylton 2010, p. 247). Should ordered pairs – distinct from sets – be included amongst the types of entity to which a theory ought to be ontologically committed? Quine's answer is 'No'. He argues persuasively that on the basis of mathematical demonstrations by Wiener et al., the resources of set theory are sufficient to systematically account for the

---

[7] Quine's primary objection to analyticity is based on the putative synonymy relation presupposed as the foundation of an analytic truth (Quine 1951a [1980]). Quine appears to modify his attitude toward analyticity in work published after *Two Dogmas* (see Hylton 2010, pp. 63-64).

notion of ordered pairs (Quine 1960 [2013], Section 53 pp. 238-39). Thus, the notion of an ordered pair can be explicated in terms of set theory.

Quine's method of explication is linked to the enterprise of philosophy as an academic discipline. For Quine, philosophers begin their enquiries as physical objects embedded in a physical world. His philosophical ambition is "to ponder our talk of physical phenomena as a physical phenomena, and our scientific imaginings as activities within the world that we imagine." (ibid., Section 1 pp. 4-5) This is a departure from Carnap's notion of explication as a philosophical method. Although he shares Quine's predisposition that favours the language of empirical science, Carnap argues that explication is best understood as a form of philosophical clarification (Carnap 1962, pp. 3-5). For Quine, on the other hand, explication is a process by which we eliminate expressions that obstruct our understanding of ourselves as a physical phenomenon (Quine 1954 [1976], pp. 228 ff.). This radical conception of the human condition informs Quine's views of philosophical analysis – genuine analysis should focus only on the observable characteristics of language: "Sentences are observable, and dispositions to assent are fairly accessible through observable symptoms ... I begin with occasion sentences, indeed with observation sentences in my special sense." (Quine 1981b [1981], pp. 184-85) Quine's approach to language differs from that of Carnap. For Carnap, philosophical analysis should aid the empirical sciences, i.e., language is a tool in need of clarification by way of philosophical analysis. For Quine, however, language is – at least in part - a physical phenomenon. The previous sentence requires qualification as Quine does acknowledge that sentences are also a type of abstract object or universal. Sentences can be analysed – explicated – in terms of sets or ordered pairs: they consist of sequences a1, a2 ... aφ or sets of φ-pairs {a1, 1}, {a2, 2} ... {aφ, φ}. The elements of these ordered pairs are the characters and phonemes of the sentence uttered; understood as concrete instances of sound or inscription. Unuttered abstract sentences are also accommodated as sequences of ordered pairs, the elements of which are a concrete observable phenomenon. Language is a concrete, observable phenomenon because sentences are analysed as ordered pairs or sets whose elements are concrete observable phenomenon (Quine 1960 [2013], Section 40 p. 178). Quine's theory is ontologically committed to sets as abstract types of entity on the grounds of 'indispensability'. That is, sets are an indispensable part of our best 'total theory' of the world (§ 8.3.2) (Quine 1954 [1976], p. 244).

For Lewis, the philosophical study of modality is grounded neither in language nor thought (Lewis 1983a [1983], p. xi). The metaphysical implications of the modal translation scheme are conceptually distinct from the semantic thesis (§ 5.3). As an idiom of ordinary language, the phrase 'ways things could have been' appears to be an indexical term. By **S1**, this phrase is itself a paraphrase of an earlier expression 'things could have been *different* in countless ways'. That is, 'different' from how they actually are. Hence, by criterion (a) of a genuine paraphrase, I propose that the phrase 'ways things could have been' should include the subordinate clause 'but are not'. The truth-value of sentences that include the phrase 'ways things could have been' partially depend on how things actually are. As an indexical phrase, it is doubtful that the phrase could be constitutive of an 'eternal sentence' of canonical notation, however. Are indexical terms conducive to paraphrase into canonical notation? How comprehensible would a language free of indexical terms be? I now examine the proposal that 'ways things could have been' *is* an indexical phrase and amenable to canonical notation.

2.5 Ways things could have been [but are not]

Lewis accepts that the quantificational idioms of ordinary language may – dependent on the context of utterance – satisfy the **QC** (§ 2.2). Does this legitimacy extend to the modal idioms of ordinary language? Granting quantification, do the modal idioms of **S1**, such as 'ways things could have been,' refer to a type of entity? Could these forms of modal idiom be explicated or eliminated from ordinary language? Could they be eliminated in favour of terms more conducive to 'eternal sentences'? I proceed on the supposition that although modal idioms are *not* eliminable, they are nonetheless reducible. As a *partial* test case, I examine the modal idiom 'ways things could have been' [but are not].[8] If the term 'actual' – and its cognates – are indexical (see Lewis 1986a, pp. 92 ff.), then I argue the phrase 'ways things could have been' is indexical. We can *only* identify the 'way things could have been' [but are not] on the basis of how things actually are. If a phrase of ordinary language is interpreted as an indexical then by implication, it could not be constitutive of an 'eternal sentence' (Quine 1960 [2013], Section 40 pp. 177-78: Kaplan 1977 [1989], p. 506). As a paraphrase of 'ways things could have been' the complex term 'possible world' appears to be prohibited from any meaningful role in an 'eternal sentence'.

Semantically, indexical phrases appear to be a type of singular term or referring expression (Braun 2017). Singular terms, such as pronouns, function as expressions that 'pick out' particular things. Unlike most singular terms, however, the things 'picked out' by indexical expressions vary with the context of utterance – the same expression can pick out different objects at different times and places. A sensitivity to the context of utterance appears to distinguish

---

[8] By S1, reference to a difference at the actual world is analysed – in part – by an ontological commitment to non-actual worlds.

indexical expressions from other types of singular terms, such as proper names and descriptions. For example, the phrase 'I am thirsty' can be used to refer to different people, i.e., it 'picks' me out when I say it and you out when you say it. A puzzling aspect of indexical terms can be illustrated by way of Frege's theory of sense and reference (Frege 1892a [2001]). In brief, the sense or 'mode of presentation' of a word determines its reference. Hence, if two phrases share a sense, then they must share a reference, e.g., 'neurologist' and 'brain-doctor'. In contrast, if two phrases differ referentially, then they must differ in a sense, e.g., 'Pope in Rome' and 'Pope in Avignon'.

As an avowed "descriptivist" (Lewis 1968 [1983], pp. 32-33), it might be supposed that Lewis would be sympathetic to a Fregean analysis of indexical terms. However reasonable, the supposition is problematic. Take, for instance, the Fregean analysis of the first-person pronoun 'I'. If the reference of 'I' is determined by the sense of a sentence in which it occurs, then the sense of 'I' changes with the context of utterance. As in the case of the pontiff, if the referent of the word 'I' is indeed context-sensitive in this way, then the sense of the sentence that contains the word must change. Intuitively, however, the use of the same word (even by different people) should share some common feature or meaning. The problem of identifying a 'common meaning' distinct from a Fregean sense is further demonstrated by the terms 'here' and 'now'. The common meaning of these indexical-type expressions approximates respectively to 'the place of this utterance' and 'the time of this utterance'. The referents of these phrases are context-sensitive, i.e., 'the place of this utterance' could be London, Paris, or Rome. If the referents change with the context of utterance, then the Fregean sense of 'here' cannot be invariant, *mutatis mutandis* for 'now'. Therefore, the common meaning of these indexical terms cannot be identified with their Fregean sense. I argue that the interpretation of the modal phrase 'ways things could have been' [but are not] shares the indexical features of 'here' and 'now'. Does the paraphrase of 'ways things could have been' by 'possible world' entail a 'common meaning' beyond a Fregean sense?

David Kaplan (Kaplan 1977 [1989]: cf. Evans 1981 [1985]) isolates two elements of indexical sentences that together constitute a common meaning. Neither element corresponds to a Fregean sense. The first element of common meaning is the proposition expressed by a sentence. Propositions are to be construed in the Russellian manner; that is, as composed of objects and their associated properties. When I utter the phrase 'I am thirsty,' I express a *different* proposition from your utterance of the same phrase because the person denoted by 'I' is different in each case. However, the proposition expressed by the phrase 'You are thirsty' – uttered by you of me – is the *same* proposition expressed by my utterance of the phrase 'I am thirsty'. Again, because the subject of the predicate 'x is thirsty' is the same person, me. Hence, the same

Russellian proposition can be expressed by the use of different words, e.g., the person denoted by 'I' and 'You' is the same. The second element of 'common meaning' is the 'character' of an indexical-type sentence.

> The character of an expression is set by linguistic conventions and, in turn, determines the content [proposition] of the expression in every context ... it is natural to think of it as *meaning* in the sense of what is known by a competent language user. (Kaplan 1977 [1989], p. 505)

The character of an indexical expression is standardly considered to be a function from possible contexts of utterance to contents or propositions. That is, it is the character of the expression that determines its content or proposition in various contexts of utterance. Hence, my utterance of the sentence 'I am thirsty' has the same character as your utterance of the same sentence. The utterance of 'You are thirsty' – said by you of me – has a *different* character – but the same content or proposition – as my utterance of the phrase 'I am thirsty' by dint of context-sensitivity.

I argue that – by Lewis' counterpart theoretic interpretation – the indexical phrase 'ways things could have been' [but are not] may be used to express *different* propositions dependent on the context of utterance – the relevant feature of the 'context' in these circumstances being the world at which the phrase is uttered (Lewis 1980 [1998], pp. 24-25). Thus interpreted, the proposition expressed by this phrase is composed of the objects and properties of the world in which it is uttered, i.e., the 'actual world'. A change anywhere in the actual world is analysed (in part) as a change of world. Objects and their properties differ dependent on which world is taken as 'actual'. Therefore, different objects and properties entail different propositions. The character of the expression 'ways things could have been' [but are not] determines the content or proposition expressed in the context of utterance. By Lewis' interpretation in the context and content or proposition of an expression relate to the world at which the expression is uttered. For example, the proposition expressed by the use of the phrase 'there is no more beer' is composed of the objects and properties of the fridge, which change with the context of utterance – from household to household. By parity of reason, a proposition expressed by way of the expression 'ways things could have been' [but are not] is composed of the objects and properties of the actual world, which change with the context of utterance – from world to world.

Kaplan argues that indexical sentences are typically those whose content varies with context (Kaplan 1977 [1989], p. 506). Although he denies that 'actual' is an indexical term, I believe that Lewis is able to avail himself of Kaplan's analysis of indexical-type sentences in order to argue that the cognate phrase 'ways things could have been' [but are not] is an indexical term.

Arguably, the interpretation of the ordinary language expression 'ways things could have been' has been secured as an indexical phrase. Thus understood, I now turn to the use of this phrase in canonical notation. Quine postulates a number of different sentence-types. Eternal sentences are those whose truth-value is generally invariant. Their truth-value does not change with the vagaries of our knowledge or beliefs. They include arithmetic sentences or sentences that specify the laws of nature. Eternal sentences are contrasted with standing sentences whose truth-value is subject to variation. Standing sentences include 'George W. Bush is President' [years] and 'It is Friday' [days]. Occasion sentences represent a third type of sentence. The truth-values of occasion sentences change with the circumstances and context of their utterance (Hylton 2010, p. 112). Occasion sentences are those which include but are not limited to indexical expressions. Indexicals or 'indicator words' may be substituted by regimented paraphrase into canonical notation in the form of specific objects, places, times, etc. These specifications establish 'systems of reference' to a particular space or time, e.g., latitude and longitude at Greenwich Mean Time. Canonical notation is motivated by a desire to render explicit the truth-values of context-dependent terms (ibid., p. 271). In addition to indexical expressions, context-dependent terms include 'tensed verbs', which relate to past or future events and can be regimented by way of explicit indicators of time (Quine 1960 [2013], Section 36 p. 155). Quantifiers, on the other hand, are treated as timeless. The interpretation of the quantified phrase 'Aristotle is mortal', for instance, includes Aristotle in the domain of discourse regardless of whether he did, does, or will exist (Hylton 2010, pp. 271-72).

With these preliminary points in mind, the question becomes: can the indexical phrase 'ways things could have been' be eliminated from ordinary language, say, as a component of an 'eternal sentence'? "So we need to show how we could replace the context-dependent sentences which are actually uttered with eternal sentences, true or false once for all." (ibid., p. 271) The problem with this type of endeavour is one of generality. A language wholly free of indexical terms could only be used to express general sentences. For example, we may wish to refer to an object by way of a predicate (see § 1.2). Unfortunately, the same predicate may hold for multiple objects that share a property or relation. How can we refer to a *unique* object in a language stripped of indexical terms? Logical constants and definite descriptions are dissolved through Quinean analysis. As suggested in the previous paragraph, reference to a unique object might be secured by the use of terms that render the object's spatiotemporal location explicit. A system of reference based on a location by way of latitude and longitude at Greenwich Mean Time. This solution is unsatisfactory, however. Suppose that the unique object that we wish to refer to is the Royal Observatory in Greenwich Park. The Meridian – the line of zero degrees longitude – is partially located at the Royal Observatory. The Royal

Observatory is one of the places on the Earth's surface where the Meridian is 'nailed down'. We cannot, on pain of circularity, apply a system of reference based on latitude and longitude at Greenwich Mean Time in order to make explicit the location of the Royal Observatory. That is, state both that the Royal Observatory is located at the Meridian *and* the Meridian is located at the Royal Observatory. Alternative means of specifying the Royal Observatory might be available, but establishing the required uniqueness of reference continues to be elusive (ibid., pp. 271-72).

Quine does *not* intend 'explication is elimination' to replace the idioms of ordinary language (§ 2.2). I conclude that the modal idioms of ordinary language are indexical in the sense that their truth-value is sensitive to the context of utterance. As a cognate of the phrase 'actual world', the content of a sentence in which the phrase 'ways things could have been' [but are not] appears is constituted by the context of utterance. This is the mark of an indexical term. As modal idioms of ordinary language or paraphrase thereof, these terms fail to satisfy the precepts of an 'eternal sentence'. These modal idioms are reducible – but not eliminable – to sentences of **PL**. The regimented paraphrase of 'ways things could have been' by 'possible world' preserves the context-sensitivity indicative of an indexical phrase.

2.6 Conclusion

I argue that the existential quantifier may be used to express the serious ontological commitments of ordinary language. That is, formal translation into the canonical notation of **PL** may be a sufficient but not a necessary condition of serious ontological discourse. In a probable departure from Quine, I argue that a paraphrase need not be regimented in order to yield translations that are trivial but informative. A paraphrase of F by G is trivial because it imposes no constraints on the world viz. the 'insubstantiality thesis' (§ 5.4). The synonymy of terms is nonetheless informative because F's ontological commitment to a type of entity K is identified by way of a conceptual reduction to G. In summary, Lewis' criteria of a genuine paraphrase (a-c) are identified. Modal idioms of ordinary language can indeed be paraphrased into the extensional idioms of ordinary language but is the paraphrase a genuine one? *If* these extensional idioms result in an ontological commitment to a controversial type of entity, then we may have breached one of the conditions of genuine paraphrase, condition (c). If a community of ordinary language users would *not* endorse an ontological commitment to possible world(s), then **S1** has failed to satisfy a necessary condition of a genuine paraphrase. In the alternative, I distinguish the paraphrase of 'ways things could have been' from an ontological commitment to possible worlds. The **S1** paraphrase of 'ways things could have been' may still pass criterion (c) on the grounds of linguistic convenience.

Lewis stipulates that one phrase – accepted by a community of ordinary language users – be abbreviated to a second, novel term of art. As the term 'possible world' can be interpreted in a number of different ways, this paraphrase manoeuvre seems to be innocuous (chapter five). An ontological commitment to a type of entity or 'possible world(s)' is another matter. The incredulity oft provoked by this commitment surrounds a particular interpretation of the term employed by the genuine realist (chapters three and four). In light of this distinction, I now attempt to identify the source of the incredulous stare that threatens the theoretical desideratum of accord with common sense judgement.

3

Beyond belief

"The question is this: is it crazy enough to be true?" Niels Bohr[1]

3.1 Introduction

Lewis' third criterion of a genuine paraphrase echoes a theoretical virtue often cited as a decisive reason to reject genuine modal realism **(GMR)**. The third criterion states that the proposed paraphrase be endorsed by a community of ordinary language-users. The usual – and perhaps normal – reaction to one's first encounter with **GMR** is incredulity. Sider, for example, comments: "Perhaps I speak for the majority when I say that I don't really know why I find the incredulous stare compelling; I only know that I do." (Sider 2003 [2003], p. 194) In this chapter, I examine the role played by common sense judgement – and the role that it *ought* to play – in the assessment of the theoretical virtues. I argue that Lewis' commitment to theoretical conservatism is a breach of his naturalist epistemology. Incredulity ought to prompt the reply made by Peter van Inwagen: "it seems to be the practice of scientists (one we philosophers should adopt) not to reject the only workable theory simply because that theory is (or seems to be) incredible." (van Inwagen 1986 [2001], p. 227) Naturalised epistemology maintains that there is no non-arbitrary distinction to be made between philosophy and science. As an advocate of naturalised epistemology, Lewis ought to deny common sense judgements a place at the table of reflective equilibrium. He consistently argues that the scientific picture of the world is not only *correct* but *complete* (Lewis 1994 [1999], p. 292). As a consequence, the only theoretical virtues we ought to consider in the philosophical process of reflective equilibrium are those of the natural sciences, especially physics. To object to the use of Bohr's quote – above – as misplaced in a philosophical thesis is to ignore Lewis' 'materialism'. As a materialist, Lewis states that "if we optimistically extrapolate the triumph of physics hitherto, we may provisionally accept that *all* fundamental properties and relations that *actually* occur are

---

[1] The quote is attributed to Niels Bohr by Marcus Chown (2001) *The Universe Next Door* Headline, p. xiv. Lewis' naturalistic epistemology commits philosophy to the same theoretical virtues as science (Nolan 2005, p. 7). I maintain that Lewis' commitment to theoretical conservatism is a breach of his naturalist epistemology.

physical." (Lewis 1994 [1999], p. 292 my emphasis: 1983a [1983], p. xi) [2] The fact that the *completeness* of physics only pertains to the *actual* world is not relevant. The important factor for my purposes is not the scope of the subject matter but the theoretical virtues that are recognised by the natural sciences: one aspect of naturalised epistemology is the thesis that there is no 'first philosophy'. There is no viewpoint 'outside' the natural sciences from which they can be critically assessed (Nolan 2005, p. 11). In the absence of a 'first philosophy', philosophers seem bound to observe the theoretical standards of the natural sciences.

Lewis argues, however, that a standard to which philosophical theories ought to be held but from which – presumably – scientific theories are exempt is theoretical conservatism. For Lewis, any philosophical theory that offends against common sense judgement incurs a defeasible cost.

> It's not that the folk know in their blood what highfalutin' philosophers may forget. And it's not that common sense speaks with the voice of some infallible faculty of 'intuition'. It's just that theoretical conservatism is the only sensible policy for theorists of limited powers, who are duly modest about what they could accomplish after a fresh start. Part of this conservatism is reluctance to accept theories that fly in the face of common sense. But it's a matter of balance and judgement. (Lewis 1986a, p. 134: 1983a [1983], p. x: 1996a [1999], p. 433: cf. Cappelen 2012)

What 'type of case' is the theoretical postulation of a plurality of worlds? Does an 'infallible faculty of "intuition"' supply an indefeasible reason to dismiss the notion out-of-hand? Is there a more nuanced view that grants common sense judgement a defeasible plausibility? These are the questions to be addressed in this chapter. How certain is the 'intuition' that renders the postulation of a plurality of worlds incredible? Do the folk know in their blood what the highfalutin' philosophers have forgotten? I aim to identify the source of Sider's incredulity and satisfy Lewis' third criterion of genuine paraphrase.

Incredulity toward a plurality of worlds can be demonstrated by way of three sentences. Three types of sentences can be distinguished on the grounds of their – putative – assertion of a common sense judgement:

---

[2] Lewis shares Quine's naturalism in respect of the correctness and the completeness of the scientific world view (Nolan 2005, pp. 7 ff.). Recent commentators appear to concur; Williamson argues in favour of "a conception of theories in logic and metaphysics as scientific theories, to be assessed by the same overall standards as theories in other branches of science." (Williamson 2013, p. 27) Williamson explores the implications of these preliminary remarks in chapters three, six and Afterword of that work.

A1: It is possible that talking donkeys exist

A2: There are no actual talking donkeys

A3: There is a talking donkey at a possible world

A1 is an assertion of genuine realism and common sense judgement. **A2** also appears to be an assertion of genuine realism and common sense judgement, given an indexical understanding of the term 'actual' (§§ 2.5 & 5.3) (Lewis 1986a, pp. 97-101: cf. Soames 2007).[3] **A3**, on the other hand, is true by the lights of genuine realism but false by the lights of common sense judgement. The divergence of opinion at **A3** is based on the postulation of a plurality of worlds other than the actual world. **A3** is an assertion by the genuine realist of what common sense judgement denies, namely the existence of non-actual talking donkeys premised on the existence of non-actual worlds.

Lewis maintains that common sense *knowledge* can be philosophically relevant in one of two ways (Lewis 1996a [1999], p. 418): firstly, in the context of everyday conversation, we all know many things. I know that pandas eat bamboo. I know that there were only four TV channels available in the United Kingdom, but now there are many more. I know that Hull FC won the 2016 and 2017 Rugby League Challenge Cup finals. We each possess a reservoir of context-sensitive knowledge. The 'folk knowledge' that we all possess in the context of everyday life can evaporate with a change in context, e.g., from the Clapham Omnibus to the philosophy seminar. Hence, Lewis acknowledges a second type of knowledge that no philosophical argument can dislodge. Indubitable knowledge of a 'Moorean fact' is immune from the vagaries of sceptical doubt in virtue of the principle of differential certainty: we are more certain of the truth of a Moorean fact than we are of any premise of a philosophical argument deployed in order to cast doubt upon it (cf. Unger 1975: Stroud 1984). For the purpose of exposition, I stipulate that Moorean facts constitute the core of our knowledge, while broader folk knowledge pertains to those facts that are non-Moorean. I distinguish, therefore, three types of common sense judgement: indubitable knowledge of Moorean facts, defeasible or folk knowledge of non-Moorean facts, and a peripheral 'web of belief'. In order to identify the source of Sider's incredulity, I must first identify against which of these three categories the postulation of a plurality of worlds offends.

Lewis argues that **GMR** offers the *best* philosophical explanation of our common sense modal beliefs (cf. Stalnaker 1976/1984 [2003], pp. 26 ff.). I begin

---

[3] Alternatively, Stalnaker accepts the indexicality of the term 'actual' as a semantic thesis but rejects the metaphysical thesis of a plurality of concrete worlds (§ 5.3) (Stalnaker 1976/1984 (2003), pp. 27 ff.)

by identifying the type of theoretical conservatism endorsed by Lewis (§ 3.2). In order to isolate the source of Sider's incredulity, I examine the claim that 'there is only one world or universe' qualifies as a Moorean fact. The degree of certainty associated with knowledge of a Moorean fact is 'negational absurdity'. In short, to deny a Moorean fact is absurd. I find that the denial of the claim is not absurd and does not meet the certainty required of a Moorean fact. I then scrutinise the criterion of 'negational absurdity' through the prism of the cautious man (§ 3.3). I then examine an alternative source of the incredulity. If the claim 'there is only one world or universe' is *not* a Moorean fact, does it count as folk knowledge. I stipulate that folk knowledge can be identified – in part – as knowledge that *is* dependent on specialised or technical terminology. Genuine realism does depend on specialised or technical terminology and so the claim may be an instance of folk knowledge (§ 3.4). The final alternative in the search for the source of incredulity is the 'web of belief'. I argue that Lewis' philosophical interest in common sense belief is not in terms of any potential evidential value but is rather an attempt to align *his* beliefs or intuitions with reality (Lewis 1983a [1983], p. x) (§ 3.5). I conclude that the incredulity objection is misplaced. The claim that 'there is only one world or universe' is merely one aspect of a shared belief about a non-Moorean fact. As such, the claim is defeasible in the face of countervailing factors such as theoretical simplicity. Common sense beliefs are subject to change, say, on the basis of the introduction of new terminology (§ 3.6).

3.2 Moorean facts and theoretical conservatism

The claim that *some* statements, namely those used to express our common sense knowledge of the world, are philosophically significant can be traced back to antiquity.[4] The claim is adopted by G. E. Moore (Moore 1925 [1993]: 1939 [1993]) in his attempt to demonstrate that he knew with certainty the truth of a number of contingent propositions. That is to say, 'contingent' propositions that we know with certainty to be true. The certainty ascribed to these propositions contrasts with the certainty demanded by Descartes. Certain truth in the Cartesian sense is immunity from *all* doubt. The set of contingent propositions that Moore holds with certainty to be true, on the other hand, are those insulted against philosophical theories – such as Scepticism and Idealism

---

[4] Aristotle, for example, argues: "As with other topics we must first set out how things appear to be, and then, after developing the problems '*aporia*', go on to prove the truth, if possible, of all the common beliefs '*exdoxa*' about the matters in question, or failing that, of the majority of them and the most authoritative. For if we can solve the problems while leaving common beliefs untouched, we shall have proved the case sufficiently" (cited in J. L. Ackrill (1981) *Aristotle the Philosopher* Clarendon Press, page 12).

– employed to cast doubt on them. Moore opens "A Defence of Common Sense" with a diverse list – designated List (1) – of propositions that relate to his mind, his body, and other physical objects that he claims to know with certainty to be true (Moore 1925 [1993], pp. 107-08). They include the propositions that "There exists at present a living human body, which is *my* body … Ever since it was born, it has been either in contact with or not far from the surface of the earth;" (ibid., p. 107). He then states – as a single proposition (2) – that many other people share in respect of their own minds, their bodies, and other physical objects a similar reservoir of propositions that they know with certainty to be true (ibid., pp. 108-09). Moore concedes that although he knows with certainty that many of these contingent propositions are 'truisms' he does not know *how* he knows them. His defence of common sense is not, therefore, foundational in the epistemological sense (ibid., p. 118).

It seems probable (Nolan 2005, p. 208), that Lewis adopted the notion of a 'Moorean fact' from Armstrong (cited in Lewis 1983d [1999], p. 20). Lewis includes amongst the instances of a Moorean fact the fact that we enjoy numerous instances of "folk knowledge" (Lewis 1996a [1999], p. 418). Furthermore, we have knowledge of the sameness of type, e.g., that two objects share the same shape (Lewis 1983d [1999], pp. 20 ff.), that language has a broadly determinate interpretation (ibid., p. 47) and that any attempt to deny the law of non-contradiction "should be dismissed just because the hypothesis it invites us to entertain is inconsistent." (Lewis 1982 [1998], p. 101) In addition, our knowledge of the psychophysics of colour is – approximately – true; we know that objects are coloured, that they retain their colour – as a property – even when they are not observed, and that colour is determined by sense perception (Lewis 1997 [1999], p. 333). Hence, there is a core of contingently true propositions knowledge of which qualifies as knowledge of Moorean facts.

Do these candidates share a common feature or characteristic? Although a canonical definition has proven elusive, a number of potential features have been suggested as indicative. Logical truths – at least those that are knowable – are prime candidates. As a formal criterion, however, logical truth fails to capture the peculiarity of the contingently true propositions enumerated by Moore. The claim that 'the Earth has *not* existed for more than 100 years' may be odd, but it is not logically inconsistent. Armstrong suggests that a Moorean fact is "one of the many facts that even philosophers should not deny, whatever philosophical analysis they give of such facts." (cited in Lewis 1983d [1999], p. 20) Armstrong's criterion is unsatisfactory, however; "presumably, *any* truth has some claim to be something that 'even philosophers should not deny'." (Nolan 2005, p. 208) Elsewhere, Lewis suggests that to deny a Moorean fact is symptomatic of a "philosophical (or scientific) error" (Lewis 1997 [1999], p. 333) and "to doubt [a Moorean fact] would be absurd" (Lewis 1996a [1999], p. 418). Shortly,

I will distinguish the notions of 'error' and 'absurdity' in order to explicate the notion of a Moorean fact. I argue that to deny a Moorean fact results in absurdity, not error. It is the absurdity of denial that gives the test of differential certainty its epistemic bite: "[a Moorean fact is] one of those things that we know [with certainty] better than we know the premise of *any* philosophical argument to the contrary." (ibid., p. 418 my emphasis) Before I embark on this endeavour I examine the notion of theoretical conservatism.

Lewis advocates a *weak* form of theoretical conservatism. Theoretical conservatism is a principle of philosophical methodology that states that pre-philosophical judgements ought to be accorded a privileged status even *after* our deliberations are complete. Theoretical conservatism is a standard that grants philosophical theory its plausibility. Thus predisposed, a philosopher presented with the ontological commitments of **GMR** is likely left incredulous. That is, **GMR's** analysis of modality generates a set of beliefs in the existence of entities that have nothing to do with common sense judgement. I designate Lewis' theoretical conservatism 'weak' because it is defeasible in the face of other theoretical virtues weighed in the process of reflective equilibrium.

It may be objected that as a virtue theoretical conservatism is flawed. The flaw pertains to the notion of reliability. The problem of reliability is best illustrated in respect of a common sense *belief*. Christensen, for example, invites us to consider the case of the opinionated coin-flipper (cited in Daly 2010, p. 21). The coin-flipper flips what he believes to be a fair coin and, without looking at the outcome, forms the opinion that it has landed on heads. The mere fact that he has formed this opinion does not justify his belief that the coin did land on heads. He is simply dogmatic. Theoretical conservatism, however, states that the coin-flipper has a reason to hold this belief and that his belief is justified. The coin-flipper's unreliable belief that the coin landed on heads certainly has a cause, say, his obstinate attitude. The causal origins of his belief do not generate a justification for his holding it, however. Additionally, under a traditional conception of knowledge – as justified true belief – the coin-flipper's belief does not qualify as knowledge and so cannot amount to knowledge of a Moorean fact (cf. Lewis 1996a [1999], p. 421).

As a counter-example to theoretical conservatism, the case of the obstinate coin-flipper is based on the problem of reliability. Its potency is mitigated if we adjust to instances of knowledge claims based on common sense judgement. Knowledge of a Moorean fact is indubitable by way of differential certainty: it outweighs, so to speak, the certainty of any premise of an argument deployed in order to cast doubt upon it. Hence, if knowledge of 'there is only one world or universe' is knowledge of a Moorean fact, then Lewis' method of reflective equilibrium is in vain. There is – in principal – no philosophical or scientific argument that could be used to cast doubt upon it. However, Lewis acknowledges both Moorean facts and theoretical conservatism as a theoretical virtue. This suggests that 'there is only one world or universe' is *not* a Moorean fact, in his opinion. If, on the other hand, the claim is considered to be an instance of folk knowledge it may be true but defeasible. Understood as such, knowledge of this 'fact' appears to be a prime candidate of weak theoretical conservatism (Lewis 1986a, p. 134). Folk knowledge of this fact is defeasible since it might be overturned in the presence of countervailing theoretical virtues. Hence, my examination of the incredulous stare turns on an evaluation of this putative 'fact' as an instance of one of three types of common sense judgement: as knowledge of a Moorean fact, as folk knowledge of a non-Moorean fact, and as the content of a shared belief.

3.3 The absurdity of denial

All Moorean facts are indubitable. Not indubitable in the Cartesian sense of doubt, as a species of thought, but in the sense of differential certainty. I must now discharge a possible equivocation in regard to Moorean facts as either a case of Cartesian 'necessity' or Moorean 'contingency' – together with their respective scare quotes. Any putative fact must be epistemically 'necessary' in order to qualify as a Moorean fact. That is, a 'fact' is counted as Moorean in those circumstances were if it is known by anybody, then it is known by everybody. Furthermore, Lewis' weak theoretical conservatism admits to countervailing virtues that are irrelevant in the case of a Moorean fact. I will proceed on the supposition that **MF** is a Moorean fact:

MF: There is only one world or universe

I also offer **T1** as a definition of the core membership of the common sense *weltbild*:

> **T1:** A proposition p is a core member of the common sense weltbild – and thereby S knows with certainty that p is true – if, and only if, the truth of p is made true by a Moorean fact. (Moore 1925 [1993], p. 119)[5]

---

[5] I do not address many of Lewis' substantial contributions to philosophy in this chapter. My concern is to identify the source of the incredulous stare expressed by critics of GMR. Lewis' philosophical analysis of knowledge, belief, proposition or truth-maker draws upon the resources of GMR as a component of the analysans. I therefore remain silent in respect of these contributions: for example, Lewis (1998, 2001) initially is suspicious of the Truthmaker Principle on Humean grounds – an 'innocent' but required assumption of a necessary connection between wholly distinct existents – that a proposition p is made true by a thing t whose mere existence necessitates the truth of p. Lewis subsequently embraced a version of the principle by way of the 'qua' locution (Lewis 2003 [2003], pp.

If the object of knowledge – that which is known – is a Moorean fact, then we cannot fail but to know it (ibid., p. 119). This high standard of epistemic privilege secures immunity from 'reasonable doubt': we are more certain of the truth of **MF** than of any premise that could be deployed in order to doubt it. To illustrate, consider two lists of sentences as potential candidates for core membership of the common sense weltbild (Stroll 1994, pp. 33-34):

List A:

1. The Universe is very old
2. My desk is made of wood
3. I am a human being
4. Blood flows through my body
5. Human beings experience emotion: they can be happy, sad, worried, hopeful, etc.

List B:

1. The Universe is 13.8 billion years old
2. There exist many different things in the Universe, all of which are constructed from elements listed in the Periodic table
3. The Universe is expanding
4. The Magna Carta was signed in 1215
5. Human life begins fourteen days after conception

In order to distinguish Moorean facts I employ the notion of 'negational absurdity' (Wittgenstein 1953 [1969], G.E.M. Anscombe & G.H. von Wright (eds.) *On Certainty* Blackwell: Sections 185-190). Wittgenstein employs the technique of negational absurdity in order to distinguish a mistake from an aberration. A mistake or error occurs when we follow the normal procedure but go astray at some point: I am asked to count the chairs in the auditorium. I complete the task and calculate that there are 299 chairs when in fact, there are 300. The circumstance of a mistake is distinguished from the case of a paranoid who believes that her drink has been poisoned by an unknown assailant. She has not made a mistake when she discovers that her drink is, in fact, safe. Rather, she is suffering from a conceptual aberration or misunderstanding. Moore claims to know that the Earth has existed many years before he was

---

30-31). The 'qua' locution may generate a more demanding form of the counterpart relation relative to which A is essentially such that A is F (Beebee & McBride 2015, pp. 227-30 for further discussion).

born. How does he know? Moore is unable to justify this type of knowledge claim. In the absence of a justification, is the counter-claim warranted – that the Earth sparked into existence 150 years ago? Possibly, although we presume that the counter-claim is false, it remains logically possible. Moore concedes the point but maintains that the counter-claim is nonetheless absurd. A claim to know is negationally absurd if "it runs counter to what we all know, that is, runs counter to that sort of primordial proposition we call the common sense view of the world" (Stroll 1994, p. 45). The first point to notice here is that Stroll restricts the phrase 'we all know' to knowledge of Moorean facts. If he had not, then the denial of *any* knowledge claim that 'we all know' would be negationally absurd! Instead, any proposition – whose truth is determined by a Moorean fact – subsequently discovered to be 'false' would render the world incomprehensible. Hence, the denial of any proposition whose truth is determined by a Moorean fact has this property of negational absurdity. The denial of any proposition in List A is negationally absurd, for example. The propositions of List A are amongst the core members of the common sense weltbild. The denial of a proposition in List B, on the other hand, is *not* negationally absurd and so they are not numbered among the core members of the common sense weltbild.

Does **MF** satisfy the criterion of negational absurdity characteristic of a Moorean fact? Consider the denial of **MF** designated **(dMF)**;

dMF: (It is not the case) that there is only one world or universe

At first blush, **dMF** appears to be a little odd. There is, however, an interpretation of theoretical physics which states that even though **dMF** is odd, it is nonetheless true. The Everett interpretation of quantum mechanics indicates that: "when we do take it [quantum mechanics] literally, the world turns out to be rather larger than we had anticipated: indeed, it turns out that our classical 'world' is only a small part of a much larger reality." (Wallace 2012, p. 13) The Everett interpretation of quantum mechanics is believed to be true albeit by a minority of physicists. One implication of the Everett interpretation is that there are many universes. Hence, the scientific postulation of many universes is a plausible one. As a consequence, even if the truth of **dMF** is disputed, it is not absurd (by the Everett interpretation of quantum mechanics). **MF** is denied by a faction of the scientific community without absurdity, and so by the standard of negational absurdity, it does *not* express a Moorean fact.

Does this example of a scientific interpretation of quantum mechanics establish my conclusion? Aren't we more certain of **MF** than of any premise of a scientific argument deployed to refute it? In order to establish the veracity of a scientific interpretation to challenge the status of **MF** as a putative Moorean fact, recall List A. I propose that any scientific or philosophical theory that denied the truth of a proposition in List A would be widely rejected. "If a science were to develop, as some eliminativist materialists suggest, which flatly denied that people have feelings, are or have ever been in love, and so on, such a 'science' would be discredited. Here common sense is dominant." (Stroll 1994, p. 35) If **MF** were indeed a proposition at the core of the common sense weltbild then knowledge of its truth would be indubitable on the grounds of differential certainty. "If there is a role for science in this domain, it is to add to and not subtract from that which everyone knows." (ibid., p. 35) Unlike eliminativist materialism, the Everett interpretation of quantum mechanics supplements theoretical physics with a multiverse that is coherently believable. If **MF** were indeed a Moorean fact, then this interpretation of quantum mechanics would be incoherent.

In reply, it might be objected that the criterion of negational absurdity does not carry the philosophical weight I require of it. An alternative third way, between mistake and aberration, might be available to confound the criterion of negational absurdity. Crispin Wright offers a thought experiment that could provide a safe passage between the Scylla of mistake and the Charybdis of aberration – the Cautious Man. The origins of the Cautious Man are found in Wright's critique of a supposed 'special' faculty used in the recognition of a necessary truth. The faculty under investigation is one of "a *special* certainty [enjoyed], at least in a wide class of fundamental cases, by our apprehension of necessity, it is easy enough to call it into question; rather harder to see how it might actually be demonstrated to be wrong." (Wright 1980, p. 446) The cautious attitude is intended to show that this alleged faculty does not exist. To illustrate the point, Wright suggests that we consider a relatively straightforward case of necessary entailment – the rule of conjunction elimination (**CE**). The rule of **CE** justifies the inference of a conjunct from a conjunction in which it appears, e.g., 'P' from 'P & Q'. Wright invites us to consider the following conditional statement of **CE**: ((P v Q) & (P v R)), therefore P v Q. "In order intelligibly *not* to accept such a proof, a person does not have to do anything which will indicate a lack of understanding or misunderstanding or a mistake. A quite different possibility will be his adoption of … [a] cautious attitude to the thing." (ibid., pp. 452-53) Traditionally, **CE** is logically valid. There is – and indeed could not be – a valid counter-instance of **CE**: if the premise is true, the conclusion *must* be true. However, the Cautious Man is reluctant to assert the logical *necessity* of that entailment.

Is the Cautious Man's reluctance the result of an error or mistake? No. The Cautious Man is aware of the correct procedure to follow in regard to **CE** – just as I was aware of the correct procedure when counting chairs in the auditorium. Hence, his reticence is not a mistake on procedural grounds. He is simply reluctant to assert the kind of necessity usually associated with logical entailment. He understands the basis of the proof, the process by which we arrive at the conclusion and accepts the outcome. His 'failure to follow the proof' is simply a reluctance to assert the logical necessity that we presume holds between the individual steps – basis, process, and outcome.

> He would [simply] refuse to regard the capacity of a proof apparently to survive arbitrary close scrutiny as a sufficient ground for saying that such a conditional expresses an *essential* truth; his acceptance of proofs would always be provisional in the way our acceptance of any hypothesis is provisional - proofs would never impress him as possessing the special cogency with which they impress other men. (ibid., p. 453)

If, on the other hand, there is no mistake or error then could a reluctance to assert the necessity of logical entailment be an aberration? Almost certainly not. The Cautious Man is willing to accept the correctness of each individual step in the proof; he grants the obscurity of any attempt to 'correct' **CE** on procedure grounds and concedes that repeating the proof would yield the same conclusion. He – merely – "dispute[s] that there is anything in all that which justifies him in claiming to have apprehended any essential connection between basis, process and outcome" (ibid., p. 455). The Cautious Man's reluctance to assert the necessity of **CE** is not an aberration. The mere possibility of the cautious attitude in the case of a logical necessity indicates that a similar reluctance to assert the *truth* of a Moorean fact may *not* result in absurdity. The criterion of negational absurdity is weakened. **MF** may still qualify as a Moorean fact. A reluctance to assert – rather than flatly deny – the 'necessity' of logical entailment need not result in absurdity (see chapter six).

Sider's incredulity appears to originate in the indubitability of a particular Moorean fact, **MF**. As such, no premise of any philosophical or scientific argument could dislodge the certainty of **MF**. It might be anticipated, therefore, that Sider would prefer a 'strong' type of indefeasible conservatism. That is a type of conservatism defined as indefeasible or immune from any philosophical or scientific doubt. Lewis advocates a 'weak' form of conservatism, however; one defeasible in light of alternative virtues. His approach is indicative of a repudiation of **MF** as a possible Moorean fact.

I now turn, therefore, to an exploration of the second supposition; that **MF** falls into the category of 'folk knowledge'. In this section, I examined one proposed criterion of a Moorean fact – negational absurdity. By this criterion, the denial of **MF** should result in absurdity, but it does not. Although the truth of the Everett interpretation is disputed by scientific experts, it is not intellectually absurd. In the alternative, the Cautious Man's attitude in the case of the logical necessity of entailment suggests that my preference for negational absurdity as a criterion is at least questionable. If assent to examples of logical necessity can be coherently withheld, then perhaps the denial of a Moorean fact – an epistemic necessity – may *not* result in absurdity. It is unlikely that

Lewis would be persuaded by Wright's thought-experiment, however. Lewis' 'weak' theoretical conservatism implies that knowledge of **MF** is defeasible, and so is not subject to the test of differential certainty.

3.4 The criterion of specialised or technical terms

Lewis argues that common sense knowledge is not limited to knowledge of Moorean facts. In the context of everyday life, we know many things that are not factive in the Moorean sense, e.g., that Hull FC won the 2016 and 2017 Rugby League Challenge Cup finals.

> **T2:** A proposition p may be a member of the common sense weltbild – and thereby S may or may not know that p is an instance of folk knowledge – if, and only if, the truth of p is *not* made true by a Moorean-fact. (Lewis 1996a [1999], p. 418)

The 'common sense weltbild' is the common sense conception of the world. **T2** can be utilised to test a new supposition; that **MF** is a non-Moorean fact. I may know a non-Moorean fact even if you do not know it – and vice versa. To reflect this change, I re-designate **MF** as **FK.**

> **FK:** There is only one world or universe

FK should be understood as an instance of folk knowledge. A number of criteria have been proposed, the satisfaction of which identify a particular fact as Moorean. In the previous section, I employed the criterion of 'negational absurdity'. This criterion was subsequently blocked by the 'cautious attitude' outlined by Wright. I now propose new criteria from which to derive the means to identify a non-Moorean fact. Although the common sense conception of the world includes Moorean facts, my intention in this section is to examine those facts that are an element of this conception but *not* Moorean. The criterion I adopt is derived from William Lycan's criteria of a Moorean fact. The criterion will help to identify the defeasible knowledge of non-Moorean facts: 'folk knowledge' of facts that *partially* constitute the common sense weltbild.

Lycan nominates a number of criteria that he argues are individually necessary and collectively sufficient to identify a Moorean-fact (cited in Daly 2010, pp. 18-19):

1. It is 'about something noted by someone at a particular time and place'
2. That the claim is an instance of a more general claim that most people would accept if it were put to them
3. That neither the claim nor the generalisation use any specialised or technical terms
4. That it is difficult to give up accepting the generalisation

5. That it would sound strange to assert the generalisation because it is so obvious, and

6. That it would be peculiar to deny the generalisation

I propose to identify a *non*-Moorean fact on the basis of a criterion derived from the above list. That is, a claim to know that p will be an instance of 'folk knowledge' if, and only if, at least one of Lycan's criteria is *not* satisfied: specifically, the third criterion that precludes 'all specialised or technical terms' from the analysans of a Moorean fact. In short, in order to qualify as 'folk knowledge,' I must establish that the phrase 'possible world' *is* a specialised or technical term. Lycan's third criterion deals explicitly with the use of language. My interest is in the use of the phrase 'possible world' as a philosophical term of art. I argue that the phrase is either a technical or semi-technical term, and so my criterion of folk knowledge – derived from Lycan's third criterion – is satisfied. **FK** is an example of folk knowledge. Lewis' weak form of theoretical conservatism permits the incredulous stare objection to detract from genuine realism without being decisive against it.

I allow for the possibility that a specialised or technical term may be explicable by way of ordinary language. This admits the possibility that an ordinary language predicate F may be derived from expert terminology (chapters one and two). Recall the true propositions of List B (§ 3.3). Some of these sentences include the use of specialised or technical terms, the meaning of which is established by scientific research programmes: "The average person comes to acquire these pieces of information not by any investigation he or she has pursued but secondhand, as it were, for example, by hearing or reading news accounts of such inquiries." (Stroll 1994, p. 34) The truth of these propositions is established by a community of experts (cf. Williamson 2007, pp. 94 ff.). Contrast the sentences of List A that do not employ specialised or technical terminology and whose truth is not established by experts.

In addition, recall that Lewis' original paper (1968 [1983]) is motivated by a desire to retain our normal practice of translation – that is, of ordinary language into predicate logic (**PL**) instead of by way of quantified modal logic (**QML**). Provisionally, I discount Lewis' modal translation scheme as a candidate of 'folk knowledge'. As a normative discipline, the correct use of formal logic requires a degree of expertise that can only be acquired through training (Williamson 2007, pp. 103 ff.). Formal languages, such as **QML** and **PL**, are the preserve of experts. The interpretation of logical notation requires a degree of expertise. Despite the 'ignorance' of the man on the Clapham Omnibus and if we eschew fatalism[6] modal notions are nonetheless embedded in the language and thought of everyday life. Reality is more than a collection of entities with varying properties and relations – reality includes what could or could not be, what must or must not be, and what should or should not be. We may fear or hope for the future, celebrate or regret the past, adopt a healthier lifestyle, develop our intellectual abilities, educate the young, construct roads and bridges, etc. In the context of everyday life, we 'project' a wide spectrum of modal knowledge and beliefs that pertain to how the world must, could or should be. Modal notions may be expressed in the idioms of ordinary language, e.g., **A1** 'It is possible that talking donkeys exist' (§ 3.1). What of sentences such as **A3**; 'There is a talking donkey at a possible world'? That is, sentences that are couched in the idioms of ordinary language *and* function as the analysans of **A1**? Do the artificial expressions of formal logic, such as the predicate expression 'Wx', derive their meaning from ordinary language or vice versa (§ 2.2)?

GMR employs a number of specialised or technical terms that are the preserve of experts. Several technical 'primitive' concepts are employed in order to explicate the conceptual, ontological, and semantic implications of possible world talk: *individual, set, part of, similar to* and *spatiotemporally related to* (Divers 2002, p. 46). If the artificial symbols of formal logic derive their meaning – interpretation – from ordinary language, then Lewis provides a 'semi-technical' explication of modality conducive to **FK** (Lewis 1986a). For example, take a primitive concept of genuine realism; 'similar to'. Lewis argues that the counterpart relation can be understood in terms of the primitive concept 'similar to'. He also claims that our ability to recognise 'sameness of type' is a Moorean fact (§ 3.2). It might be tempting to conflate these two concepts; especially if the latter is understood as a case of qualitative identity. This temptation should be resisted, however. Clearly, the relational term 'sameness of type' is not equivalent to the counterpart relation of 'similar to'. Identity or sameness is transitive, similarity is not (Lewis 1968 [1983], p. 28). The Moorean fact that we recognise that three distinct objects are of the 'same' type is not equivalent to the recognition that three distinct objects are of a 'similar' type.

If, on the other hand, the meaning of ordinary language terms is derived from the artificial symbols of formal logic, then Lewis could be said to offer a 'technical' explication of modality conducive to folk knowledge. That is, 'technical' in the sense that the meanings of logical symbols are conceptually prior to their meaning in ordinary language (§ 2.2). Again, let the primitive

---

[6] Forbes argues that the plausibility of fatalism is based on the failure to distinguish the invalid (p→□p) from the valid □ (p → p) (Forbes 1985, p. 7).

concept 'similar to' act as an exemplar; Lewis provides a number of principles that we ought to observe whenever this concept is employed, e.g., the rule of accommodation (Lewis 1986a, p. 251). With respect to a counterfactual statement, for example, we may truly assert that Caesar would have used the atomic bomb – if he had one. Alternatively, we may truly deny that he would have used the atomic bomb and assert that he would have preferred the use of catapults (Lewis 1973, p. 67: 1970 [1983]: 1979 [1983]). The context of utterance affects not only the precision of what is asserted but also the weight we ascribe to each point of comparative similarity. The genuine realist's reservoir of primitive concepts may be deemed as either 'technical' or 'semi-technical'. *If* the technical terms of counterpart theory derive their interpretation – meaning – from the artificial symbols of formal logic, *then* we require a context of utterance in order to evaluate their use, e.g., **A2** 'There are no actual talking donkeys' may be deemed indexical (§ 2.5).

Hence, the phrase 'possible world' and the predicate expression 'Wx' or 'x is a possible world' may be interpreted in one of two ways. If the predicate expression derives its interpretation – meaning – from the ordinary language phrase, then the modal translation scheme employs a semi-technical vocabulary. If, on the other hand, the phrase derives its interpretation – meaning – from the logical predicate, then the translation scheme employs a technical vocabulary. Either way, the use of the ordinary language phrase proceeds on the basis of folk knowledge. A non-specialist may use phrases that are derived from the vocabulary of experts to express folk knowledge. The number of universes may be a point of contention among the folk just as it is among highfalutin' philosophers!

It might be objected that scientific and philosophical terminologies are the product of two quite different types of enterprise. To conflate the 'specialised or technical terms' of science with those of philosophy is erroneous. What reason is there to suppose that the endless deliberations of armchair philosophers should be accorded the plausibility of theoretical physics? Moore, for example, argues that there is "no good reason to suppose" (Moore 1925 [1993], pp. 119-20) that any 'physical facts' logically or causally depend on 'mental facts'. Broadly, Idealism is a philosophical theory that invokes a reduction of the physical qualities and spatial relations of objects to the subject's experience (e.g. of sense data). Most non-philosophers would be baffled by this analysis – what are sense data? Do sense data require the existence of physical objects? The 'ordinary' man or woman would consider Moore's common sense claims far more plausible than the Idealistic analysis of them! However, this criticism has no traction. Most journeymen on the Clapham Omnibus would find Moore's common sense claims more plausible than the explanation of them presented by theoretical physics, i.e., that 'atoms mostly consist of empty air'.

The philosophical-scientific dichotomy is false. Those persuaded that theoretical conservatism is a virtue require a non-arbitrary distinction between philosophy and science to support the idea that conservatism *should* apply in the former case but not the latter. A distinction might be drawn on the basis of methodology, for example. It might be argued that the natural sciences employ empirical investigation, which is capable of debunking common sense 'knowledge'. The highly abstract arguments of philosophers, on the other hand, enjoy a degree of immunity from empirical discovery. In the absence of the possibility of empirical falsification, the burden of proof placed on philosophy before the tribunal of common sense judgement is greater than that of science. Unfortunately, this distinction is ad hoc, i.e., absent a principled reason that grants the results of empirical inquiry epistemic authority. The methods employed by natural scientists, particularly theoretical physicists, include thought experiments and abstract argument. Erwin Schrodinger would soon have exhausted his supply of cats were he required to replicate his thought experiment with actual felines! By parity, Lewis' explanation of *how* we know that a non-actual cat would suffer the same fate is based on reasoning from first principles and imagination (Lewis 1986a, pp. 113-14).

I argue that the modal translation scheme can be expressed in the idioms of ordinary language. The primitive predicate expressions of modal translation can be considered to be 'technical' or 'semi-technical'. The use of specialised or technical terminology is a breach of Lycan's third criterion of a Moorean fact. I conclude, therefore, that the use of a specialised/technical term is indicative of knowledge of a non-Moorean fact. If we admit common sense judgements as a theoretical virtue, it appears that Lewis' weak form of conservatism supports this conclusion. The source of the incredulous stare is a pre-theoretical claim to know **FK** as an instance of folk knowledge: knowledge defeasible in the light of countervailing theoretical virtues. I have examined and (potentially) identified the source of the incredulous stare. Knowledge of the fact (if a fact it be) that 'there is only one world or universe' may be Moorean or folk. These two types of knowledge are mutually exclusive and collective exhaustive. However, Lewis' famous **S1** declaration does not pertain to knowledge but to a shared belief. It is a shared *belief* in a type of entity, namely, the 'ways things could have been' that prompts the argument from paraphrase. Is the paraphrase of 'ways things could have been' innocuous? I defer an answer to this question for later (chapter four). Meanwhile, I address the alleged methodological role of belief in philosophical theory. Does a shared belief in 'possible worlds' constitute *evidence* in favour of **GMR**? "It is the reasonableness of modal beliefs which I think Lewis's extreme realism cannot account for." (Stalnaker 1976/1984 [2003], p. 31)

3.5 The evidential value of modal beliefs

S1 is perhaps one of the most famous – or, if you prefer, notorious – statements in modern philosophy. What is the status – in respect of common sense judgement – of beliefs that pertain to the 'ways things could have been'? It is tempting to infer that Lewis cites his shared belief in a type of entity as *evidence* in support of **GMR**. He argues that beliefs are intuitions (Lewis 1983a [1983], p. x). This minimalist account is supported by Peter van Inwagen: "Our 'intuitions' are simply our beliefs – or perhaps, in some cases, the tendencies that make certain beliefs attractive to us, that 'move' us in the direction of accepting certain propositions without taking us all the way to acceptance." (van Inwagen 1997 [2001], p. 149) If this is correct, then a dependency on intuition is not the exclusive preserve of philosophy. Scientific progress is fuelled by the intuitions of scientists (Williamson 2007, p. 215). Despite this commonality, the allegation that intuitions play or should play an evidential role in the ontological commitment to a plurality of worlds is problematic. Why should Lewis' idiosyncratic doxastic states justify such a bizarre metaphysical claim? The answer is simple – they shouldn't, and they don't.

Lewis refuses "to take language as a starting point in the analysis of thought *and of modality*." (Lewis 1983a [1983], p. xi my emphasis) As a materialist, Lewis holds that there is a mind-independent reality composed of stuff. The metaphysical theories we construct are the result of a process of reflective equilibrium where mature 'post-theoretic' intuitions are generated.[7] To suggest that Lewis postulates a plurality of worlds because that is what his pre-theoretical intuitions tell him is to put the cart before the horse; rather, his *best* philosophical theory – partially composed of his intuitions – is aligned with a pre-existing, mind-independent reality consisting of a plurality of worlds. Hence, Williamson's general concern over a conceptual gap between the content of our intuitions and their putative truth does not apply in Lewis' case (Williamson 2007, p. 215).

The evidential value of intuitions might be weakened to one of mere consistency. That is, plausible philosophical theories should be consistent with our shared intuitions. The plausibility of a philosophical theory is measured by

---

[7] The 'belief in' procedure that I defend is best summarised by Quine: "My point is not that ordinary language is slipshod, slipshod though it be. We must recognize this grading off for what it is, and recognize that a fenced ontology is just not implicit in ordinary language. The idea of a boundary between being and nonbeing is a philosophical idea, an idea of technical science in a broad sense. Scientists and philosophers seek a comprehensive system of the world, and one that is orientated to reference even more squarely and utterly than ordinary language. Ontological concern is not a correction of a lay thought and practice; it is foreign to the lay culture, though an outgrowth of it." (Quine 1981a (1981), p. 9)

way of an accord with common sense judgement (Lewis 1986a, p. 134). Generally, 'consistency' is a relation that exists between items, e.g., propositions (Williamson 2007, p. 209). Williamson does observe that an asserted proposition may be true and yet *inconsistent* with the evidence – understood as our shared intuitions. Indeed, this is the status of **GMR**: a 'belief in' the existence of a type of entity K is true and *inconsistent* with common sense judgements. If the content of a belief is the proposition P that 'there is only one world or universe', then P is both consistent with common sense judgement and false, by **GMR** lights. Thus, the proposition Q that 'P is false' is true, by **GMR** lights. It is, therefore, a mistake to place any theoretical value on *consistency* with common sense judgements as a guide to veracity (Williamson 2007, p. 209). I am inclined, therefore, to dispense with the perceived scientific-philosophical value of an accord with common sense intuition.

3.6 Conclusion

In this chapter, I identified the source of the incredulous stare oft provoked by the postulates of **GMR**. I argued that two types of incredulity are possible. Firstly, incredulity provoked by the denial of a Moorean fact, **MF**; a fact indefeasible on the grounds of differential certainty. Ted Sider et al. appears to endorse a 'strong' form of theoretical conservatism: a degree of certainty in the truth of **MF** that is greater than the premise of any argument deployed in order to cast doubt upon it. I challenged the presumption that **MF** is a Moorean fact by arguing that the criterion of 'negational absurdity' is not satisfied. In the realm of science, the Everett interpretation of quantum mechanics denies **MF** without absurdity. I acknowledge that the criterion of 'negational absurdity' may itself be problematic, however. Wright's Cautious Man dilemma can be mitigated by the observation that the cautious attitude does not demand a flat denial of the relevant modal claim but merely a refusal to assent to it. A second source of incredulity is prompted by claims that **GMR** breaches folk knowledge. As a supposed instance of folk knowledge, **FK** is not insulated against doubt and is susceptible to revision based on further scientific or philosophical argument. I distinguished **FK** from **MF** on the basis of specialised or technical terminology; specifically 'Wx' or 'x is a possible world'. Lewis' adherence to a weak form of conservatism suggests that **FK** is indeed a claim of folk knowledge. As a pre-theoretic 'knowledge' claim, it is judged to be false by the genuine realist given a preponderance of theoretical virtues. Finally, I argued that Lewis' famous **S1** declaration of a personal – but shared – belief in 'ways things could have been' should not be interpreted as *evidence* in favour of a 'belief in' possible worlds. It should rather be understood as an attempt to align his beliefs with a mind-independent reality (§ 4.6).

Doubts linger, however. Have I successfully identified the true source of the incredulity provoked by **GMR**? Is the incredulity provoked amongst philosophers truly prompted by an innocuous paraphrase of 'ways things could have been'? Sober philosophers need not object to the indexicality of the term 'actual' as a *semantic* thesis (Stalnaker 1976/1984 [2003], p. 27). I now turn to examine a particular interpretation of the term 'possible world'. This interpretation may be where the trouble lies. That is the concept of a 'possible world' interpreted as a discrete, spatiotemporal continuity much like this world, i.e., the homogeneity thesis (cf. van Inwagen 1986 [2001], pp. 224-25).

4

Theoretical parsimony

"entium varietates non temere esse minuendas" (translated – "the variety of entities should not be rashly diminished") (Kant 1781 / 1787 [1929], p. 541, A 656 / B 684)

4.1 Introduction

In chapter three, I examined Lewis' defence against the incredulity objection. It is not the argument from paraphrase that provokes the incredulity but the genuine realist interpretation of the term 'possible world'. The interpretation of possible worlds as discrete spatiotemporal individuals much like the actual world, i.e., the homogeneity thesis. As a materialist, Lewis should ignore the 'incredulous stare' as a theoretical irrelevance, but he does not. Later, I defend genuine modal realism **(GMR)**, not from the incredulity provoked by the homogeneity thesis but from an entailment thereof. **GMR** has been challenged on the grounds that it entails, say, that talking donkeys and one million-carat diamonds necessarily exist! I postpone an examination of these consequences (§ 7.4) but note here that they arise by way of a prior belief in non-actual worlds. In this chapter, I address another problem raised by the homogeneity thesis; that **GMR** is engaged in an unjustified ontological inflation (§ 2.3). The simplicity of a theory can be assessed in one of two ways: first, by the elegance or syntactic simplicity of a theory's basic principles, and second, by parsimony which pertains to the number of the *types* of entity postulated. Parsimony as a virtue is determined by a theory's meta-ontology or to the number of types of things that the theory *says* exist. These two aspects of elegance and parsimony can "pull in different directions. Postulating extra entities may allow a theory to be formulated more simply, while reducing the ontology of a theory may only be possible at the price of making it syntactically more complex." (Baker 2013, Section 1) In order to avoid the fallacy of 'respect neglect', I will restrict my remarks to the parsimony of genuine realism – or lack thereof (Lewis 1973, p. 87).[1]

---

[1] 'Respect neglect' defined as "a prominent instance of the broader fallacy of illicit amalgamation, which consists in treating as a single uniform unit something that in fact involves a diversified plurality of separate issues. Specifically, it has the form of treating a

Before I commence, a further distinction in regard to theoretical parsimony ought to be acknowledged. Parsimony can be interpreted as either an epistemological or methodological virtue. Epistemological parsimony states that if theory X is simpler, i.e., postulates fewer types of entity than theory Y, then it is rational to believe X over Y. Methodological parsimony states that if theory X is simpler, i.e., postulates fewer types of entity than theory Y, then it is rational to accept X as one's preferred theory for the purpose of philosophical investigation. I will restrict my examination of simplicity to methodological parsimony: given the number of types of entity postulated, which philosophical theory is it rational to accept? I will attempt to define, distinguish and justify on *a priori* grounds the methodological principle of parsimony (§ 4.2). For those not persuaded by an a priori justification, I also offer a naturalised justification of the principle based on evidence selected from case studies in the history of science. This evidence offers an alternative *a posteriori* justification of the principle of methodological parsimony (§ 4.3). Lewis (1973) distinguishes qualitative from quantitative parsimony and discounts the latter as a theoretical virtue. Is this dismissal warranted? I examine Daniel Nolan's argument that Lewis' dismissal is premature and quantitative parsimony is worthy of consideration (§ 4.4). The quantifier-predicate model of analysis aims to reflect the 'structure' of reality. As such, one precursor to evaluating the ontological costs of genuine realism is an explanation of the notion of a 'property'. What are the 'joints' at which nature is to be carved? (§ 4.5) If 'natural properties' are understood to demarcate these joints, then do the predicate expressions of the quantifier-predicate model secure agreement as to where the knife should be placed? (§ 4.6) Lewis' philosophical conception of a 'property' is pivotal to the type of parsimony he invokes – qualitative or quantitative – and the theoretical costs accrued. I conclude that qualitative parsimony favours **GMR** whilst quantitative parsimony does not count against it (§ 4.7).

4.2 Ontological parsimony, defined

I adopt the following criterion of ontological parsimony in respect to theory choice:

Ontological Parsimony (OP): Other things being equal, if T1 is more ontologically parsimonious than T2, then it is rational to prefer T1 over T2

(Baker 2013, Section 2)

---

feature *F* as a unified property that things do or do not have, whereas in fact *F* has several respects, and things can have *F* in one respect and lack it in another." (Rescher 2006, p. 45)

The clause 'other things being equal' is critical. It renders **OP** comparatively weak as a theoretical virtue set against other desiderata. As previously noted, Quine's quantifier criterion (**QC**) of ontological commitment is intended to identify the types of entity to which a theory is committed. Hence, if T1 and T2 are otherwise equivalent in their satisfaction of theoretical desiderata, but T2 is also committed to a type of entity G and T1 is not, then T1 ought to be accepted on the grounds of **OP**.

With all due deference to Kant's caveat, theoretical simplicity is a multi-faceted virtue. It was decisive with respect to theory choice amongst philosophers of science in the twentieth century. Theoretical simplicity can be assessed in a number of different ways, however. Is the expressive simplicity of a theory, i.e., the economy of the conceptual apparatus required for its formulation, compatible with its instrumental simplicity, i.e., the mathematical apparatus required for its formulation? If not, which type of simplicity should be granted precedence? Furthermore, how are these forms of simplicity related in turn to a theory's pedagogical simplicity or the ease with which it can be taught or understood? An analogy with motor vehicle manufacture might be instructive. Individual motorcars may vary in their complexity in respect to manufacture, maintenance, ignition systems, and driver friendliness. These characteristics may conflict: a car that is easy to manufacture might be horrendous to drive. In addition, each characteristic is subject to further refinement. The characteristic of 'driver friendliness' can vary with the weather conditions: a vehicle may be 'friendly' in dry conditions and positively 'hostile' in icy conditions. "With automobiles, simplicity is critically respectival. And the simplicity of theories is in much the same situation. ... Here one cannot appropriately speak of simplicity *tout court*." (Rescher 2006, p. 47)

Lewis resists the fallacy of 'respect neglect'. He unpacks the notion of theoretical simplicity into one of elegance *and* parsimony. He further delimits parsimony in terms of quantitative and qualitative parsimony. In comments criticised for their brevity,[2] Lewis concedes that **GMR** is guilty of an ontological inflation only in respect to *quantitative* parsimony. This concession ought to have no bearing on theory choice, however: "I subscribe to the general view that qualitative parsimony is good in a philosophical or empirical hypothesis; but I recognise no presumption whatever in favour of quantitative parsimony." (Lewis 1973, p. 87) The only offence committed by genuine realism against parsimony is quantitative, not qualitative: it postulates a *plurality* of a *single*

---

[2] See James Woodward (2003) *Making Things Happen: A Theory of Causal Explanation* Oxford University Press.

type of entity.[3] Hence, the homogeneity thesis should be endorsed as a theoretical boon, and quantitative parsimony deemed to be irrelevant in regards to theory choice.

Lewis' remarks can be expanded. He acknowledges that ontological parsimony is a theoretical virtue but only in respect of how many types of entity are postulated by a theory. He agrees that **OP** is partly constitutive of rationality. Indeed, a priori 'justifications' of **OP** as a theoretical virtue appear to be ubiquitous. The word 'justification' must here suffer the indignity of scare quotes because the rationality of a methodological principle need not require that the principle be justified (Strawson 1952). The principle may be understood either as admitting of no proof, i.e., as axiomatic, or not standing in need of proof, i.e., as self-evident. If the demand that a methodological principle ought to be justified is accepted then a priori or a posteriori grounds appear to be prime candidates.

I begin with a priori justification. In the latter part of the twentieth century, a priori justifications fell into disfavour among analytic philosophers. The disfavour was a consequence of the rise of empiricism that was suspicious of metaphysical systems. Lewis, however, bucked the trend and adopted an ontological parsimony of kinds **(OPK)** based on the wider principles of rational enquiry. As previously noted, Lewis supports methodological conservatism as a theoretical virtue (§ 3.2): "A worthwhile theory must be credible, and a credible theory must be conservative." (Lewis 1986a, p. 134) The **OPK** principle is a component of methodological conservatism embraced by the broader scientific community engaged in the rational enterprise of empirical investigation. This fact viz. the scientific community's endorsement of **OPK** as partly constitutive of rationality insulates Lewis from censure from empirically-minded, analytic philosophers. Unfortunately, a priori justifications of **OPK** tend to share a common flaw: "it can be difficult to distinguish between an *a priori* defence and *no* defence (!)" (Baker 2013, Section 3) The problem is that **OPK** can be accepted as 'constitutive of rationality' in a number of different ways, e.g., as axiomatic, as self-evident or on pragmatic grounds. To accept any one of these options is to risk-reducing **OPK** to the status of a methodological 'article of faith'. Absent a priori justification, it is difficult to persuade a sceptic of the rational legitimacy of **OPK** without simply inviting further controversy (ibid., Section 3: Kuhn 1977). Why is **OPK** partially constitutive of rational enquiry? How does a prospective methodological principle actually qualify as rational? How does a methodological principle qualify as irrational e.g. Kant's Principle

---

[3] Daniel Nolan (1997) critically examines the comparative ease with which Lewis – and others – dismiss the theoretical significance of quantitative parsimony.

of Plenitude? Do methodological principles ever conflict? What meta-principles should be invoked to adjudicate these conflicts? Do these principles constitute rational enquiry or do they merely reflect the presumptions of those engaged in the scientific or philosophical enterprise?

4.3 A naturalised justification

In light of these doubts about an a priori justification of **OPK** I now turn to the alternative. A justification based on a posteriori or naturalistic grounds may prove more fruitful. Naturalistic epistemology views the enterprise of philosophy as contiguous with that of the natural sciences (§ 3.2). Simplicity or parsimony may be cited as a theoretical virtue on the grounds of historical evidence related to the acceptance or rejection of theories by the scientific community. **OPK** might be justified on the basis of evidence gathered from episodes in the history of science, for example. Has **OPK** ever proved decisive in respect of theory choice? The stock example of Einstein's special theory of relativity and the role it played in the falsification of the existence of the electromagnetic ether – to use the modern spelling – illustrates the *relative* strength of **OPK**. In brief, if the speed of light c is constant then the Earth's movement through the ether should affect c; as the speed of a sailing ship is affected by the direction of the currents in the ocean, e.g., sailing against the current has a drag effect on the speed of the ship. The Michelson-Morley experiment demonstrated that the "measured speed of light is the same in the direction of the Earth's motion as it is at right angles to the direction of the Earth's motion." (Gribbin 2002, p. 437) The speed of light is not affected by the direction of the Earth's motion so the ether does not exist! However, even if **OPK** is set aside special relativity enjoys a host of other theoretical virtues that grant rational acceptance over any alternative explanation e.g. the Lorentz-Poincare theory.[4]

The plethora of theoretical desiderata enjoyed by special relativity makes it a poor option in terms of illustrating **OPK's** decisiveness in respect of theory choice. In short, special relativity is a case of *ceteris non paribus*. A more persuasive example of **OPK** as a theoretical virtue involves a comparison of

---

[4] "But there are two classes of experimental facts hitherto obtained which can be represented in the Maxwell-Lorentz theory only by the introduction of an auxiliary hypothesis, which in itself – i.e. without making use of the theory of relativity – appears extraneous." (Einstein 2001, p. 52) Hence, the addition of ad hoc hypotheses to match the explanatory power of special relativity clouds the issue of theory choice on the basis of OPK alone. The addition of ad hoc hypotheses is sufficient to justify a preference for SR simply on the grounds of theoretical elegance.

alternative theories that are otherwise equivalent in terms of explanatory value (Baker 2013, Section 4).

With this constraint of parity duly acknowledged, I offer Buffon's Law as an illustration of **OPK** (Gribbin 2002, pp. 221-26). Buffon observed a number of examples of animal and plant species diversification in different geographical regions that share similar environments. These observations became known as Buffon's Law (Baker 2013, Section 4). Two otherwise incompatible theories emerged to explain the pattern of species variation. The Darwin-Wallace model states that there are two causal mechanisms in effect that explain the phenomenon. First, 'dispersal', in which species gradually migrate to new geographic areas, and second, 'evolution by natural selection' in which species evolve over a period of time. As a consequence of these two factors, different animal and plant species may evolve in geographically similar but distinct environments. Alternative theories in the 'extensionist' tradition, on the other hand, reject a core presumption of geographic stability found in the Darwin-Wallace model. Proponents of extensionism argue that areas of land or 'land bridges' are exposed by either a fall in sea level or by plate tectonic shift. These 'land bridges' are the primary causal mechanism in play. A 'land bridge' is an isthmus that connects two separate geographic areas which animal and plant species may cross. As a result, the extensionist model is ontologically committed to more types of entity than the Darwin-Wallace theory. Extensionist theory postulates additional types of entity implied by geographic and tectonic instability. "The debate over the more parsimonious Dispersal theories centred on whether the mechanism of dispersal is sufficient on its own to explain the known facts about species distribution, without postulating any extra geographical or tectonic entities." (ibid., Section 4)

Can the case of Buffon's Law be used to extrapolate a general framework of the **OPK** debate? The evidence is shaky. Historically, otherwise incompatible scientific theories have been exalted and condemned on the basis of **OPK**. Theories that postulate *more* types of entity are condemned for their proliferation of kinds, particularly in the absence of evidence. Theories that postulate *fewer* types of entity are condemned for their inability to fully explain the observed facts. As such, any attempt to provide an a posteriori justification of theoretical parsimony faces a number of cogent objections. Even *if* we are able to grant naturalism a privileged methodological status, extracting principles of rationality from science in order to apply them to philosophy is no straightforward matter. How do we identify the underlying methodological principles of the scientific enterprise? Some philosophers reject the very idea of a scientific method, and even those who don't may still reject the notion that this method is *unified*. Furthermore, even if we discovered an avenue out of this impasse, obstacles remain. How do we dissect 'nature at the joints' and secure an *accurate* determination of the types of entity to which 'total theory' should be committed? Identifying a theory's ontological commitments to a type of entity presupposes a method of identification. What is to count as a 'type of entity'? The quantification-predicate model appears to endorse properties as a basis of identification. But which properties? How do we distinguish abundant from sparse properties? "The abundant properties may be as extrinsic, as gruesomely gerrymandered, as miscellaneously disjunctive, as you please." (Lewis 1986a, p. 59) Before I address the problem of joint-selection, however, I will attempt to tackle an antecedent problem. Why does Lewis consider the *quantitative* conception of **OP** to be irrelevant in respect of theory choice? Why does the number of tokens posited of a particular type of entity cast no shadow of doubt over a theory's *rationality*?

4.4 Quantitative parsimony, rehabilitated

Lewis accepts a lack of *qualitative* parsimony as a theoretical cost but rejects the 'cost' associated with a lack of *quantitative* parsimony (Lewis 1973, p. 87). The only potential cost incurred by **GMR's** ontological commitments is to how many types of entity are postulated, not the number or tokens of those types. Is there really no theoretical cost incurred by the number or tokens of each type of entity postulated? A proliferation of worlds ought to play some role in theory choice, shouldn't it?

In "Quantitative Parsimony" Daniel Nolan tests the cogency of Lewis' distinction: "I motivate the view that quantitative parsimony *is* a theoretical virtue: ... we should also minimize the *number* of entities postulated that fall under these kinds." (Nolan 1997, p. 329 my emphasis). Nolan does not offer an account of how competing virtues should be weighed, nor does he argue that quantitative parsimony is a primitive virtue. Indeed, he argues that quantitative parsimony is essentially dependent on qualitative parsimony. It is understood not just as a calculation of "the total number of things, but how many things *of each type* there are is relevant." (ibid., p. 340) Nolan's primary aim is to demonstrate that quantitative parsimony ought to be amongst the desiderata of theory choice. He presents two case studies from the history of science in pursuit of this goal. I will examine one of these studies. The particular case relates to the discovery of the neutrino, a fundamental particle revealed during the process of Beta-decay. Beta-decay occurs when the nucleus of an atom ejects an electron and is transformed into an atom formerly 'adjacent' to it on the periodic table (Gribbin 2002, pp. 524-26). Enrico Fermi's (1901-1954) mathematical model demonstrates that Beta-decay is caused by the influence of a new field of force – the weak nuclear force. "His model described how, in addition to the strong nuclear force ... there was a weak, short-range force which could cause a neutron to decay into a proton and electron *plus* another, uncharged particle, which he dubbed the 'neutrino' (from the Italian for 'little neutron')." (ibid., p. 525) The point germane to parsimony is that physicists' concluded a single new type of particle is emitted from the atom during Beta-decay. There are, however, several plausible hypotheses each capable of explaining the observed phenomenon:

1. One neutrino with a spin of ½ is emitted in each case of Beta-decay

2. Two neutrinos each with a spin of ¼ are emitted in each case of Beta-decay

3. (More generally for any positive integer n) n neutrinos, each with a spin of $1/2n$ are emitted in each case of Beta-decay

(Baker 2013, Section 6.1)

Why should physicists' posit just one emitted neutrino rather than, say, fifty-five? Why is the former explanation more *rational* than the latter? Each hypothesis is an adequate explanation of the observed phenomenon. The only material difference appears to be the postulated number of neutrinos sufficient to secure explanatory adequacy. Despite this parity, however, physicists were drawn to the first hypothesis as the obvious choice. Quantitative parsimony is the methodological principle that favours the first hypothesis over equally viable alternatives. Therefore, quantitative parsimony *must* be a theoretical virtue!

A general principle of quantitative parsimony **(QP)** can be extrapolated from the historical case of Beta-decay. A provisional suggestion is:

QP: We should not admit any entities into our theory that lack explanatory power.

(Nolan 1997, p. 338)

Nolan concedes that, as it stands, **QP** requires some refinement. To begin with, explanatory power is a necessary but not sufficient criterion of a theoretical virtue. Why should hypothesis one enjoy a privileged status if each hypothesis is equivalent in terms of explanatory power? In the 1930s, numerous experiments were conducted to investigate the phenomenon of particle decay. None yielded an example of a missing particle with a spin of ⅕ or ⅙ or ⅛. In the absence of an observed emitted particle with fewer fractional spins hypothesis one emerged as the preferred candidate. It is consistent with the simple explanation that no particles are emitted during Beta-decay with a spin other than ½. Although hypothesis two shares this consistency, it is purchased at the price of postulating particles with spins that have never been observed. Hypothesis one is able to explain this absence and the presence of particles with a spin ½. "It seems intuitive to me, and I hope to the reader, that postulating seventeen million neutrinos in each case of Beta decay produces a theory that is less plausible and attractive than the theory proposed by Pauli and Fermi." (Nolan 1997, p. 334) Nolan acknowledges, however, that **OPK** is only a precondition of **QP**: the kinds of entity postulated by a theory must first be identified before a 'head count' of their respective number is taken (ibid., p. 341).

As a general principle, **QP** favours **GMR** as a philosophical analysis of modality. As a theory, **GMR** is ontologically committed to a type of entity or possible world understood as a discrete spatiotemporal continuity. In addition, it postulates a plurality of that type. In the alternative, say, actualist realism **(AR)** favours an ontological commitment to two types of entity; the actual world understood as a discrete spatiotemporal continuity and sets of maximally consistent propositions. This numerical difference in the *core* ontologically commitments of each account of modality does little to advance my main thesis, however. Although not a core commitment of modal translation, Lewis accepts an ontological commitment to sets, and I argued – by denying the 'singularist dogma' (§ 1.5) – that sets ought to be a core commitment of 'total theory'. The exploration of **QP** relates to the scientific analysis of Beta-decay in which *one* neutrino explains the absent ½ spin. It does not pertain to the total number or cardinality of neutrinos in the universe. By parity of reason, **GMR** explains, say, a de re possibility by postulating at least one world at which that possibility is realised. It does not pertain to the total number or cardinality of worlds that populate the multiverse. Nolan explicitly cautions against broadening the theoretical scope of **QP**, however. As a theoretical virtue, **QP** should be restricted to certain subject areas. "Intuitively, the strengths and weaknesses of theories about one subject matter (such as the question of the existence of neutrinos or elemental atoms) has little to do with theories about some other subject matters." (ibid., p. 341) As a materialist, Lewis is compelled to argue that Nolan's injunction is misplaced. Scientific and philosophical enquiry share a common set of theoretical virtues and vices (§ 3.4).

Ideally, I require a procedure that identifies these shared virtues and applies to individual cases. Nolan merely hints at how this could be achieved: "after all, arguing from the practice of scientists to what norms they should follow (or what the cognitive virtues are) is by no means straightforward." (ibid., p. 331) To keep faith with Lewis, I endorse **OPK** as a theoretical virtue. Qualitative parsimony is a primary theoretical virtue, although quantitative parsimony may play a subsidiary role. The homogeneous interpretation of the phrase 'possible world(s)' grants **GMR** an advantage over rival theories on the grounds of **OPK**. There is one type of interpretation that best explains a possible world, i.e., a spatiotemporal continuity. There are numerous instances of this type of thing, i.e., many tokens of this particular type. This outcome viz. quantitative parsimony, is not peculiar to **GMR**: **AR** also posits numerous instances of a certain type, i.e., sets of maximally consistent propositions. I conclude that qualitative parsimony favours **GMR** whilst quantitative parsimony need not count against it. However, regardless of whether quantitative parsimony is accepted as a theoretical desideratum, a method of identifying the 'joints' at which nature is to be 'carved' is required. Critical to this endeavour is the quantification-predicate model of philosophical analysis which is employed to reflect the 'structure' of reality. Hence, the search for this method begins with properties.

4.5 The creatures of the night (what sweet music they make!)

A consensus in regard to the explication of properties has eluded philosophers since antiquity. Initially, the notion of a property – at least the properties of material objects – appears unproblematic. A red apple has the properties of [redness] and [appleness]. "Properties (also called 'attributes,' 'qualities,' 'features,' 'characteristics,' 'types') are those entities that can be predicated of things or, in other words, attributed to them." (Swoyer & Orilia 2014, Section Introduction) Dig a little deeper, and philosophical problems quickly emerge. The problem I address in this section relates to the claim that properties are the 'entities that can be predicated of things'. If we suppose that the meaning of a predicate is the set whose members share a common property, then that property can be defined by way of set-membership. Quine rejects this proposal on the grounds of identity conditions; that is, by way of the principle 'no entity without identity'. There are, he argues, distinct properties that share the same instances. Standard examples include the properties [creature with a heart] and [creature with kidneys]. It just so happens that every creature with a heart also has kidneys and vice versa. On the proposed set theoretic model of properties, the same set will denote two distinct properties, which would make these properties identical! Little wonder that he dismisses the notion of properties – indeed all intensional notions – as "creatures of darkness" (Quine 1956 [1976], p. 188). Despite these misgivings, philosophers have considered the notion of properties to be a useful one in the resolution of what might otherwise be intractable problems. In addition to epistemology and semantics, there are metaphysical benefits to be found in the postulation of properties. For example, the explanation of resemblance and recurrence can be facilitated by way of the notion of properties. We are able to classify the world in objective ways based on the similarity of objects that furnish it. We explain the resemblance of two objects based on the attribution of a property or constellation of properties, for example. Lewis concurs: "the proposed constraint is that referents are to be eligible ... the traditional realism that recognises objective sameness and difference, joints in the world, discriminatory classifications not of our own making." (Lewis 1983e [1999], p. 67) The search for a cogent explanation of qualitative similarity and difference may motivate a realist account of properties as universals.

Lewis' account of properties is reductive i.e. he reduces properties to the unrestricted sets of their instances (Lewis 1986a, pp. 50 ff.). The inclusion of non-actual worlds blocks Quine's objection about the same set being used to identify distinct properties. Recall the phrase 'it just so happens' from the previous paragraph. As a contingent matter of fact, *in this world* creatures with a heart are coextensive with creatures with kidneys. "It is contingent whether two properties have the same this-worldly instances. But it is not contingent whether they have the same instances *simpliciter*." (ibid., p. 51) Lewis' defence is premised on an apparent equivocation in the notion of set-membership. An equivocation between the subset of talking donkeys restricted to this-world and the set of talking donkeys unrestricted to this or any particular world, understood *simpliciter*. Membership of the second set does not vary *simpliciter* from world to world. Membership of this set is a matter of necessity. Suppose 'Eeyore' is a talking donkey who inhabits a non-actual world. It is a contingent matter whether or not he talks – some of his counterparts do whilst others do not. If Eeyore does talk then he is a member of the unrestricted set of talking donkeys, *simpliciter*.

Lewis acknowledges that his account is incomplete (ibid., p. 59). Hence, properties that are instantiated relative to something else are to be excluded. In such cases, the property instantiated is not equivalent to the set of its instances. Hunger, for example, is a property relative to a particular time i.e. a property that I may instantiate at one time but lack at another (§ 2.5). Despite this concession, doubts continue to linger as to whether the move to a set-theoretic model of properties holds – even *simpliciter*. Some properties, say those found in mathematics, are necessarily instantiated and appear to qualify as properties *simpliciter*. However, distinct mathematical properties can be instantiated by the same object and are identical by virtue of set-membership. For example, the mathematical properties [triangularity] and [trilaterality] (ibid., p. 55). Even *simpliciter*, these distinct properties are rendered necessarily identical by the set-membership model. Each property is instantiated by every triangle. In order to extricate his argument from this difficulty, Lewis invokes the role that properties fulfil: "which entities, if any, among those we should believe in, can occupy which versions of the property role?" (ibid., p. 55) The answer to this question is central to Lewis' philosophical strategy. A partial role is assigned to possibilia: that is, the types of entity that partially fulfil the 'property' role as members of sets *simpliciter*.

Alternatively, the notion of a property can be aligned with the *meaning* of a predicate. This option may restore the distinction between otherwise 'identical'

– that is, necessarily coextensive – properties on semantic grounds: in English, the predicate 'trilateral' means to have three sides whilst the predicate 'triangular' means to have three angles. However, to switch from properties to meanings is to jump out of the frying pan and into the fire. A consequence of this manoeuvre is to ascribe *structure* to properties – linguistic expressions have syntactic structure, so we might be tempted to ascribe a quasi-structure to properties. A quasi-structural model of properties and relations could be constructed utilising sets of possibilia *simpliciter*. In addition to properties and relations, we might posit a higher-order *unstructured* relation – as a set of pairs – that holds between them. Consider A and S as unstructured relations:

- Let A be the relation of [being an angle of]

- Let S be the relation of [being a side of]

- Let T be the higher-order unstructured relation that holds between an unstructured property F of individuals and an unstructured relation G of individuals iff F is the property of being something that exactly three things bear relation G to.

(Lewis 1986a, p. 56)

Hence, the structured property of [triangularity] is the higher-order relation ⟨T, A⟩ whilst the structured property of [trilaterality] is the higher-order relation ⟨T, S⟩ (ibid., p. 56). The relations A and S differ, and the distinction between necessarily co-instantiated properties is restored.

Thus far, I have disregarded Lewis' views on *natural* properties. I concluded § 4.3 by noting that some properties – the natural properties – identify the 'joints' at which nature ought to be 'carved'. Lewis argues that natural properties constitute the objective features of reality (Lewis 1986a, p. 61). The objective features used to determine similarity and difference are not a matter of contingency. Hence, classification of the natural properties is not a contingent matter. Although non-contingent, naturalness may still admit of degrees. Blue things, for example, may instantiate different shades of blue more similar to each other than they are to, say, red things. Set-membership is arbitrary in the sense that it can be determined in any one of an infinite number of ways. How do we distinguish between the resemblance of objects that I thought about last Friday and the resemblance of objects that are atoms of platinum? The 'similarities' and 'differences' amongst the objects I thought about last Friday appears to be arbitrary – certainly, there appears to be no natural feature that they all share – a feature not shared by the objects that I did *not* think about last Friday. Platinum atoms, on the other hand, do appear to share a natural feature. How is this demarcation to be explained? For Lewis, the idea that some properties are 'natural' is absent prior to his "New Work for a

Theory of Universals". As late as Lewis (1983f), he spurns the distinction: "*Any* two things stand in infinitely many relations, share infinitely many properties, and are both included as parts of infinitely many aggregates." (Lewis 1983f [1999], p. 394) Lewis' *volte-face* was prompted by conversations with David Armstrong (1978a, 1978b). Persuaded by some of Armstrong's arguments in favour of universals (Lewis 1983d [1999], p. 8), the demarcation of natural properties became a central feature of Lewis' theory of mind (ibid., pp. 52-53), to the 'exact match' of the intrinsic duplicates/properties of two worlds' spatiotemporal regions (ibid., p. 27) and to the 'tenability' of Humean supervenience (Lewis 1986b [1986], p. xi).

Lewis is committed to methodological naturalism as a theoretical desideratum. The structure of the quantification-predicate model reflects the structure of reality. Lewis' change of heart suggests that the 'qualitative joints' at which nature should be carved are determined by natural properties. A form of ontological realism is presupposed but are the predicates of the quantification-predicate model wholly unambiguous? I adopt Sider's definition of ontological realism as "the claim that the world's distinguished structure includes quantificational structure." (Sider 2009, p. 407) If philosophers agree on their interpretation of the quantifiers (§ 1.3), must they also agree on the interpretation of the predicates? I now turn from a discussion of properties to a discussion of predicates.

4.6 Ontological realism

Recall the question posed at § 4.3. The decision to select the quantifier as a criterion of ontological commitment leaves the validity of various inferences as an open question (§ 1.3). For example, the problems raised by the exclusion of the 'empty domain' from the standard Tarskian interpretation of **PL**. As a consequence, universal quantified sentences turn out to have existential implications. I now turn to contrast the predicate expressions of the quantification-predicate model with an alternative notion of plural predication. For present purposes, I employ the central notion of a 'structure': does the structure of the quantification-predicate model reflect the structure of reality, specifically in regard to predicate expressions? (Sider 2009, pp. 397-402). In this section, I examine the predication side of the quantification-predicate model.

In "Ontological Realism," Ted Sider argues that ontological realism is a common presumption – perhaps the definitive presumption – of analytic philosophy. "A certain core realism is, as much as anything, the shared dogma of analytic philosophers, and rightly so." (ibid., p. 399) Imagine that two philosophers are presented with a table. The first, DKL affirms what the second, PVI denies[5]:

EQ: This table exists

Sider initially considers ontological deflationism as a potential explanation of their apparent disagreement. In brief, the deflationist argues that DKL and PVI are actually talking past one another. **EQ** is being used to express two different propositions. As a result, DKL and PVI both assert a proposition that is true – by their own lights – on the grounds of meaning variance. DKL makes a mereological assertion of his 'belief in' a table composed of simpler entities. PVI makes a non-mereological assertion of his 'belief in' a 'table' understood as a collection of simple entities arranged *tablewise*. PVI is thereby able to deny what DKL affirms: that there is a table which exists in addition to a collection of simpler entities from which it is composed.

As a sentence, the syntactic structure of **EQ** is the same for both DKL and PVI. The disparity, therefore, would appear to be rooted in either their respective use of the predicate expression 'x is a table' or in their use of the quantifier 'x exists'. Sider immediately sets aside one possible source of disagreement; ambiguity. The interpretation of some predicates, e.g., 'set' or 'bank', is open to ambiguity. The sentence 'John walked by the bank' could be interpreted in at least one of two ways: 'bank' could be interpreted to mean either a riverside or a financial institution. Ambiguity does not apply in this case, however. In the present context, DKL is speaking on behalf of those "immersed in the business of ordinary life" (van Inwagen 1990, p. 1), where the truth of **EQ** is assured by the triviality of language. If **EQ** were ever uttered in ordinary life, then its truth would be assured by the scope of the quantifier as determined by the domain of discourse: "They (DKL and PVI) agree on the condition ϕ that a thing must meet in order to count as a table; their disagreement is over whether there exists anything that meets that condition." (Sider 2009, p. 388) PVI does not dispute the meaning of the quantifier but rather the existence of a particular type of entity, a table, i.e., understood as something distinct from a collection of simples arranged *tablewise*. The plural quantification-predication model of a 'collection' of simples arranged *tablewise* is not equivalent to the claim that a table exists (ibid., pp. 388-89). PVI's denial is consistent with the assertion of **EQ** because it is made in an extraordinary context; the philosopher's study (van Inwagen 1990, p. 2).

---

[5] Sider's argument is loosely based on the actual work of David Lewis and Peter van Inwagen. I say 'loosely based' because Peter van Inwagen, for example, accepts a thesis rejected by PVI, namely, the existence of 'composite' living things (Sider 2009, p. 389 fn. 17).

Does a distinction based on context sensitivity make sense (§ 2.5)? As previously noted, Lewis' argument is premised on a notion of properties – specifically, natural properties – that demarcate 'the joints of nature'. In contrast, PVI may argue that there are no privileged lines of demarcation. Even if we accept that nature's 'joints' are to be identified on the basis of the natural properties the spectre of arbitrariness remains: that any one group of properties can be just as 'natural' as any other. Nelson Goodman, for example, argues that the relation of similarity is determined by objects that share a property, any old property (Goodman 1972, pp. 443-44). He denies that reality enjoys an objective structure: any two arbitrary objects might be judged to be 'similar'. Object 'a' that instantiates property F is 'similar' to object 'b' that instantiates property G because 'a' and 'b' instantiate the disjunctive property, F-or-G! How does Goodman's objection apply to PVI's denial? The arguments in van Inwagen's *Material Beings* are sophisticated and illustrated with vivid analogies throughout. For example, he invites us to imagine that a predicate 'bliger' is used by a linguistic community – the Pluralians – to refer to the black tigers they occasionally espy from a distance moving through the jungle (van Inwagen 1990, p. 104). After centuries of native use, an expedition of foreign zoologists determine that bligers do not actually exist. The creatures, thought to be bligers by the Pluralians, are actually a composite of six other creatures that are arranged *bligerwise*: four monkey-like creatures for 'legs', a sloth-like creature for a 'trunk', and a type of owl for a 'head'. Only by careful study are the zoologists able to expose the widespread Pluralist misattribution of bligerhood. "That is, it does not follow that six animals arranged in bliger fashion compose anything, and that is what I mean to deny when I say that there are no bligers." (ibid., p. 104) PVI's bliger-denial, however, remains consistent with an assertion by the Pluralians that 'there is a bliger crossing that field'. By implication, the Pluralians are ontologically committed to a certain type of entity, bligers. Does this consistency rank PVI's denial of bligerhood alongside Goodman's arguments? The consistency of an existential claim asserted-in-context-a and denied-in-context-b appears to render the property of bligerhood an irrelevance in regard to the objective structure of reality (ibid., pp. 1-2). There is no privileged set of natural properties to demarcate the 'joints of nature'.

Lewis argues that the structure of reality – at this world – is determined by the arrangement of natural properties and relations (Lewis 1983d [1999]: 1986a pp. 59-69). Natural properties and relations serve two functions; 'similarity-determiners' and 'content-determiners'. They are 'similarity-determiners' insofar as "perfectly similar objects, for example, are those objects over whose parts the natural properties and relations are isomorphically distributed." (Sider 2009, p. 400) They also function in respect to language and thought as 'content determiners' (Lewis 1983d [1999], p. 53). Consider the content of my thoughts and language. How should an ideal interpreter decipher the meaning of my sentences? What information might she draw upon in order to interpret my remarks? One way to understand my sentences is to examine how I actually *use* them: "Think of this as determining a set of sentences, ∏, such that the interpreter ought, other things being equal, to interpret my words so that the members of ∏ come out true." (Sider 2009, p. 400) This set of sentences may include those sentences that I consider to be analytic or that comprise the content of those beliefs that I hold to be true. It has been cogently argued, however, that this condition – that the sentences of ∏ ought to be interpreted such that they are all true – is not a sufficiency condition of interpretation.[6] Suppose the interpreter mistakenly accepts a sentence F that is false but consistent with ∏: by this supposition "if there are enough objects then there will be an interpretation that makes all the sentences of ∏ plus *F* as well true." (ibid., p. 400). An interpreter, whose resources are limited to *the facts of my use* of a sentence may misinterpret F as true (see § 3.5 in respect to the content of belief). In order to avoid misinterpretation, Lewis argues that in addition to 'the facts of my use' the interpreter must also have access to *the facts of 'naturalness'*. That is, the interpreter should – all things being equal – assign natural properties and relations to my use of predicate expressions. Natural properties and relations also function as "reference magnets" (Lewis 1983d [1999], p. 47) that warrant the interpretation of my sentences in novel circumstances. They prevent the over-generation of meaning to which the interpretation of my sentences might – otherwise – be susceptible.

Lewis' modal translation scheme is an application of the quantification-predicate model that reflects the structure of reality. "The point of metaphysics is to discern the fundamental structure of the world. That requires choosing fundamental notions with which to describe the world. No one can avoid this choice." (Sider 2009, p. 420) I have made my choice; the **QC** of the quantification-predicate model.

4.7 Conclusion

Lewis endorses the ontological parsimony of kinds as a theoretical virtue. The additional virtue – if virtue it be – of quantitative parsimony is wholly derivative. He argues that the **OPK** is partially constitutive of rationality. It is a methodological principle whose justification is located in the history of the natural sciences. The history of science is replete with episodes of theory choice in which the pragmatic principle of **OPK** has played a pivotal role. Lewis also supports the notion of natural properties, which constitute the qualitative

---

[6] See Putnam's model theoretic argument (Putnam 1978, Part IV: 1980 [1983]) and Kripke's interpretation of the later Wittgenstein (Kripke 1982).

'joints' at which nature is 'carved'. The quantification-predicate model reflects the structure of reality. Unrestricted quantification extends beyond the boundary of the actual world to encompass everything that exists. "Our idioms of existential quantification may be used to range over everything without exception, or they may be tacitly restricted in various ways. In particular, they may be restricted to our own world and things in it." (Lewis 1973, p. 86) The postulation of a plurality of worlds can be justified on the grounds of qualitative parsimony. Quantitative parsimony, on the other hand, is likely to become problematic for the genuine realist if the content of common belief is restricted to the furniture of the actual world. In these circumstances, the postulate *may* conflict with Lewis' criterion c of a legitimate paraphrase. Lewis' criterion c states that the relevant paraphrase should be endorsed by a community of ordinary language-users. I maintain that it is *not* the **S1** paraphrase of 'ways things could have been' that places quantitative parsimony in jeopardy but the genuine realists' interpretation of that paraphrase as a discrete spatiotemporal entity. The detrimental effects of admitting quantitative parsimony as a theoretical virtue can be mitigated: first, with the recognition that **QP** is derived from **QPK** and, secondly, that a 'materialist' such as Lewis ought to accept the theoretical values of the natural sciences. The paraphrase of 'ways things could have been' may strike a discordant note with common belief, but the theoretical benefits are worth the earache. I now advance the argument that the paraphrase of 'ways things could have been' by 'possible world' is innocuous. Indeed, the paraphrase is *partially* constitutive of an analytic truth, viz., the modal translation scheme.

5

Analyticity

5.1 Introduction

Previously I enumerated the logical, semantic, and expressive benefits accrued by the genuine realists' quantification-predicate analysis of modality (§ 1.1). They are: (1) the logical benefits of the simplification of resources by way of the substitution of modal expressions by their 'worldly' equivalents; (2) the semantic benefits of dispensing with intensional semantics by discarding modal operators as logical primitives; (3) finally, the expressive benefits that include an enhanced ability to articulate modal concepts by lifting the restriction of sentential modal operators and 'actualist' quantification. Advocates of genuine realism allege that taken in combination, these desiderata establish that the modal translation scheme is an analytic truth (Divers 1997, p. 142). This entitlement appears to be a departure from the traditional semantic account of analyticity. A philosophical analysis is true if and only if it is analytically true. If the analysis offered by the modal translation scheme is analytic, then it is true because of the meanings of its terms. In this chapter, I examine the idea that the modal translation scheme *is* an analytic truth; not on the grounds of the theoretical benefits it secures but in virtue of the meaning of its terms. It should be noted that this is not Lewis' position: although the logical form of the translation scheme is a universalised biconditional, the truth linking the analysandum and analysans is contingent.

I will restrict the scope of this ambitious enterprise to the claim that a single term of the translation scheme is a stipulated synonym. Specifically, the **S1** paraphrased term 'possible world' i.e. $\lozenge$ p iff $\exists$x ... Wx .... I begin with an examination of analyticity as the notion is unpacked by Lewis (§ 5.2). I then contrast the genuine realist analysis of modality with that of Robert Stalnaker. Stalnaker defends a form of liberal Platonism in which the semantic thesis is distinguished from the metaphysical theses. Newly distinct, Stalnaker claims to provide modal translation in semantic terms devoid of the onerous metaphysical implications of genuine realism (§ 5.3). What type of analyticity is operant in the case of the modal translation scheme? I examine two forms of metaphysical analyticity identified by Timothy Williamson. I conclude that the paraphrase cited at **S1** is Frege-analytic (§ 5.4). As an instance of a genuine paraphrase, the relevant expressions face the problem of stipulation. How could the meta-semantic act of a stipulation ground a semantic synonymy? I locate an answer in the form of a linguistic convention (§ 5.5). I conclude the chapter by returning to the problem posed by Stalnaker: if we restrict modal translation to a semantic thesis, can we enjoy the analytical benefits of translation without the associated metaphysical cost? (§ 5.6)

5.2 Defending a dogma

Traditionally, philosophical analysis imposes a number of criteria the satisfaction of which legitimise the proposed analysis as philosophical (see § 7.4). One such criterion is analyticity. A philosophical analysis of the form '$\forall x \, (Fx \leftrightarrow Gx)$' must be an analytic truth. "Hence if the analysis is true, it is analytically true – true in virtue of the meaning of the terms involved." (Daly 2010, p. 45). Quine famously rejects this traditional account of philosophical analysis (Quine 1951a [1980]). Lewis' commitment to naturalised epistemology might suggest that he shares Quine's scepticism in regard to the analytic/synthetic distinction. Lewis accepts, however, a form of analyticity that grants meaning a pivotal role:

> I have tried to make sense of analyticity. Or, rather, I have tried to make sense of two different analyticities. In Chapter V.3, I defined analyticity in a possible language L; in Chapter V.5, I defined analyticity in a population P of language users. The latter analyticity depended on the former analyticity and on the conventional relation between a possible language and a population. If I have succeeded in rescuing the platitude that language is conventional, have I thereby succeeded in rescuing analyticity and its kin? I believe I have. (Lewis 2002, p. 203: 1975 [1983], p. 163)

A linguistic community counts as speaking a language L only if it has a convention of truthfulness and trust in L (§ 5.5). But how is a given convention established within a given community? The problem is particularly acute for those who argue that conventions link possible languages to a particular language community; in order to establish a particular convention, the members of a language community must first reach an accord as to which conventions to adopt and which to abandon. But how is this agreement reached? Presumably by way of language, a language regulated by established conventions based on a prior agreement ... so on *ad infinitum* (Quine 1935 [1976]). The language-agreement-convention cycle can be broken by the admittance of conventions that are non-linguistic. Occasionally, conventions just 'spring up' without the need for negotiation. For Lewis, the conventions of language likely originate in this way – implicit in the sense that they are not arrived at by way of an explicit agreement. Generally, a convention is a regularity in the behaviour of a population that emerges in response to a coordination problem. Coordination problems "are situations of interdependent decision by two or more agents in which coincidence of interest predominates and in which there are two or more proper coordination equilibria." (Lewis 2002, p. 24)

I argue that Lewis' modal translation scheme is based on a synonymy of linguistic 'pragmatism' (§ 1.3). The translation of modal sentences into sentences of counterpart theory does not yield an analytic truth in the sense of a traditional synonymy of meaning but rather in the sense of a stipulated synonymy on pragmatic grounds (cf. Beebee & McBride 2015, p. 230 ff.). In order to establish this thesis, I must explore the notion of language – or rather, languages. Lewis argues that convention is the bridge between a possible language and the use of an actual language by a community. My intended destination is the analytic truth of a particular element of the modal translation scheme, viz. the paraphrase term 'possible world'. In order to make this journey, I must first 'clear the rubble'. It might be objected that as a wholly semantic notion, the analytic truth of the scheme could be secured without the metaphysical proliferation of worlds. We could dispense with the controversial ontological commitments of genuine realism and still secure the theoretical benefits acquired by the modal translation scheme. The first step in this endeavour would be to divorce the semantic component of modal translation from its metaphysical implications. This is Stalnaker's liberal Platonism.

5.3 Liberal Platonism

In "On What Possible Worlds Could Not Be" Robert Stalnaker objects to the thesis of indexicality as it is advanced by genuine realism (§ 2.5). He argues that the genuine realist's interpretation of the term 'actual world' mistakenly conflates two distinct theses:

1. The semantic thesis is that claims about what is possible or necessary should be analysed as claims about what is true in some or all of the appropriately individuated parts of reality.

2. The metaphysical thesis is that there exists a plurality of parts of reality individuated in this way – a plurality that is full enough to make true many of our ordinary beliefs about what is possible and necessary when those beliefs are interpreted in accordance with the semantic thesis.

(Stalnaker 1996 [2003], p. 40: 1976/1984 [2003])

Stalnaker accepts the indexical interpretation of the phrase 'actual world' as a semantic thesis but denies the metaphysical thesis, which states there is more than one world. By parity of reason, one may accept an indexical analysis of tense and yet endorse the thesis that the past is mere memory and the future mere anticipation (Stalnaker 1976 / 1984, [2003], p. 29). There is, for Stalnaker, a conceptual link between the nature of a thing and the ways that we know about that thing. Lewis denies this conceptual link. For Lewis, knowledge of actual people and objects is personal because it is indexical. All impersonal knowledge of de re contingency, including knowledge of non-actual people and objects, is a priori. How can genuine realism hope, asks Stalnaker, to explain our ordinary, practical modal deliberations? How can objects causally isolated from us – worlds and their inhabitants – be relevant to our everyday modal thoughts and language? The query echoes a problem faced by the Platonist in the field of mathematics. In "Mathematical Truth", Paul Benacerraf (1973) raises a dilemma for the Platonist in respect of mathematical truth and knowledge. Benacerraf exposes a tension between what mathematical statements *say*, on one hand, and the way in which we can *know* what they say is true, on the other. Statements of, say, number theory purport to be statements about a domain of objects – numbers – that have no spatiotemporal characteristics and hence no causal relation to us. If this is so, then how can a Platonist account for our knowledge that true mathematical statements are, in fact, true? In reply, Lewis' draws a favourable analogy between mathematical and modal knowledge (Lewis 1986a, pp. 108 ff.). He does so by grasping one horn of Benacerraf's dilemma: we accept the truth-conditions of a 'straightforward' semantic theory and deny the requirement of a causal link between knower and what is known. "Causal accounts of knowledge are all very well in their place, but if they are put forward as *general* theories, then mathematics refutes them." (ibid., p. 109)[1]

Stalnaker concedes that a mathematical realm of objects in the Platonist model is compatible with the view that knowledge of *this* particular realm need not be causal. He concurs with Lewis' dissolution of Benacerraf's dilemma but rejects the analogy with the modal case. The challenge Stalnaker now faces is how to explain why the proposed mathematical-modal analogy is false. In short, to establish that there is no plausible analogy between "reference to and knowledge of numbers and reference to and knowledge of cabbages, kings, and croquet games that are alleged to exist in spatio-temporally disconnected parts

---

[1] Lewis rejects the epistemic distinction of an a priori (abstract realm) and an a posteriori (concrete realm). The true distinction, he argues, is one based upon objects that are contingent and those which are necessary. Independently, there appear to be 'objects' that are abstract and contingent: "those objects, like the Equator, whose existence is contingent upon the existence and behaviour of concrete objects." (Dummett 1991, p. 239) Does the converse hold true? There are, according to genuine realism, 'countless concrete objects causally isolated from us' that comprise the furniture of a plurality of worlds. By analogy with the mathematical case, the existence of these worlds is a matter of necessity. Hence, we acquire knowledge of these worlds and their inhabitants through a priori, non-causal reasoning. This appears to licence the inference that 'objects' such as the Equator (abstract but dependent upon contingent objects e.g. the actual world) fall within the purview of a posteriori knowledge and should be juxtaposed with the existence of 'objects' (that are concrete but dependent upon necessary objects e.g. possible worlds) fall within the purview of a priori knowledge.

of reality." (Stalnaker 1996 [2003], p. 43) If Stalnaker can establish a mathematical-modal disanalogy, then he can assert non-causal knowledge in the former case whilst denying it in the latter (ibid., p. 41). What is Stalnaker's strategy; how does he separate the mathematical wheat from the modal chaff?

The strategy employed is one of 'liberal Platonism', which seeks to *limit* the proposed reconciliation between 'straightforward' semantics and epistemology to the mathematical domain. Stalnaker begins with an endorsement of Quine's injunction; "to ponder our talk of physical phenomena as a physical phenomenon, and our scientific imaginings as activities within the world that we imagine." (Quine 1960 [2013], Section 1, pp. 4-5: Stalnaker 1996 [2003], p. 45) (§ 2.4) Hence, the context in which a speaker refers to a certain object or person by name and the relation in which that speaker stands to the object or person is *itself* the subject of empirical enquiry. The liberal Platonist maintains that in order to refer successfully to a person or object, the speaker must be related to the referent in an appropriate way. In the case of mathematical discourse, any putative act of reference to, say, numbers, sets, or functions is guided by established rules and procedures. These rules and procedures also guide assertion, falsification, inference, and mathematical argument. Initially, Stalnaker is tempted to argue that the existence of mathematical entities such as numbers is *constituted* by the fact of an operative, legitimate practice of structured mathematical discourse. The statements produced in the context of a mathematical discourse satisfy the standards of correctness that *are* numbers (Stalnaker 1996 [2003], p. 44).

On reflection, Stalnaker decides to abandon this approach; if true, it would mean that the existence of non-contingent numbers depends on the contingent practice of mathematical discourse. Instead, he chooses to revise his initial position. "The point is rather that the commitment to numbers is just constituted by the endorsement of the practice with this structure and standards." (ibid., p. 45) The practice of mathematical discourse is itself to be the subject of empirical enquiry, in line with Quine's injunction. This enquiry has led to the conclusion that there is a domain of mathematical entities.

How does this conclusion advance Stalnaker's overall aim to establish a mathematical-modal disanalogy? In both cases, a 'straightforward' truth-conditional interpretation of semantics entails the capacity to refer to objects that stand in non-causal relations to us. However, Quine's injunction appears to be applicable to both the modal and mathematical case. His concerns about the de re modal status of irrational cyclists and hopping mathematicians aside, what are the actual operative, structural rules of modal discourse?[2]

Stalnaker's adopted strategy simply begs the question. Lewis' modal translation scheme supplies counterpart theory with the structure of predicate logic (**PL**) and established rules and procedures of valid inference. A schism in the mathematical and modal case is not immediately evident. The next step in Stalnaker's argument is, therefore, essential:

> The liberal Platonist says that the legitimacy of the practice does not presuppose that there is any story to be told, in our empirical theory of the practice, about an external relation between acts of reference and the referents ... The point is rather that the commitment to numbers is just constituted by the endorsement of the practice with this structure and standards. (Stalnaker 1996 [2003], p. 45)

Unfortunately, the manoeuvre is unsuccessful. Stalnaker attempts to embed the relation between the act of reference and a putative referent within a practice of rules and procedures and thereby generate a commitment to mathematical entities. It equivocates between two positions that are equally unpalatable for the liberal Platonist. Of course, Stalnaker is aware of the danger and attempts to mitigate each end of the oscillation. First, in regard to the claim that Stalnaker appears to be committed to a realist ontology. In what sense is the liberal Platonist a Platonist? Stalnaker considers a number of alternatives to a realist ontology that are more conducive to the liberal case. A liberal Platonist might askew a realist ontology and find a safe harbour in a fictionalist account of modality, for example. She might propose an analogy between a general account of truth in fiction and modality. The truth of some sentences, it might be argued, such as 'Professor Moriarty died at the Reichenbach Falls', should not be taken at face value. They are truncated sentences; explicitly true only in the context of a wider fiction. They can only be truly asserted in the context of an utterance that compels their interpretation as sentences, which begin with a latent operator, i.e., 'according to such and such fiction'. Despite initial

---

[2] Beebee & McBride (2015, pp. 224 ff.) argue that Lewis concurs with Quine insofar as the determination of the modal attributes of a thing x is context-dependent. Rather than share Quines 'bewilderment' in respect of the attribution of de re modal properties, however, Lewis advanced a multiplicity of counterpart relations that enables him to accept the inconstancy of ordinary modal discourse (Lewis 1986a, p. 252). Although often inconstant and vague the practice is still rule-governed viz. Wittgenstein's analysis of the concept 'game': "In one context we may favour the counterpart relation that (e.g.) weighs being two-legged more heavily than being rational, but in another context we may reverse the relative weighing of these respects of similarity, and so on." (Beebee & McBride 2015, p. 225: Lewis 1986a, p. 254: 1983b [1983], p. 42).

appearances, these sentences impose no commitment to quantify over a domain of objects within the scope of the 'fiction' operator. Although initially appealing, Stalnaker rejects this option: "a fictionalist position requires a commitment to the intelligibility of a thesis that, if true, would make the fiction fact." (Stalnaker 1996 [2003], p. 46) Alternatives to a realist ontology that are viable in the Platonist sense appear to be in short supply (see § 6.3).

Second, and more seriously, how is the liberal Platonist to distinguish her theory from genuine modal realism **(GMR)**? In what sense is the liberal Platonist a liberal? Specifically, how is liberal Platonism to demonstrate the alleged mathematical-modal disanalogy? The mathematical case of a non-causal account of epistemology and semantics needs to be distinguished from the modal case. Isn't the liberal Platonist nothing more than a realist 'wolf in sheep's clothing'? Stalnaker is quick to anticipate Lewis' response:

> If our most plausible semantic hypothesis tells us that a certain bit of discourse is about things that speakers are not causally connected to, and if epistemological principles that seem on reflection to be reasonable tell us that we can know about such things, then there is no reason that we should not accept both the semantics and the epistemology. Isn't that just what your liberal Platonist thinks? (Stalnaker 1996 [2003], p. 47: Lewis 1986a, pp. 113-15)

Stalnaker accepts that identifying the grounds for a plausible distinction is difficult. A preliminary step is to acknowledge that the liberal Platonist is allied to a diluted form of verificationism. The allegiance is 'diluted' because it is restricted to the ways in which epistemology ought to constrain ontology. The 'diluted' verificationist case unpacks as follows. The genuine realist claims to know that there are people and objects that exist despite their causal isolation from this world. People and objects that exist in space-time but not *our* space-time. Given this analysis, how are modal beliefs to be justified if we are causally unrelated to these entities? How can we determine that these people and objects resemble us in certain respects? As mentioned earlier, for Stalnaker, it is the very nature of the entities, to which the genuine realist claims to have epistemic access that thwart his claims to know. The liberal Platonist argues that in order to acquire knowledge about people and objects, we must be causally related to them. Thus a diluted form of verificationism offers the liberal Platonist a route to the elusive mathematical-modal distinction: it is the very nature – de re contingency – of people and objects that impose a causal relationship between the knower and what is known. It is the absence of epistemological constraint that needlessly inflates the genuine realists' ontology (Stalnaker 1996 [2003], p. 49: cf. Dorr 2011).[3]

I have arrived at an impasse. Although committed to a naturalised epistemology (see chapter three), Lewis' rejects the claim that ontology should be constrained by epistemology. There *are* constraints on the ontology of genuine realism, but they are not epistemological. Instead, the ontological commitments of **GMR** are constrained by methodological principles. There ought to be no conceptual link between the nature of a thing and the ways that we know about that thing. All impersonal knowledge of de re contingency, including knowledge of non-actual people and objects, is a priori. Knowledge of actual people and objects is personal because it is indexical (§ 2.5). I defer an exploration of the realist distinction between the semantic and metaphysical theses for chapter six. Meanwhile, I turn to examine one consequence of the proposed distinction: if we separate the semantic and metaphysical theses do we reduce analytic truth to an insubstantial truth?

5.4 A metaphysical conception of analyticity

In **S1**, Lewis' argued that the term 'possible world' is a paraphrase of 'ways things could have been' (§ 2.5). It appears that Lewis stipulates a synonymy of two predicate expressions that partially render the modal translation scheme an analytic truth. The semantic-metaphysical distinction highlighted in the previous section would appear to impose an insubstantiality thesis on any potential account of analyticity. The type of analyticity most amenable to the insubstantiality thesis is metaphysical analyticity. I now examine two forms of metaphysical analyticity: modal-analyticity and Frege-analytic (Williamson 2007). Although, as a general conception, modal-analyticity is appealing, I reject the account. An obvious cloud of vicious circularity lingers over modal-analyticity in relation to Lewis' modal translation scheme. Frege-analyticity, on the other hand, does appear to be more promising. If it is combined with a descriptivist understanding of meaning, it appears to satisfy the 'synonymy' relation of *some* predicate expressions. Timothy Williamson is sceptical about

---

[3] Eventually, Stalnaker concedes that he is unable to offer a general principle of distinction that the genuine realist is obliged to accept. Furthermore, Lewis denied a premise on which Stalnaker's argument depends: namely, a conceptual connection between the way in which we know a thing and our conception of its nature. On Dummett's proposed 'fifth way' (see Dummett 1981, *Frege: Philosophy of Language* Duckworth 2nd edition, pp. 471-511) intended to distinguish concrete and abstract entities, for example, Lewis comments: "Even if this fifth way succeeds in drawing a border, as for all I know it may, it tells us nothing directly about how the entities on opposite sides of that border differ in their nature." (Lewis 1986a, p. 82 fn. 56)

the Frege-analytic conception on the grounds of the insubstantiality thesis. His doubts are illustrated by way of a further distinction that he argues is too often ignored; a distinction between meta-semantic and sematic fact.

In *The Philosophy of Philosophy*, Williamson subjects a number of accounts of analyticity to scrutiny. Those that compose the metaphysical form of analyticity are united by a common thread: "They impose no constraint on the world, not even on that part of it which consists of words and concepts. ... Analytic truths are less substantial than synthetic ones because the latter do impose constraints on the world, which it may or may not meet." (Williamson 2007, p. 52) Metaphysically analytic truth is marked by the lack of constraint imposed by the world on the truth of the sentence. Williamson endorses the semantic notion of synonymy as a point of departure from which to explore the notion of analyticity. The difficulty, in respect of analyticity, is Kripke's 'widely accepted' differentiation of analytic, a priori and necessary truth on semantic, epistemological and metaphysical grounds (Kripke 1980, p. 39). Kripke argues that analytic entails both a priori and necessary. In addition, he argues that neither a priori nor necessary entail one another. It follows – by the transitivity of entailment – that neither a priori nor necessary entail analytic. The notion of analyticity is thereby relieved of the epistemological burden of the a priori and the metaphysical burden of the necessary. There is reason to suppose, however, that the notion of analyticity still has work to do.

Let us suppose that 'ways things could have been' and 'possible world' are synonyms. In short, that 'possible world' is a genuine paraphrase. Traditionally, the proposed analytic truth expressed by the modal translation scheme should be based on an equivalence in meaning. That is, the modal translation scheme is not just true but analytically true – in part because these two predicate expressions share a common meaning. Contrast this with synthetic truth – truth in terms of the meaning of the expression *and* how the world accords with that meaning. For example, 'John Mortimer is a barrister' is a synthetic truth because it means that Mortimer is a barrister and he *is*, in fact, a barrister. This is the crux of the insubstantiality thesis: the truth-value of an analytic sentence is wholly determined by the meaning of the words and not by the nature of the world. Williamson is not persuaded by the insubstantiality thesis (Williamson 2007, p. 58). He is unconvinced, therefore, that the insubstantiality thesis can supply a route to an accurate notion of analyticity in the metaphysical sense. There is, he argues, in addition to the meaning of the words, an element of *presumed* truth that partially explains the analytic truth of sentences such as 'all solicitors are lawyers'. Specifically, a presumed truth that underwrites the *fact* – in terms of how the world is – that all solicitors are lawyers! "For any true sentence *s* whatsoever, a canonical explanation of the truth of *s* takes the overall form '*s* means that P, and P.'" (ibid., p. 59). If the insubstantiality thesis is not a necessary condition of analytic truth might it be a sufficient condition? The meaning of an expression will be "*sufficient for truth* just in case necessarily, in any context any sentence with that meaning is true." (ibid., p. 60) Clearly, the use of 'necessarily' in Williamson's remark invokes a modal notion. Indeed, Williamson designates this definition of analyticity 'modal-analyticity'.

What are the implications of modal-analyticity? Let a non-indexical proposition p be a necessary truth. Any sentence s that expresses the actual meaning of p in any context is true. Let sentence s meet the proposed sufficiency condition and be a modal-analytic truth. "But how little has been achieved in so classifying it!" (ibid., p. 61). Nothing is yet established in regard to whether s is/is not:

   a.   a deep metaphysical necessity discovered only after detailed a posteriori investigation

   b.   just 'verbal' or 'insubstantial' in a pre-theoretical sense

   c.   a mathematical truth.

The paucity of theoretical ground secured by adopting the clause 'in virtue of meaning' as a sufficient condition can be illustrated by way of an analogy: "call a meaning *temporally sufficient for truth* just in case at all times, in any context any sentence with that meaning is true." (ibid., p. 61) The quantifier expressions 'at all times' and 'in any context' are to be understood non-modally, i.e., as restricted to the actual world. Any sentence that expresses an eternally true proposition – no matter how contingent – has a meaning sufficient to be true. Designate this type of sentence 'temporally-analytic', e.g., 'no automobile has ever had a million seats'. There remains no valid inference, however, from temporal-analyticity to insubstantiality (ibid., p. 61). Hence, a desired route to the insubstantiality thesis [and metaphysical analyticity] is blocked by the notion of modal-analyticity.

Arguably, it seems that there are some modal-analytic sentences that do not necessarily express true propositions, e.g., contingent a priori. Further, not all necessarily true propositions are modal-analytic, e.g., necessary a posteriori. It is reasonable to suppose that there is a core of true propositions constituted by modal-analytic truths, however. By **S5** modal logic – the possible is non-contingently possible, and the necessary is non-contingently necessary. Questions such as 'is it necessary or possible that p?' prompt answers that are themselves necessarily true. In addition, if these answers can be expressed in terms that are non-indexical, then they are modal-analytic. Despite this, the recognition that a true sentence is modal-analytic still fails to unlock the epistemology of that sentence's analyticity. That is, although the conventional meaning of such sentences may reliably be asserted, the reliability invoked is not a sufficient condition for knowledge. A mathematical truth, for example, may rest on a 'theorem' that is suspect. A competent language user may use a true sentence s to express a proposition p that is modal-analytic. This is not equivalent to either knowing or holding a justifiable belief in the truth of s, nor does it supply insight into the truth of s. I raise but will not attempt to answer these important concerns because there is a darker storm cloud on the horizon. To resort to an explanation of analyticity based on the notion of modal-analytic truth appears to be viciously circular, at least on its face. The proposed analytic truth of the paraphrase found in **S1** as one component of the modal translation scheme can hardly rest *itself* on a notion of modal-analyticity. For this reason, I – abruptly – discontinue this line of enquiry in order to turn to a second possibility raised by Williamson. The possibility that the paraphrase is an example of Fregean-analyticity.

"A sentence is Frege-analytic just in case it is synonymous with a logical truth … roughly speaking because everything of the form 'All F is F' is true." (ibid., p. 63). For example, 'all bachelors are lazy' is not equivalent to a logical truth because not every sentence of the form 'All F are G' is a logical truth. Most sentences of this latter form do not meet the standard of Fregean-analyticity. Those that do include the sentence 'all bachelors are unmarried men', which *is* equivalent to the logical truth 'All F is F' after a substitution of synonyms, e.g., 'bachelors' and 'unmarried men'. In "Two Dogmas," Quine concedes that analytic statements include those that are logically true (Quine 1951a [1980], p. 22); so *if* the notion of synonymy is admitted, then so should the notion of a Fregean-analytic truth. By **S1**, Lewis expresses a preference for the term 'possible world' as a paraphrase of 'ways things could have been' (Lewis 1973, p. 84). Does Lewis' argument from paraphrase establish a Fregean-analytic truth? Various forms of analyticity can be distinguished on the basis of syntactic category: a sentence, a singular term or a predicate expression (Hylton 2010, p. 55). In our case of predicate expressions, the relevant linguistic form of analyticity unpacks as follows:

i. Two predicates, F and G, mean the same just in case "All Fs are Gs and vice versa" is not merely true but analytic (ibid., p. 55)

The 'not merely true but analytic' clause is important. Recall Quine's objections to the set theoretic interpretation of properties due to their identity conditions (§ 4.5) (Quine 1951a [1980]). Any attempt to explain the synonymy of predicate expressions by way of their inter-substitutivity *salve veritate* in all contexts also fails (ibid., p. 27). This is because the proposed condition fails to deliver the 'cognitive synonymy' required of analyticity. The co-extension of predicate expressions may simply turn on the contingent facts rather than meaning, e.g., 'creature with a heart' and 'creature with kidneys'. As a descriptivist – with a fine-grained view of meaning – Lewis' preferred paraphrase entails only linguistic competence *and* rationality. Proponents of descriptivism usually argue in favour of a loose semantic connection between a proper name and a cluster of descriptions. By avoiding a strict synonymy between a proper name and a single description, they hope to dodge a host of persuasive counter-arguments marshalled by Kripke et al. (cf. Williamson 2007, p. 69). In the case of modal translation, the predicate expression – or descriptive phrase – 'possible world' is offered as a synonym of the descriptive phrase 'ways things could have been', which I abbreviate as 'WTCB' (ibid. p. 68 ff.). By (i) above:

A.   'All possible worlds are WTCB (and vice versa).'

Sentence (A) does not appear to be a logical truth by any standard conception of classical logic – unless 'possible world' and 'WTCB' are interpreted as logical constants. Indeed, the logical form of (A) has instances that are false: 'All Ps are Es (and vice versa)' is false in the case of 'All Parisians are Ethiopians (and vice versa)'. The damage caused to my argument by such counterexamples is minimal, however. Frege-analytic sentences include a range of expressions that include but are not limited to logical truths. Suppose, for a moment, that 'possible world' and 'WTCB' had the same intension – understood as a function from circumstances of evaluation to extension in every context of utterance. Even this generous supposition does not supply synonymy, however. The semantic structure of the phrase 'possible world' is finite and is not a proper part of the semantic structure of the phrase 'ways things could have been' (Williamson 2007, p. 69). These two expressions also differ in their syntactic structure. Quite aside from these difficulties, Williamson's central problem with the proposal – to establish a Fregean-analytic truth by way of a stipulated synonymy – is grounded in a distinction of semantic and meta-semantic facts (ibid., pp. 71-2).

Semantic facts are those that are systematised by a compositional theory for any given language. Semantic facts pertain to what a given expression means; for example, the common noun 'dog' means the species dog. Meta-semantic facts, on the other hand, are the facts upon which the semantic facts supervene. Meta-semantic facts include the fact that the presence of a dog will often prompt the utterance 'dog'. By parity of reason, it is a semantic fact – if fact it be – that the predicate expression 'possible world' means the way things could have been. However, the fact that the meaning of the phrase 'possible world' is introduced by Lewis in the form of a stipulation is meta-semantic. The manner in which a term is introduced to the lexicon of a language is semantically irrelevant (ibid., p. 72). The problem is that Lewis' declared preference for 'possible world' over 'way things could have been' does not make a possible world *be* a way things could have been. That would be to make the way things could have been be the way things could have been. Clearly, Lewis' act of stipulation does not make the way things could have been be the way things could have been. The way things could have been – literally – existed whether

Lewis' stipulates the synonymy or not. "The peculiarity of the case is all at the meta-semantic level; the use of stipulative definitions as paradigms does not yield a *semantic* notion of analyticity." (ibid., p. 72)

Traditionally, the modal translation scheme would require an equivalence 'in virtue of meaning' of our two predicate expressions. As a necessary condition of analyticity, the insubstantiality thesis is confounded by the worldly assessment of truth required of some analytic sentences. As a sufficiency condition of analyticity, the insubstantiality thesis may enjoy some success with the modal form of metaphysical analyticity. Unfortunately, in the case of the modal translation scheme, the deployment of the modal-analytic explanation is circular. However, an alternative variety of metaphysical analyticity is found in Fregean-analytic sentences. Absent a synonymy in ordinary language, the predicate phrases 'ways things could have been' and 'possible world' demand a stipulated synonymy. That is, a simple declaration for a preference; that by 'F', I shall mean 'G' – and vice versa. Quine admits that a novel term of art might be introduced for the sake of brevity or in order to teach (Quine 1951a [1980], p. 27: 1960 [2013], Section 40 p. 175). The problem with Lewis' preferred paraphrase of the 'ways things could have been' is that synonymy cannot be established by stipulation alone. Williamson argues persuasively that a synonymy by stipulation is apt to confound two types of fact. In order to defend Lewis' preferred paraphrase, therefore, I require a bridge to link the meta-semantic fact of stipulation with the semantic fact of synonymy. Fortunately, Lewis provides the materials for the construction of such a bridge in his account of linguistic meaning – semantic fact – based on convention – meta-semantic fact.

5.5 Analytic truth by convention

I argue that Stalnaker's demarcation of the semantic and metaphysical theses is correct. This distinction facilitates my endorsement of the insubstantiality thesis of analyticity that is opposed by Williamson. An analytic truth is true by virtue of meaning *alone*. Analytic truth is true regardless of how the world is. The term 'bachelor' is a synonym of the phrase 'unmarried man' whether there are any actual bachelors or not. The term 'dodo' is a synonym of the phrase 'a large flightless bird, *Raphus cucullatus*, formerly native to Mauritius', whether there are any actual dodos or not. The term 'unicorn' is a synonym of the phrase 'animal with the body of a horse and a single straight horn projecting from the forehead', whether there are any actual unicorns or not. Hence, the predicate expression 'possible world' is a synonym of the phrase 'ways things could have been' whether there are any ways things could have been or not. Importantly, the view entails that the complex term 'possible world' has no metaphysical implications. A possible world could be a discrete, spatiotemporal continuity or a set of consistent and complete unactualised propositions or a recombination of actual world properties or a convenient fiction, and so forth. In this section, I address Williamson's main objection to this form of analyticity. How does a meta-sematic act of stipulation establish a semantic synonymy?

Lewis' preliminary remarks on convention relate to how they must hold in order that a population P speak a language L (Lewis 2002: 1975 [1983]). The notion of a convention is subsequently developed in two ways. First, conventions are to be understood as a regularity not just in action but also in belief. Second, an earlier condition of conventionality is diluted. A 'preference shared by almost everyone in a community' is replaced by '(almost) every agent has a reason to conform when they believe others will also conform'. This 'reason to conform' may be a practical one when conformity relates to action, knowledge, or belief. Lewis' initial account of linguistic convention relates only to a regularity among the speakers of a language. The adjusted account includes the hearers as well as the speakers of the language. Intuitively, Lewis' mature analysis aligns his account with the actual practice of a population: linguistic conventions resolve coordination problems between speakers of a language and their hearers. As a consequence of these adjustments, a population P use a language L only if it has a *convention* of 'truthfulness and trust' in L (Lewis 1992: cf. Hawthorne 1990, 1993).

1. Truthfulness in L; "To be truthful in L is to act in a certain way: to try never to utter any sentences of L that are not true in L. Thus it is to avoid uttering any sentences of L unless one believes it to be true in L." (Lewis 1975 [1983], p. 167)

2. Trust in L: "To be trusting in L is to form beliefs in a certain way: to impute truthfulness in L to others, and thus to tend to respond to another's utterance of any sentence of L by coming to believe that the uttered sentence is true in L." (ibid., p. 167)

Lewis' earlier account took convention to be rooted in coordination between the speakers of a language. The English-speaking community utter English sentences in, say, London because they intend and expect their sentences to be understood by the inhabitants – community – of that city. However, this analysis fails to account for a basic form of communication: two-way coordination between a single speaker – convention to speak truly in L – and a single hearer – convention to trust in L. Naturally, exceptions to the conventions of truthfulness and trust in L exist. People don't always intend to tell the truth. In addition to dishonesty, people can be mistaken or misapply sentences. As a result, we do not always believe what people say. However, Lewis' account of conventions in language represents a default position. In a sense, the possibility of dishonesty or mistake is conceptually 'parasitic' on the predominantly honest and reliable practice of a linguistic community. As

Gilbert Ryle noted, the idea of a counterfeit £10 note is conceptually dependent on the idea of a genuine £10 note.

Any putative synonymy of terms is embedded in the conventions to speak truly, and trust in L. Lewis' initial definition of a convention repeatedly makes use of the notion of conformity to R or R' (Lewis 2002, p. 78). Later, with respect to language, he cites the 'rules of composition' and 'rules verbal expression'. Provisionally, I propose that 'conformity to R' should be interpreted as a meta-semantic component of linguistic convention, e.g., an act of stipulation. A meta-semantic act of stipulation is supplemented by the rules of 'composition' and 'verbal expression'. Provisionally, these rules comprise the semantic component of a putative linguistic convention. Combined, the meta-semantic 'conformity to R' and the semantic 'following a rule R' warrant the synonymy of our two predicate expressions. The **S1** paraphrase of 'ways things could have been' by 'possible world' is licensed by a bridge constructed on the basis of a distinction between conformity to a rule and following a rule. How are 'conformity to R' and the rules of composition and verbal expression combined in practice? Consider an example long favoured by philosophers, the game of chess:

> (B): The Knight in chess first moves two squares in a straight line, then one square to the side.

In order for a chess player to comprehend (B), she must first understand certain practices and facts about the game of chess. What is a Knight in chess? What is a square in chess? What is a move in chess? In this context, (B) could be said to have the following canonical reading:

    i.   (B) formulates a rule in chess

However, (B) can be understood in different ways:

    ii.   An inductive generalisation regarding the permitted movement of an object called the 'knight in chess', or

    iii.   An empirical hypothesis about the activity of moving the knight in chess, or

    iv.   An expression of an indirect command to a player of chess

"That (B) has these different usages is something that continues to be relevant to its application even *after* its inception." (Juhl & Loomis 2010, p. 122) A person ignorant of the difference between i and iii would be unable to correct a player who mistakenly moved a knight 'bishop-like' along the diagonal, for example. If (B) is indeed just a hypothesis – as at iii – then the movement of the knight along the diagonal is not incorrect; it is simply the falsification of a hypothesis. In an actual game of chess, however, a player who moves the knight along the diagonal has not merely falsified a hypothesis or refuted an empirical generalisation. They have made an illegitimate move. They would be open to censure by their opponent. The stipulation-hypothesis distinction clearly rests on a difference between following a rule and mere conformity with a rule (Wittgenstein 1958, Sections 138-242). Wittgenstein's passages on 'rule-following' offer a normative account of language:

> From the point of view of a normative conception of meaning such as Wittgenstein defends, a behaviouristic conception like Quine's is simply no conception of meaning at all, not even an ersatz one (fn. 19). Indeed, it is no conception of *language*, for a language stripped of normativity is no more language than chess stripped of its rules is a game. (Hacker 1996, pp. 15-16)

Hacker's comments demonstrate the folly of ignoring Wittgenstein's distinction (§ 2.4). The folly is amplified if there are independent reasons that favour it. Indeed, there are independent reasons that favour the distinction; a ticking clock, a set of traffic lights, and waves lapping on a seashore are among numerous examples of conformity to a regularity. A set of traffic lights, for example, can be said to conform to the rule 'show a green light only after a red and amber light are shown together'. It is inappropriate to say that the set of traffic lights follows this rule, however. Absent Wittgenstein's distinction we are left with an invidious choice between two implausible alternatives: either nothing is an instance of rule-following, or every regularity is an example of rule-following.

Mere conformity to a linguistic rule is insufficient to establish a stipulated synonymy of terms amongst a community of language users. A community must also 'follow a rule' in order to satisfy the demands of actual language use. The meta-semantic act of stipulation can establish a semantic synonymy if the convention guiding the stipulation is non-linguistic. A stipulated synonymy warrants Lewis' preference for the paraphrase of 'ways things could have been' by 'possible world'. However, even if the paraphrase is genuine (§ 2.3), it remains only one component of the overall modal translation scheme. The introduction of the predicate phrase 'possible world' as a novel term of art may generate a number of theoretical advantages, e.g., the semantic benefits accrued by the use of a 'worldly' extensional language (§ 1.1). In combination, these theoretical desiderata may justify the claim that the modal translation scheme is an analytic truth (Divers 1997, p. 142). If successful, one component of the scheme is indeed a paraphrase of an ordinary language expression. I reiterate, however, that no metaphysical implications accompany the success of this endeavour. The truth of a traditional analytic sentence is wholly trivial or insubstantial. Nonetheless, the bridge between semantic synonymy and the meta-semantic act of stipulation is constructed. The truth value of a sentence in L is determined in part by convention. Conformity to a rule of language – a meta-sematic fact – is combined with following a rule of language – a semantic fact – to establish a genuine paraphrase of 'ways things could have been'. Hopefully, I have (at least) partially allayed Williamson's primary concern.

5.6 Conclusion

Stalnaker's dislocation of **GMR's** semantic and metaphysical theses indicates that the analyticity of the modal translation scheme need not entail an ontological commitment to a plurality of concrete worlds. Hence, this ontological commitment needs to be justified on independent grounds (chapter four). The notion of metaphysical analyticity implies that analytic truth is insubstantial. I argue that insubstantiality does not meet a necessary condition of analytic truth. There are analytic truths whose truth is based on a presupposition about how things stand in the world. As a sufficient condition, the insubstantiality thesis was tested against modal-analyticity. I was compelled to set aside modal-analyticity on the grounds of circularity. A second conception, Fregean-analyticity, was then adopted. Williamson doubts the plausibility of this new form of analyticity on the grounds that it fails to observe the meta-semantic/semantic distinction. I accept the distinction but argue that it might be bridged by Lewis' account of linguistic convention. Lewis offers a systematic account of how linguistic meaning is generated by social convention. Adjusted to recognise Wittgenstein's 'following a rule', Lewis is able to establish a synonymy by stipulation of his preferred paraphrase of 'ways things could have been'. These gains do not banish Stalnaker's semantic-metaphysical distinction, however. Indeed, they presuppose that distinction. This is to invite danger. Do semantic explanations of modality enjoy the theoretical benefits of the quantification-predicate model without the need to postulate a plurality of Lewisian worlds? I turn to examine an alternative to **GMR** that exploits Stalnaker's semantic-metaphysical distinction, John Divers' worldly agnosticism.

6
Modal agnosticism

6.1 Introduction

The topic of this chapter is Divers' modal agnosticism in respect of an ontological commitment to a type of entity, possible worlds. The antirealist interpretation of modal discourse is based primarily on an ontological distinction.[1] Broadly, the modal realist asserts that there is a mind-independent plurality of worlds that constitute the domain of non-modal discourse. The type of world varies depending on the type of realism employed. The genuine modal realist **(GMR)** asserts the existence of a plurality of concrete individuals or worlds whilst the actualist realist **(AR)** asserts the existence of a plurality of abstract entities or worlds. The antirealist, on the other hand, denies the realist interpretation of the relevant domain of discourse (Divers 2002, p. 3).

Antirealism is contrasted with **GMR** analysis. The analysis usually presented as the viable alternative to **GMR** is **AR**. Divers, however, argues that both varieties of realism suffer from a parallel defect. Whether they be concrete individuals or abstract entities, 'worlds' are causally isolated from the actual world. This causal isolation prompts Divers to reject both types of realism on epistemic and semantic grounds (cf. Sosa 2002) (§ 6.2). I briefly consider the motivation behind antirealist interpretations of modal discourse (§ 6.3). I examine one variety of modal antirealism, worldly agnosticism **(WA)**. I consider one criticism of **WA**; an assertibilty – and belief – deficit. Divers' offers the worldly agnostic three strategies intended to mitigate this criticism. They are each loosely based on the rational dispensability of the – disputed – class of belief in a de re possibility (§ 6.5). I conclude that although modal agnosticism presents a cogent alternative to **GMR,** it cannot match the latter's reserve of assertible – and belief – modal sentences (§ 6.6).

I previously identified a number of theoretical advantages associated with the quantificational-predicate model of modal analysis (§ 1.1). Divers hopes **WA** can acquire the advantage of inferential validity without incurring the cost of

---

[1] The ontological distinction in respect to the demarcation of realism is not unanimously endorsed. Grayling argues that since it is mind-independence that demarcates the realist position the distinction should be based on epistemological grounds. "Realists and their opponents do not disagree about what exists, but about how we are epistemically related to what exists." (Grayling 1997, p. 288)

an ontological commitment to a plurality of worlds. The thread of inferential validity runs through the weave of Divers' argument to establish worldly agnosticism as a viable alternative to **GMR** (Lewis 1986a, p. 174). If successful, Divers' **WA** would secure both the theoretical benefit of valid logical inference (§ 1.1) and criterion b of a genuine paraphrase (§ 2.3).

6.2 Realism and possible worlds

We inhabit a world populated by people and objects that possess properties and stand in relations of various kinds. Standard predicate logic **(PL)** allows us to quantify over people and objects and assign to them properties and relations. Recall **GMR** extends the ability to quantify over what actually exists to include that which does not actually exist. This 'unrestricted' domain of quantification aims to facilitate a reductive analysis of modality (§ 2.3). When we discuss what could, might, or ought to happen, we are talking about a possible world in which what could, might, or ought to happen, did happen. We are able to translate intensional modal talk of necessity and possibility into extensional talk about possible worlds where the relevant necessity or possibility is realised. The biconditional schema of modal translation unfolds as follows:

A.   It is necessary that P iff P is the case at all worlds

B.   It is possible that P iff P is the case in at least one world

C.   It is impossible that P iff P is the case at no world

Hence, modal translation exploits a logical equivalence between the modal operators and quantificational expressions. It avoids the problems associated with sentences of intensional language by translating them into sentences of extensional language (§ 2.2). There are significant theoretical benefits associated with this philosophical technique, e.g., valid logical inferences (Divers 2004, p. 665).

Many philosophers consider the price attached to securing these benefits too high. As a result, they have sought alternative routes to the same destination: to enjoy the inferential power of modal translation whilst eschewing the ontological commitment to a plurality of worlds. Divers' preferred alternative route is *moderate* **WA** which is "agnostic about the existence of any entities that are characterized as unobservables, *except when some further characterization gives grounds for disbelief in the entities in question.*" (ibid., p. 669) In contrast, radical agnosticism retains its agnostic stance about unobservable entities 'no matter how they are otherwise described'.[2] However, despite this licence to the

---

[2] The moderate-radical contrast allows for a further characterisation that might supply a warrant to deny / disbelieve the content of an otherwise 'agnostic' assertion or belief. For

modal inferences of the genuine realist, **WA** suffers from a deficit of otherwise warranted modal belief. The charge of an assertibility – and belief – deficit against worldly agnosticism can be made on logical grounds.

As a preliminary, I explore Divers' enumerated reasons to reject two varieties of modal realism. The realist-antirealist demarcation is drawn on the basis of their respective ontological commitments to a type of entity, K. Realism is marked by a commitment to non-actual worlds, although the ontological nature of those worlds differ, dependent on the type of realism. The postulates of **GMR**, for example, state that possible worlds are mind-independent, discrete spatiotemporal individuals. By implication, each world is causally isolated, one from the other. Consider the following standard translation of a modal sentence:

> **GMR 1:** It is possible that dragons exist iff there is a world at which a dragon exists

Formally, the analysans [right side, biconditional] of the above analysandum [left side, biconditional] is:

> **GMR 2:** $\exists x \, \exists y$ (Wx & Iyx & Dragon y)

Pitted against genuine realism is a view espoused by Robert Adams et al. designated by Divers actualist realism **(AR)**. Philosophers perplexed by an ontological commitment to a plurality of concrete worlds suggest a different interpretation of the phrase 'possible world'. Adams, for example, argues that possible worlds are determinate but abstract, maximally consistent sets of propositions. Worlds are 'determinate' when they are able to satisfy two conditions:

> [That] (1) For every possible world, w, and every pair of contradictory propositions, one member of the pair is true in w and the other member is false in w. (2) Each possible world, if temporally ordered at all, is a complete world history and not a momentary stage of one (Adams 1979, p. 191).

The genuine realist *appears* to enjoy a number of theoretical advantages over his **AR** counterpart. On the presumption that theoretical reduction is a desideratum (Divers 2002, p. 181 fn. 1: cf. Stalnaker 2012, p. 4), any attempt to provide a reductive analysis of modality by **AR** is in vain. The analysans of **GMR** translation is satisfied – in part – by a plurality of worlds that exist with or without our knowledge or belief in them (§ 3.5). This objectivity renders them immune to the vagaries of our doxastic state – in terms of what we believe is

---

example, a moderate agnostic about the existence of God may discover a contradiction derived from the presupposition of His existence and change her agnosticism to denial.

necessarily or possibly true. Worlds are understood to be independent of our notions of modality and are described in non-modal terms (§ 1.1). **GMR** analysis supplies a reductive and non-circular account of modality. Although **AR** analysis shares the objectivity of **GMR** (sets of propositions exist independently of our belief and knowledge), they do not offer a reductive explanation of modality. Adams' account, for example, is based on the 'consistency' of a set of propositions that collectively constitute a possible world. Hence, it must be possible for all of the propositions of the relevant set to be collectively true. Clearly, to explicate the notion of a possible world based on the 'consistency' of a set of propositions is to employ a modal notion as an element of the analysans. I am entitled to conclude, therefore, that **AR** analysis is circular and illegitimate.

On the other hand, **AR** does enjoy the theoretical advantage of a "safe and sane ontology" (Divers 2002, p. 227). If we are predisposed to accept propositions as amongst the ontological commitments of 'total theory', then we avoid an ontological inflation. Divers, however, is not persuaded that the ontological commitments of **AR** are so innocuous. Any ontological commitment to either sets of propositions or a plurality of concrete worlds is prone to a common flaw: causal isolation. **GMR**, for example, postulates a plurality of discrete, concrete worlds that are causally isolated one from the other (§ 5.3). How do we acquire modal knowledge of possible worlds and their inhabitants? Modal knowledge is not acquired a posteriori since, by stipulation, each world is causally isolated. The epistemological problem is particularly acute for de re possibilities. Humphrey's defeat in the 1968 US Presidential Election could have been otherwise. Humphrey might have won. **GMR** analysis states that Humphrey could have been victorious because he has other-worldly counterparts who defeated the counterpart of, say, Nixon in a counterpart election. For the genuine realist, possible people and objects are people and objects. The problem of causal isolation originates in the genuine realists' requirement that different epistemic relations justify what we know about entities of the *same* kind. Why should there be an epistemological difference based on our causal relations to Humphrey and his counterparts? Humphrey and his counterparts are contingent people. In respect of Humphrey, a posteriori knowledge of his electoral defeat is based on my causal relation to the 1968 election. In respect to Humphrey's counterpart, a priori knowledge of his electoral victory is based on my non-causal relation to a counterpart of the 1968 Presidential election. To understand what it *is* to be a person or physical object is *in part* to understand how one is epistemically *related* to that person or physical object (Stalnaker 1996 [2003], pp. 48-49). How should epistemological considerations constrain the ontological commitments of a theory?[3] For the genuine realist, the answer is simple; they shouldn't and they don't (§ 4.1).

AR fares a little better. **AR** postulates the existence of abstract entities, i.e., propositions and sets of propositions that are causally isolated from us. Again, how do we acquire knowledge of abstract entities? "**AR** ontology is not safe and sane because its causal isolation from us renders it semantically and epistemologically queer" (Divers 2002, p. 230). In terms of their causal isolation from the actual world, Divers argues that both **GMR** and **AR** are tarred with the same brush. Each postulates an ontology that is difficult to reconcile with our ordinary claims to know or debate modal truths. In these circumstances, why should we endorse either type of realism? Why not simply abstain in regard to a belief in causally isolated possible worlds? Abstention is the doxastic stance adopted by worldly agnosticism **WA** (Divers 2004, p. 668).

6.3 Antirealism and possible worlds

Antirealism in the modal sphere is based on a general strategy of securing the theoretical benefits of **GMR** whilst avoiding an ontological commitment to a plurality of worlds (Divers 2004, pp. 662-63). The strategy can be illustrated by the modal translation of **GMR 1**, [right side, biconditional]: 'there is a world at which a dragon exists'. *Prima facie,* when we assert this sentence – and so imply its truth – we are committed to the existence of at least one non-actual world that has a dragon as a part – granting, of course, that there are no actual dragons. In order to avoid asserting an analysans with a realist interpretation and associated commitments to non-actual worlds, the antirealist may employ one of two stratagems: either deny that the sentence means what it appears to mean or accept the sentence's apparent meaning but deny that it is true (ibid., p. 663).[4] The problem with the first stratagem is that denying the apparent meaning of a sentence is to risk sacrificing the theoretical benefits – such as inferential validity – that a prima facie interpretation of meaning helps to secure. In the alternative, adopting the second stratagem secures the antirealist the theoretical benefits of **GMR**. That is, a prima facie interpretation of the meaning of the sentence provides an analysis in the form of truth conditions and

---

[3] Recall §5.3: for Lewis, knowledge of contingent physical objects is acquired in a way that does not require a causal relationship between knower and what is known. Knowledge of actual contingent physical objects is to be distinguished not by the nature of the thing [contingency] but by the fact that it is indexical [personal]. Indexical in the sense that we stand in a particular relation to it (§ 2.5) (see Stalnaker 1996 [2003], p. 49: Vaidya 2017, Section 1.2.3).

[4] For example, Fictionalism (Rosen 1990), Modalism (Forbes 1985) and Expressivism (Blackburn 1984).

conceptual content that is central to inferential validity. The relevant sentences are meaningful but false. The stratagem allows the antirealist to accept the straightforward meaning of the sentence whilst rejecting the truth of the realist 'assertion' and so avoiding an ontological commitment to non-actual worlds (ibid., p. 666).

The second stratagem of non-assertion can itself be pursued in one of two ways. The antirealist may allege that the existential assertions made in possible world discourse are *systematically* false – that is, they are not assertions at all. Alternatively, the antirealist may refuse to acknowledge that *any* particular existential assertion of possible world discourse is true.[5] **WA** "offers a vindication of our modalizing without requiring that we abandon the view that our modal beliefs frequently satisfy the full-blooded cognitive norms of truth and knowledge." (ibid., p. 667) The difficulty with the second stratagem is one of a perceived assertibilty, or belief gap: if the biconditional [right side] is not true or assertible, then the biconditional [left side] is not true or assertible!

6.4 Worldly agnosticism and possible worlds

Divers' begins his advocacy of worldly agnosticism with a distinction:

1. The Epistemological Thesis: there is no warrant to believe in any world other than the actual world

2. The Semantic Thesis: no statement that entails the existence of any possible world other than the actual world is assertible – no such statements may be *held true*, even though, for all we know, some *are true*.

    (Divers 2004, p. 668)

Combined, (1) and (2) express a 'natural epistemological attitude' toward modality. Lewis presents a utilitarian justification for his shared belief in non-actual worlds by way of an implied a priori justification for their existence (chapter three). In the alternative, Divers advocates a moderate form of **WA** that is *not* committed to a comprehensive agnosticism about modality. A moderate agnostic may legitimately claim modal knowledge based on necessity or impossibility, for example. These claims may be justified on the grounds of logical validity, language, or the laws of nature. Divers, for instance, is able to characterise necessity and impossibility on the basis of the application of unrestricted negative existential content (ibid., p. 670).

---

[5] The first sub-stratagem is associated with error theory whilst the second is associated with agnosticism about the existence of non-actual possible worlds.

Hence,

> **GMR** Necessity – It is necessary that A iff at all worlds A

Becomes

> **WA** Necessity – It is necessary that A iff there is no world at which not-A
> (ibid., p. 669)

I will confine my discussion of Divers' antirealist argument to moderate agnosticism. Parallel forms of logical inference may justify a raft of agnostic claims to modal knowledge. "What the agnostic about other worlds knows to be true of *no* individual, she knows – a fortiori – to be true of no part of any world, and crucially, she knows these things without knowing whether there exists any world other than our own." (ibid., p. 670) Further, since actuality implies possibility (if A is actually the case then A is possibly the case), any warrant we have to make assertions about the actual world counts as a warrant to make possibility claims. This is the case for both de dicto and de re possibility. Additional claims to modal knowledge may be warranted by way of an analytic truth, that nothing is both male and a vixen, for example. Beyond the realms of logic and analyticity, agnostic claims to modal knowledge become more controversial. A worldly agnostic, persuaded by Kripke et al., might claim to know modal truths warranted by the laws of nature; to know that nothing is water and hydrogen-free, for instance. All these justifications do raise a number of troubling epistemic questions for the worldly agnostic. Where should the worldly agnostic draw the line between knowledge and ignorance? Can the moderate **WA** enjoy epistemic parity with **GMR** without incurring the same epistemic cost?

In the previous section, I noted that worldly agnosticism may be open to criticism on logical grounds (ibid., p. 675) (§ 6.4). Despite a number of impressive claims to modal knowledge, the **WA** does not enjoy epistemic parity with her realist counterpart. There is an epistemic deficit or shortfall. Recall, modal translation is materially adequate in that it preserves the truth or falsity of the analysandum.

> **GMR 1:** It is possible that dragons exist iff there is a world at which a dragons exists

GMR 1 is a biconditional sentence of the form P iff Q. If the **WA** professes agnosticism in respect to the analysans Q [right side, biconditional], specifically, in the form of a reluctance to assert the existence of non-actual world(s), she is obliged – on pain of logical inconsistency – to profess agnosticism in respect of the analysandum P [left side, biconditional]. That is, **WA** is obliged to be agnostic about the truth of the claim that dragons are possible. This obligation is incurred by the truth-conditions required of all biconditionals: the relevant sentences must share a truth-value, otherwise, the biconditional must be false (ibid., p. 673). As a normative discipline, logic appears to debar the agnostic from asserting the truth of P [left side, biconditional] without incurring an entailment to the truth of Q [right side, biconditional]! It is important to note that this 'criticism' is foundational to Divers' view; he cares about what modal sentences we can assert because he recognises that if one is committed to the biconditional, a commitment to modal sentences also involves a commitment to possible world claims.

The remainder of this chapter is reserved for the analyses of modal sentences of de re possibility. The assertion of sentences of de re possibility provides a fertile ground for debate. Divers argues that **WA** does possess a warrant to assert certain modal truths of de re possibility. As mentioned earlier, she may deny that A is a de re possibility by asserting that there is no world at which A. Alternatively, she may assert that A is a de re possibility on the grounds that A can be asserted of the actual world. These assertions are licenced on grounds shared with the genuine realist viz. an argument of de re representation advanced by Lewis in *Plurality*: "what is the case *at* a world is what the world represents, and a world represents (de re) of x that it is F by having a part which is a counterpart of x and is F." (Divers 2004, p. 674: Lewis 1986a, pp. 194-96) For example, on both **GMR** and **WA** analysis, 'Michael Dummett is a philosopher in the actual world' is true since the actual world has parts which are both Michael Dummett counterparts and philosophers.[6] However, the denial may also be true: Michael Dummett might *not* have been a philosopher since the actual world has parts that are both counterparts of Michael Dummett and *not* philosophers (Divers 2004, p. 674).

Matters are apt to become more contentious in further cases of de re possibility. For example, **WA** faces an assertibility – and belief – deficit in cases of the de re possibility of A when there is either no warrant to assert that there is no world at which A or no warrant to assert that at the actual world, A (ibid., p. 674). Although the worldly agnostic enjoys some degree of epistemological parity with her realist counterpart – e.g., she may assert the possibility of A on the grounds that 'A' is assertible at the actual world – Divers does acknowledge that a deficit between the genuine realist and worldly agnostic remains.

In order to be a decisive objection, however, Divers argues that the genuine realist is obliged to show that the deficit represents a significant omission (ibid., p. 676). Examples of omission are only 'significant' if the deficit has "implications

---

[6] Postulate five of Lewis' original paper prohibits this-worldly counterparts (Lewis 1968 [1983], p. 27). This prohibition is subsequently relaxed when Lewis allows – dependent on context – for this-worldly counterparts (Lewis 1983b [1983], p. 43).

for what we have reason to do, either practically or intellectually." (ibid., p. 684) Modal beliefs are 'rationally efficacious' because our assessment of what is possible has an impact on our thoughts, language, and actions. The aim of **WA** is to demonstrate that "all of those *disputed* beliefs that are rationally efficacious are also rationally dispensable." (ibid., p. 678 my emphasis) In short, Divers argues that the disputed class of beliefs in de re possibility can be abandoned without practical or intellectual loss. The genuine realist, on the other hand, must claim that the disputed class of beliefs represent an insuperable obstacle for the moderate agnostic. A failure to supply a warrant for those disputed beliefs in de re possibility leaves the agnostic with intellectual or practical gap in her rational beliefs of de re possibility.

A case in point is the circumstance in which we have reason to ϕ and where ϕ is an attempt to ψ (ibid., p. 680). How does the agnostic supply a warrant for the belief that an attempt to ψ is rational? Any rational ϕ ought to be constrained in some manner by the belief set of the agent. For example, an agent should not attempt to ψ if she believes that ψ is impossible. An attempt to prove Goldbach's Conjecture – that every even integer greater than two can be written as the sum of two prime numbers – let us suppose, is a mathematical impossibility. A belief that an attempt to ψ is impossible is one the agnostic can easily meet – it is impossible that ϕ iff there is no world at which ϕ. However, this explanation is not very robust – it amounts to the demand that disaster is not inevitable. Difficulties begin to mount when the requirement is not in a rational belief that the attempt to ψ is impossible but that the practical cost of the attempt is prohibitive. In these cases, the rational burden placed on the modal content of a belief increase. Divers selects a homely example by way of illustration (ibid., p. 681). Imagine that in normal road conditions, a driver is faced with a decision of whether or not to overtake. A more robust belief in the de re possibility of a successful manoeuvre is required than one secured by the warrant that the attempt is not impossible. This stronger requirement – a belief that overtaking is possible – is precisely the type of rational modal belief that the realist needs in order to press home the deficiency objection. That is a belief in the disputed class of de re possibility that is rationally indispensable.

6.5 In defence of worldly agnosticism

In order to block this rationally *in*dispensable belief in a de re possibility Divers' suggests that the worldly agnostic adopt one of three arguments.

Option One: The relevant type of belief is warranted on agnostic grounds.

The **WA** can argue that a warranted belief in the de re possibility to attempt ψ is compatible with a warranted belief in a this-worldly counterpart of the agent.

A rational [warranted] belief in an ability to attempt to successfully overtake is based on a warranted belief in a this-worldly counterpart, who does so (ibid., p. 681). Despite its initial promise, Divers acknowledges a potential flaw in this strategy. The reply places onerous demands on the agents' warranted beliefs about her actual world counterparts. There are too many novel situations that elude a general characterisation of modal knowledge of a this-worldly precedent to warrant a belief in the de re possibility (ibid., pp. 681-82).

These demands are not shared by **GMR,** which enjoys a reservoir of a priori beliefs in the existence of counterparts not restricted to this world (ibid., p. 682). Megan Blomfield argues that in addition to over-generating cases of 'rational efficacious' beliefs in de re possibility, the proposed strategy under-generates cases. That is, Blomfield argues that the practical and intellectual implications of 'rationally efficacious' beliefs impose a restriction too narrow to serve as a general analysis of the disputed class. Divers has significantly underestimated the size of the disputed class. Specifically, he ignores beliefs in de re possibility that A in cases where we know that 'at the actual world, not-A' (Blomfield 2008, p. 75). Consider the following translation of a de re possibility:

> MB1: It is possible for [my mind] to exist without a body iff there is a world in which [my mind] exists without a body

The translation generates two sides of a biconditional:

> MB2 Left-side: It is possible for [my mind] to exist without a body

> MB3 Right-side: There is a world in which [my mind] exists without a body

> (ibid., p. 76)

If MB2 is a member of the disputed class, then **WA** is obliged to be agnostic about the respective truth-values of MB2 and MB3. If we are persuaded that MB2 is actually true – based on, say, a Cartesian epistemology – then it expresses a belief in a de re possibility warranted by my counterpart at a non-actual world. In these circumstances, Divers' anticipated response is to claim that MB1 can be warranted on agnostic grounds, e.g., on the basis of a this-worldly counterpart. He could argue, for example, that my mind will continue to exist in this-world after the death of my body. Given the actual laws of nature, however, this reply is frustrated on the grounds that such a 'possibility' is an actual – nomological – impossibility. The Cartesian supposition that asserts the de re possibility of a [my mind] counterpart continuing to exist without [my body] is a logical truth – my 'bodiless' mind counterpart exists at *some* non-actual world. There is no this-worldly counterpart to warrant the worldly agnostic's rational belief in this de re possibility. Although unwarranted on agnostic grounds, the relevant modal belief remains a member of the disputed class. Hence, membership of the disputed class extends beyond Divers' narrow criterion of 'rationally efficacious' agnostic belief in a de re possibility.

I now turn to Divers' second option, which seeks to avoid the consequences of an agnostically 'unwarranted' but indispensable rationally efficacious modal belief in a de re possibility.

Option Two: The dispensability of the disputed belief is shown by the sufficiency of a distinct but warranted modal belief.

Divers' second option is based on the availability of a 'rationally efficacious' belief with counterfactual content that will supply the apparent deficiency of an appropriately warranted belief in a de re possibility (Divers 2004, p. 682). To return to the example of a successful attempt to overtake. A belief in this de re possibility may be warranted on agnostic grounds by way of counterfactual content, namely, that if he [Divers] were to attempt to overtake, then he would be successful. The truth-conditions of this counterfactual are met because there is no relevant world in which his counterpart's attempt to overtake is unsuccessful. Divers' argues that the invocation of a counterfactual conditional to supply the content of a belief in a de re possibility leaves the realist and agnostic interpretations in the same boat: specifically in regard to the 'similarity relation' (ibid., p. 682) (§§ 4.5, 4.6). A counterfactual alternative to a belief in a de re possibility invokes the 'similarity relation' twice over – in the selection and counterpart relations.

Broadly, by Lewisian semantics, a counterfactual conditional, e.g., if A were the case then B would be the case – is true just when at all of the closest worlds at which A is true, B is true. The closest worlds at which A is true are the 'selected' worlds. These are the worlds relevant to the evaluation of the conditional. If A and B are also de re then we need to take account of the counterparts that relevant individuals have in the selected worlds. Hence the need for two relations – selection (of worlds) and counterpart-hood. Now, suppose I wish to assert 'If A were the case, then B would be the case' when this involves a de re claim, say, about x. If this is true, then *if* there is a world at which B is false, either that world is not a selected world (not sufficiently similar to count as relevantly close) or B doesn't have a suitable counterpart (sufficiently similar to x). Hence, in the case of the overtaking manoeuvre: 'If there is a world at which an individual whose attempt to overtake is unsuccessful, then either the world in question is not relevantly similar to this one or the individual is not relevantly similar to him'. Since this is effectively the truth-condition of the counterfactual, he [Divers] can make *this* assertion instead. It is not a modal statement – it is just a material conditional about worlds that can be true on agnostic grounds. For example, if there are no non-actual worlds, then there is no world in which the attempt to overtake is unsuccessful. By the falsity of the antecedent, the whole conditional must be true.

A warrant to assert the counterfactual belief of a de re possibility can be satisfied on both worldly agnostic and genuine realist grounds. *If* there is a world at which an individual whose attempt to overtake is unsuccessful, then either the world in question is not relevantly similar to this one – genuine realism – or the individual is not relevantly similar to him [Divers] – worldly agnosticism (ibid., p. 682). A belief in the truth of a counterfactual conditional offers the agnostic a surrogate for the content of a belief in a de re possibility. This option offers **WA** a rich vein from which to mine examples of otherwise 'rationally efficacious' modal beliefs required to meet the realist's challenge (ibid., p. 682).

Does Divers second option, a belief with counterfactual content standing in place of a belief in a de re possibility, scupper Blomfield's objection? In order to be successful, **WA** requires an x such that:

MB4: If x had been the case, then [my mind] would have existed without a body

(Blomfield 2008, p. 76)

Blomfield argues that the logical possibility of her mind existing without a body is compatible with her ignorance of x. It appears, therefore, that **WA** must remain agnostic about the truth-value of some modal claims, such as MB2. "The same goes for all de re possibility claims which are translated into contested [disputed] sentences." (ibid., p. 76) A reluctance to assert the truth of a modal claim of the disputed class – the analysandum – leaves the worldly agnostic in an invidious position; she is obliged to revise in a radical fashion those modal statements generally accepted as true (Divers 2006, p. 190 fn. 6).

Blomfield now turns to examine a central assumption of **GMR**: that genuine realism is ontologically committed to the existence of a plurality of worlds. It is a failure to adhere to this assumption that leads the agnostic into difficulty with respect to the pre-theoretic truth of sentences in the disputed class. To suspend judgement about the existence of non-actual worlds, the agnostic is obliged to suspend judgement about the intuitive truth of disputed modal sentences of de re possibility (Blomfield 2008, p. 76). These two aspects of translation are inextricably linked by the truth-conditions of the biconditional: the truth of pre-theoretical modal sentences of de re possibility and an ontological commitment to a plurality of worlds. Furthermore, pre-theoretic knowledge that a disputed modal sentence of de re possibility is true entails – by **GMR** translation – knowledge of the existence of a non-actual worlds. The agnostic, in a drive to suspend a belief in non-actual worlds, must suspend belief in the judgements that we all share. The baby is lost with the bathwater. "But I do not think we should give up trying to decide whether we are correct in thinking that things might have been different ... just because we cannot know whether or not the corresponding possible worlds exist." (ibid., p. 77)

Divers' philosophical task is to explain how the inferential benefits accrued by genuine realism are compatible with a denial of the existence of a plurality of worlds. He argues that the modal translation scheme functions by matching the truth-value of modal sentences with the truth-value of existential sentences relating to a multitude of worlds. Blomfield's criticisms are mainly concerned with the truth-value of the analysandum [left side, biconditional] assigned on our pre-theoretic modal beliefs (Divers 2002, p. 107). Although a clash with intuitive modal opinion need not be decisive (chapter three), the absence of an accord risks opening the subject matter to radical reinterpretation (ibid., p. 107 fn. 3). In respect of the biconditional [right side] the truth-value relates partially to the existence of a plurality of worlds. In "Possible-World Semantics" Divers' addresses the worldly agnostic account of the syntactic structure of modal sentences that inform how they are used in a logical argument. Of primary concern are the notions of validity, completeness, and soundness. How fruitful is the **WA** analysis of modal sentences given agnosticism about non-actual worlds? Divers is optimistic:

> Thus, I believe, we have a new, and philosophically well-motivated argument to the effect that such genuine benefits as there are to be had from applied possible-worlds semantic theories can be had without either devious re-interpretation of the Kripkean semantics or commitment to realism about possible worlds. (Divers 2006, pp. 223-24).

My criticism of worldly agnosticism is not primarily related to the syntactic features of declarative modal sentences and their valid logical inferences. Instead, I question the absence of non-actual worlds from the proposed analysans [right side, biconditional] that unduly impacts the representational aspect of the analysandum [left side, biconditional]. Of course, many philosophers are unpersuaded by Lewis' translation scheme and the associated ontological commitment to a plurality of worlds, but I suspect that Divers *is* so committed.

Divers hopes to acquire the inferential benefits of genuine realism on behalf of the worldly agnostic. I argue that in order to do so, he must be committed to both sides of the biconditional. Specifically, the agnostic must be willing to assert the analysans complete with its ontological commitment to non-actual worlds; that partially licence the truth of the whole translation scheme. If the agnostic is to reject an ontological commitment to this type of entity, then she owes us an independent account of the 'worldly' primitive predicate of the quantificational-predicate model (§ 1.3). The name-bearer relation is perhaps paradigmatic of the type of semantic relation I require of the worldly agnostic. The indicative sentence 'the cat sat on the mat' can be formally translated to 'there is an x and there is a y such that x is a cat and y is a mat and x sat on y'. The canonical truth or falsity of this formal sentence is determined by how the actual world is (§ 4.6). By parity of reason, Lewis' unrestricted use of the quantifier criterion **(QC)** of ontological commitment is satisfied by individuals that may or may not inhabit the actual world. A declared agnosticism toward a plurality of worlds places the agnostic in an invidious position: sentences of belief in a de re possibility lead the worldly agnostic to an impasse especially if the belief in question is not warranted by a this-worldly counterpart or counterfactual content.

I conclude the examination of Divers' defence of **WA** with his final option intended to grant the agnostic the 'rational dispensability' of the disputed belief in a de re possibility.

Option Three: The dispensability of the disputed belief is shown by the sufficiency of a distinct but warranted non-modal belief.

Divers argues that the content of many of our beliefs are non-modal [left side, biconditional] and non-extensional [right side, biconditional]. This observation nullifies the problem of generality associated with the first option. Recall Divers proposed that the agnostic's warrant for a belief in the relevant de re possibility could be based on her a posteriori existential beliefs about the actual world. Option three replaces this a posteriori existential belief about the actual world with a "belief that in all, or more cautiously, most such cases if overtaking is attempted, it will be completed safely." (Divers 2004, p. 683) A shift in emphasis has now occurred. The agnostic's warrant to believe in a disputed de re possibility (option one) is based not on a modal belief but on a distinct and warranted non-modal belief. In these circumstances, the factors that determine the relevant assessment ought to be made explicit – that the driver is sober, the road conditions are good, there is a sufficient gap in oncoming traffic, etc., However, Divers objects that the imposition of enhanced perspicuity on the worldly agnostic is "unfair" (ibid., p. 683). The demand for perspicuity includes enhanced precision, clarity, or specificity in regard to the similarity relations of the assessment. These demands are not made of the genuine realist, hence the iniquity. The earlier criticism of worldly agnosticism, namely, that the truth-conditions of each side of the biconditional cannot simultaneously be satisfied by grounding each in an actualist ontology can be mitigated.

In 2006, Divers revised his worldly agnosticism in order to avoid the possibility of a modal collapse into fatalism,[7] but doubt should not be misunderstood as

---

[7] Modal collapse: "Most obviously, and dramatically, when such theories are restricted to one-world models, they seem bound (invariably) to validate modal collapse as represented by the formula (MC) 'If P then □P'" (Divers 2006, p. 190).

denial. He seeks to distance **WA** from one-worlders: "we distinguish the position of the agnostic antirealist, who is neutral about the existence of other worlds, from the out and out one-worlder who denies the existence of other worlds." (Divers 2006, p. 190)

Does this third strategy to replace a modal warrant to believe in a de re possibility with a non-modal warrant – to dispense with a 'rationally efficacious' belief in the disputed class – bear fruit? Initially, this option appears to place the agnostic between the hammer and the anvil. Either she accepts an actualist – and presumably one-worldly – account of the truth-conditions of the [right side, biconditional] where modal collapse looms *or* she accepts the genuine realist interpretation – and presumably a plurality of worlds – of the truth-conditions of the [right side, biconditional] where the 'unsafe and insane ontology' awaits. Divers' preferred third way – of claiming agnosticism about the [right side, biconditional] – is scuppered by his warranted agnostic belief in a de re possibility of successfully overtaking. I deliberately prefix this assessment with the words 'initially' and 'appears'. Divers might rebut these criticisms on the grounds that a genuine analysis of modal discourse does *not* rest on questions of ontology. Recall Wright's thought experiment about the 'cautious man' who is unwilling to commit to the modal aspect of an assertion, i.e., the logical necessity of conjunction elimination **CE** (§ 3.3). If the 'cautious attitude' can be extended to the *truth* (rather than the modal status) of the analysandum then it is probable that a cautious attitude could be defended in respect of the *truth* of the analysans. The application of this – admittedly – tentative strategy in regard to the truth of these sentences may warrant an agnostic belief in a de re possibility. A refusal to assert the truth of the analysandum would potentially liberate the worldly agnostic from a logical obligation to assert the truth of the analysans. Wright's thought experiment in respect of the 'cautious man' is an option Divers could exploit in defence of the logical entailments of **WA**. The common sense judgements in regard to the truth of a belief in a de re possibility would be compromised, but the logical entailment of a biconditional would be secured. The worldly agnostic could remain an agnostic about the truth of both sides of the biconditional. However, the violence done to our common sense judgements might be a price Divers is unwilling to pay.

6.6 Conclusion

In general, outside the philosophy seminar we believe that we perceive objects whose properties are independent of our perceptions of them. This presumption might lead us to question whether thought and language are related to something independent of thought and language. Ontological autonomy implies that the object or property represented by thought and language function as an independent standard of correctness. An independent standard that renders thought and language correct if, and only if, we are appropriately related to the relevant object or property. Realists frequently allege that antirealists sacrifice the independence of the standard on the altar of the relation. In reply, antirealists allege that realists sacrifice our relation to the object on the altar of independence.

Divers' published papers on **WA** are not a complete theory of modality. Although highly sophisticated, his arguments are presented as a provisional exploration of a new type of modal theory (Divers 2004, p. 684). There is no claim that these explorations are exhaustive. In consequence, Blomfield's critique of Divers – that he only considers 'rationally efficacious' beliefs – may not be entirely justified. Despite credentials that favour antirealism – such as the common sense denial of non-actual worlds – I argue that the worldly agnostic does suffer an assertibility-belief gap. That is, the realist enjoys access to a plethora of assertable modal claims not warranted on agnostic grounds. The realist can have her cake and eat it. She enjoys the theoretical advantages accrued by an ontological commitment to a plurality of worlds *and* an assertable bonanza of modal claims that relate the asserter to what is asserted. She is able to secure the theoretical benefit of valid logical inferences (§ 1.1) and the second criterion of a genuine paraphrase (§ 2.3).

Is this premature? Is there a disputed class of assertable (and belief) modal claims that are not conducive to **GMR** analysis? The next two chapters address the problem of advanced modality. Advanced modal claims are those that the genuine realist *ought* to assert and believe, but that produce post-translation an assertibility (and belief) gap! By the lights of genuine realism, modal sentences that are true translate into non-modal sentences that are false. In chapter seven, I set out the problem of advanced modality together with proposed solutions. These solutions often depend on radical adaptations to the standard translation scheme. In chapter eight, I propose a solution to the problem that retains the conceptual resources of standard modal translation.

7

The problem of advanced modality

7.1 Introduction

I argue that the theoretical benefits accrued by genuine modal realism **(GMR)** are a consequence of the quantification-predicate model of Lewis' modal translation scheme. A potential threat to the truth-value of sentences translated by the scheme is posed by advanced modal claims. That is, there are sentences of quantified modal logic **(QML)** whose 'intuitive' pre-theoretical truth is lost in a translation scheme that yields sentences of predicate logic **(PL)** that are, by **GMR** lights, false (§ 7.2).[1] Divers' solution to this problem is premised on the redundancy of the modal operators of **QML** sentences (§ 7.3). Divers is able to extricate the genuine realist from the impasse generated by advanced modal claims by discarding my central thesis: Recall,

World Relevance Principle (WRP): The analysis of de dicto modal sentences ought to be based on the assumption that modal operators both unite worlds under quantification and restrict the domains of the quantifiers that fall within their scope.

The problem of advanced modality is ongoing in philosophy (Jago 2016). Divers' original arguments are developed in his subsequent contributions to the literature (§ 7.4). I examine the problem of advanced modality under the light of a criticism raised by Josh Parsons; namely, that the 'problem' of advanced modality is a pseudo-problem. It is a consequence of a misapplication of the quantifiers of the analysans (§ 7.5). The quantifier criterion **(QC)** of ontological commitment makes Parsons' remarks particularly pertinent to my central thesis, **WRP** (§ 1.3). I argue that Parsons has misdiagnosed the problem of advanced modality. The problem remains one of genuine philosophical concern (§ 7.6). Divers' proposed solution to the problem of advanced modality is the redundancy theory. I argue that although Divers' solution is both elegant and coherent, an alternative is available. That is, an alternative solution based on a standard interpretation of advanced modal statements. My solution preserves the 'intuitive' truth-value of advanced modal claims under standard **GMR** analysis. The solution qualifies as 'standard' in the sense that it is based solely on the conceptual resources already available to the genuine realist.

---

[1] The threat relates to Lewis' first criterion of a genuine paraphrase, namely, the truth preservation of modal sentences – analysandum – under paraphrase (§ 2.3)

Specifically, it is reliant on a continued and indispensable ontological commitment to a type of entity, possible worlds. I aim to thereby secure **WRP** (chapter eight).

7.2 Advanced modal claims

Advanced modal claims can be defined as "modal claims about entities other than spatiotemporally unified individuals (perhaps, then, spatiotemporally disunified individuals, sets, numbers, properties, propositions and events)." (Divers 1999, p. 217) For **GMR,** the problem rests on an apparent reference to entities that are not unified individuals, are not 'at a world, w', and so cannot be the subject of a translated sentence of augmented **PL.** By standard **GMR** translation, the 'intuitive' truth-value of some modal sentences are not preserved. "The intention is that all GR analyses should terminate in analysans that feature only the primitive proper concepts of individual, set, part-of, spatiotemporal relatedness and similarity." (Divers 2002, p. 50) The standard **GMR** translation of a modal sentence that states the possibility of P is:

   (P) It is possible that P iff, there is some world w, such that at w, P.

The content of the analysans [right side, biconditional] is restricted to individuals that are spatiotemporally related. The bugbear of advanced modality emerges when an intuitively true analysandum is translated as false – by **GMR** lights: for example, the intuitive truth of modal sentences that pertain to, say, sets, e.g., 'each set has its members essentially' is not preserved by standard **GMR** translation. Importantly, the truth of **WRP,** which entails an ontological commitment to a plurality of worlds falls into the category of an advanced modal claim.[2] In these circumstances, Divers argues that modal sentences call for a distinctive or 'non-standard' form of translation. Preferably, this distinctive translation ought to accord with standard analysis as far as possible in order to remain a viable option for the genuine realist. Divers argues that **GMR's** preferred option ought to be a non-standard translation that simply omits talk of worlds:

   (AM) It is possible that P iff, P

---

[2] Noonan argues that the genuine realist is committed to the claim that a plurality of worlds is both a necessary truth but false by standard translation (Noonan 1994, p. 138). Intuitively, what holds of logical space would appear to be a non-contingent matter. Unfortunately, I have been unable to locate clarification in Lewis' published work on the modal status of the plurality of worlds, that is, as a necessary truth. There are passages that appear to imply this conclusion, however. Challenged to provide an account of how we know that a plurality of worlds exists Lewis cites mathematics as a precedent (Lewis 1986a, p. 111). Lewis thereby appears to align the non-contingency of modality with the non-contingency of mathematics (see Lewis 1996b [1999], esp. p. 222) (§ 5.3).

The standard translation of modal discourse adopts the normal practices of ordinary language by imposing a restriction on the scope of the 'domain of discourse' as determined by the context of utterance. The truth-value of a declarative sentence, say, that 'there is no beer' is restricted to the contents of the fridge, or kitchen, or house, or city, or country or 'world'. Hence, the truth-value of an ordinary language sentence used to assert the existence of, say, swans is interpreted as an existential claim appropriately restricted by the context of utterance, e.g., as a claim whose truth-value is restricted to the actual world (Lewis 1970 [1983]: 1975 [1983]: 1979 [1983]):

1. $\exists x \, (Ix@ \, \& \, Sx)$ where '@' designates the actual world

Advanced modal claims, however, are not conducive to an interpretation that is world-restricted. A sentence used to assert the actual existence of a plurality of worlds, for example, although entailed by **GMR** analysis, will be interpreted as false. The truth-value shift, in this case, is the result of a prohibition against the postulation of a world that has distinct worlds as parts (Lewis 1986a, Index 'overlap of worlds' p. 274: Noonan 1994, p. 138).

PW: Necessarily, there is a plurality of worlds

PW*: $\forall x \, (Wx \rightarrow \exists y \, \exists z \, (Wy \, \& \, Wz \, \& \, Iyx \, \& \, Izx \, \& \, \neg \, (y = z)))$

How can the genuine realist square this circle? **GMR** analysis of modal sentences is dependent on the truth of **PW,** and yet, by the lights of counterpart theory **PW*** is false! The modal status of the original postulates of counterpart theory and their implications are deeply problematic.

7.3 A solution: the redundancy theory

Divers argues that any – putatively – adequate philosophical explanation of modality ought to be able to accommodate at least two principles. That is, the absence of either principle incurs a significant loss of explanatory power:

PI: Possibility Introduction – p ⊢ It is possible that p, and

MU: Modal Ubiquity – For every true statement p, it is true that it is necessary that p or it is true that it is contingent that p

(Divers 1999, p. 217)

Divers' solution to the problem of advanced modality is to abandon standard **GMR** practice and interpret each advanced modal statement as a quantification that is not world-restricted (Divers 2002, p. 48). The genuine realist ought to distinguish between standard and advanced modal claims. Standard modal claims should be interpreted by way of quantifiers whose domain *is* populated by individuals whose place within the scope of the modal operator [left side, biconditional] is held by non-modal world-restricted terms [right side, biconditional]. Hence,

A. there are swans iff ∃x (Ix@ & Sx)

B. it is possible that there are swans iff ∃x (Wx & ∃y (Iyx & Sy))

C. it is necessary that there are swans iff ∀x (Wx → ∃y (Iyx & Sy))

Advanced modal claims, on the other hand, should not be interpreted in the same way. That is, in order to preserve the pre-theoretical truth-value of advanced modal claims [left side, biconditional], the genuine realist ought to discard the principle that the content of non-modal terms should be interpreted as world-restricted [right side, biconditional]. The primitive predicate 'Ixy' or 'x is in possible world y' (Lewis 1968 [1983], p. 27) should be abandoned. The genuine realist will then be able to accommodate the principle of **PI** in circumstances where she otherwise would not:

D. It is possible that there is a plurality of worlds iff ∃x ∃y (Wx & Wy & ¬ (x=y))

"There is no world-restricting element afoot in the content of [D] to sustain subsequent existential or universal generalization. In the alternative, GR can say that in such modal cases, the modal modifiers are redundant, hence the schema [**AM**] for extraordinary [advanced] possibility." (Divers 2002, p. 49) In the case of advanced modal claims, the implicit modal operator is redundant. The redundancy theory can be expanded beyond **PI** to include the cognates of possibility; namely, necessity and contingency (ibid., p. 49):

(**AN**) It is necessary that P, iff P

(**AC**) It is contingent that P, iff P and not-P (so no advanced claim is contingent)[3]

At this stage of the argument, it may be useful to pause and reflect on a principle abandoned by Divers, namely, of the quantifier restriction in relation to worlds. What is the theoretical cost incurred by this manoeuvre? Lewis argues that the restricting modifier 'at w' "works mainly by restricting the domains of quantifiers in its scope, in much the same way that the restricting modifier 'in Australia' does." (Lewis 1986a, p. 5). In other words, 'at w' has a dual-function:

---

[3] Divers distinguishes two senses in which 'It is contingent that P' can be understood (Divers 2002, pp. 307-08 fn. 16). **AC** should be understood as contingent in the factive sense. Factive in that P is the case, granting the possibility of not-P. In the alternative, contingency could be interpreted in a non-factive sense. Non-factive in the sense of whether P is the case i.e. P is neither necessary nor impossible.

it both *unites* worlds under quantification and *restricts* the domain of discourse to the scope of the modal operator. Lewis demonstrates this duality by way of analogy: the restricting modifier 'in Australia' is compared to the restricting modifier 'at a world, w'. The phrase 'in Australia, all swans are black' is normally interpreted to mean that if we ignore everything not in Australia, that is, if we unite the 'individuals' of Australia or restrict the domain of quantification to Australia, then 'all swans are black' is true. Mutatis mutandis 'at world w, all swans are magenta' is interpreted to mean that if we ignore everything not at world w, that is, if we unite the 'individuals' of world w or restrict the domain of quantification to world w, then 'all swans are magenta' is true. The phrase 'at world, w' is required by standard **GMR** analysis in order to account for the truth of the possibility – necessity, etc. – that swans are magenta (Noonan 1994, p. 138).

The remarks of the previous paragraph are qualified by the phrase 'is normally interpreted to mean'. The qualification is necessary because Lewis notes two exceptions to the general rule (Lewis 1986a, p. 6). First, not every quantifier falling within the scope of the modal operator *is* so restricted. The phrase 'in Australia, there is a yacht faster than any other' would fall somewhat short of its actual – immodest – meaning if the modifier 'in Australia' restricted both quantifier expressions, not just the first. The yachts against which the 'fastest yacht' is compared is not limited to those in Australia! Second, some restrictions on the meaning of a sentence uttered in a context are normally ignored. For example, the undoubted existence of immigrant white swans in Australian zoos can be ignored in the interpretation of 'in Australia, all swans are black'. These exceptions certainly mitigate the potential damage inflicted by the redundancy theory on standard **GMR** analysis.

7.4 The redundancy theory, revisited

Harold Noonan (2014) offers a general critique of **GMR** on the grounds that it fails to supply a traditional or – by implication – genuine philosophical analysis of modality. A philosophical analysis must do more than merely satisfy the condition of material adequacy: that 'p' is true if, and only if, p. Any interpretation of a language L must assign the value true to all and only those sentences of L that are intuitively true. However, given the weak truth-conditions for 'P materially implies Q' (and vice versa), a further condition is demanded of a traditional or genuine philosophical analysis.[4] This condition is one of strict equivalence or $\Box$ (P $\leftrightarrow$ Q); hence, in order for a biconditional to be

---

[4] The paradoxes of material implication are well rehearsed: for example, for any sentence P, if P is false then 'P $\rightarrow$ Q' is always true. Therefore, 'if grass is magenta then skunks are cuddly' and 'if grass is magenta then skunks are not cuddly' are both true.

strictly adequate, both □ (P → Q) and □ (Q → P) must be true. Further, by system **K** of **QML**, we can deduce that if □ (P → Q), then (□ P → □ Q) and mutatis mutandis for the second conjunct. This is amounts to, employing Divers' term, an 'indirect' deduction. By rule, we may deduce the necessity of the consequent on the grounds of the necessity of the antecedent. Strict adequacy demands the de dicto necessity of each side of the biconditional. Traditional philosophical analysis has the general form:

E.   ∀x (Fx ↔ Gx)

(Daly 2010, pp. 45-48)

The traditional philosophical analysis takes the form of a universally quantified biconditional that is not only true but necessarily true. A traditional philosophical analysis of language, for example, ought to apply not only to every actual language but to every possible language. The type of necessity invoked by Noonan is de dicto necessity (Noonan 2014, Section 1 p. 2 fn. 2). Noonan's general critique is directed at Lewis' (1968) translation scheme as supplemented by Divers (1999). Noonan presents the genuine realist with the horns of a dilemma: either cleave to the 1968 counterpart theoretic translation of **QML** or strict adequacy as demanded by traditional philosophical analysis. He argues that the most viable way for the genuine realist to extricate herself from this dilemma is to deny the truth of de dicto modal statements (Noonan 2014, Section 3).

I illustrate Noonan's argument by way of one example (ibid., Section 2). Noonan argues that both Lewis and the 'common man' agree that what is possible exceeds what is actually the case – recall, **A1-A3** (§ 3.1). They may agree that the England football team might have won the World Cup in 2018, for example. However, Lewis and the 'common man' diverge in respect of their ontological commitments. Lewis asserts whilst the 'common man' denies the existence of non-actual possibilia. This schism is a consequence of the 'inflated' ontological commitments of standard translation (1968). Lewis argues that a sentence that asserts the possibility of a talking donkey, say, can be translated into a true sentence of counterpart theory. For Noonan, the crux of Lewis' analysis entails that the mere possibility of a talking donkey entails the de dicto *necessary* existence of a talking donkey. That is, if standard translation is to satisfy the traditional demands of strict adequacy, then any sentence that asserts the possibility of a talking donkey entails the de dicto necessary existence of a talking donkey! Broadly, if standard translation is to meet the demand of strict adequacy, then the mere possibility of a talking donkey is false unless there is at least one talking donkey, 'at a world, w'. By Lewisian lights, the sentence 'it is possible that there is a talking donkey, but there are none' is incoherent. This is how Noonan's point is unpacked. Standard translation assigns to the predicates 'x is a possible world' and 'y is a donkey' satisfaction conditions that entail the existence of possibilia that occupy a spatiotemporal location:

a. It is possible that there is a talking donkey

b. It is possible that there is a talking donkey iff there is a world at which there is a talking donkey

c. There is a world at which there is a talking donkey if there is a talking donkey

(ibid., Section 2 p. 3)

When the demands of strict adequacy are applied to the bi-conditionals (a-c), each of which is implied by **GMR**, we deduce

d. It is necessary that there is a talking donkey (implied by a-c)

Lewis' standard translation scheme (1968) ought to assign 'false' as the truth-value of (d). This is despite the fact that (d) is a logical consequence of sentences that are not just true by the scheme but are necessarily true by way of strict adequacy! (Divers 2014, Section 4 pp. 5-6). Noonan's argument can be illustrated formally by Modus Ponens at step 16: note the <u>implied</u> premise at step 4.

1. $\Diamond \exists x\, Fx$ Premise: (Contingent Entity)

2. $\Box\, (\Diamond \exists x\, Fx)$ Premise: (Necessary Possibility)

3. $\Diamond \exists x\, Fx \leftrightarrow \exists y\, (Wy\, \&\, \exists x\, (Ixy\, \&\, Fx))$ (by Modal Translation, 1)

4. $\exists y\, (Wy\, \&\, \exists x\, (Ixy\, \&\, Fx)) \leftrightarrow \exists x\, Fx$ (by Standard Logic 3)

5. $\Box\, (\exists y\, (Wy\, \&\, \exists x\, (Ixy\, \&\, Fx)) \leftrightarrow (\exists x\, Fx))$ (by Strict Adequacy, 4)

6. $\Box\, ((\exists y\, (Wy\, \&\, \exists x\, (Ixy\, \&\, Fx)) \rightarrow (\exists x\, Fx)\, \&\, (\exists x\, Fx) \rightarrow (\exists y\, (Wy\, \&\, \exists x\, (Ixy\, \&\, Fx)))$ Def $\leftrightarrow$, 5

7. $\Box\, ((\Diamond \exists x\, Fx) \leftrightarrow \exists y\, (Wy\, \&\, \exists x\, (Ixy\, \&\, Fx)$ (by Strict Adequacy, 3)

8. $\Box\, ((\Diamond \exists x\, Fx) \rightarrow \exists y\, (Wy\, \&\, \exists x\, (Ixy\, \&\, Fx)))\, \&\, (\exists y\, (Wy\, \&\, \exists x\, (Ixy\, \&\, Fx)) \rightarrow (\Diamond \exists x\, Fx))$ Def $\leftrightarrow$, 7

9. $\Box\, (\Diamond \exists x\, Fx) \rightarrow \exists y\, (Wy\, \&\, \exists x\, (Ixy\, \&\, Fx))\, \&\, \Box\, (\exists y\, (Wy\, \&\, \exists x\, (Ixy\, \&\, Fx)) \rightarrow (\Diamond \exists x\, Fx))\, \sqcup$ Distrib, 8

10. $\Box\, ((\Diamond \exists x\, Fx) \rightarrow \exists y\, (Wy\, \&\, \exists x\, (Ixy\, \&\, Fx)))$ & E, 9

11. $\Box\, (\Diamond \exists x\, Fx) \rightarrow \Box\, (\exists y\, (Wy\, \&\, \exists x\, (Ixy\, \&\, Fx)))$ by Rule **K**, 10

12. $\Box\, (\exists y\, (Wy\, \&\, \exists x\, (Ixy\, \&\, Fx)))$ Modus Ponens: 2, 11

13. $\Box\, (\exists y\, (Wy\, \&\, \exists x\, (Ixy\, \&\, Fx)) \rightarrow (\exists x\, Fx)\, \&\, \Box\, (\exists x\, Fx) \rightarrow (\exists y\, (Wy\, \&\, \exists x\, (Ixy\, \&\, Fx))\, \Box$ Distrib, 6

14. □ ((∃y (Wy & ∃x (Ixy & Fx)) → (∃x Fx))   & E, 13

15. □ (∃y (Wy & ∃x (Ixy & Fx))) → □ (∃x Fx)   by Rule **K**, 14

16. □ (∃x Fx)   Modus Ponens: 12, 15

If sound, Noonan's argument demonstrates that the demands of a traditional philosophical analysis yield a conclusion that is intuitively false by standard translation (1968). This is despite the intuitive truth of the premises. 'Intuitive' is here understood in the sense of intuitively true or false by **GMR** lights. How does a de dicto contingent statement of ontological commitment to a certain type of entity entail the de dicto necessary existence of that entity? Noonan's argument is particularly interesting because it is not one that is restricted to advanced modality alone. The same dilemma applies to both interpretations of the analysandum – standard and advanced. "I [Noonan] argue that even when the rules of the translation scheme are modified as Divers proposes, modal realist analysis of statements of modal discourse will be strictly *inadequate* (though materially adequate) in the eyes of the modal realist." (Noonan 2014, Section 1 p. 2 my emphasis) A modal realist committed to standard translation is obliged to assert the truth – by strict adequacy – of both sides of the biconditional – at step 15 – but hold that only one side of the biconditional is true! "whether the key sentence (15 Left) / (15 Right) is one that merits the redundancy interpretation or one that does not, *one* of the strict biconditionals that Lewis* [or **GMR**] is constrained to hold true … will not come out true." (Divers 2014, Section 4 p. 7)

Noonan suggests that a genuine realist, suitably committed to the strict adequacy demanded of philosophical analysis, has but one recourse: to abandon the notion of de dicto contingency (Noonan 2014, Section 1 p. 2). Of course, the genuine realist need not accept Noonan's proposed solution. He may simply reject the traditional demands made of philosophical analysis, say, on the grounds of paradox (Daly 2010, pp. 62-66), limited success (ibid., pp. 73-74) or the problem of multiple analyses (ibid., pp. 67-68).

How does Divers propose to extract **GMR** from Noonan's dilemma viz. strict adequacy? He begins by challenging the motivation attributed by Noonan to the redundancy theory (Divers 1999, 2002): "In its unqualified form, the proposal would be that a sentence type merits the redundancy interpretation of an outer modal modifier if (and only if) its subject matter is something other than ordinary world bound individuals." (Divers 2014, Section 5 p. 8) Divers' argues that this attribution is misplaced. The redundancy theory's true motivation is "to identify systematically – which is not to say, mechanically – the range of cases across which a *charitable* construal of the modal assertion of Lewis* required the redundancy interpretation of those sentences on those occasions of their use." (ibid., Section 5 p. 8) [5] Hence, the redundancy interpretation of advanced modal sentences echoes the flexibility of the genuine realist interpretation of sentences in general. This flexibility is clearly not available to a genuine realist attempting to meet the high demands of strict adequacy. Divers then moves to engage Noonan's 'dilemma' on two broad fronts: first, he denies a requirement – implicit in traditional philosophical analysis – that **GMR** ought to provide an invariant interpretation of any sentence *type*, and second, he re-affirms the entitlement to apply either of two interpretations to putatively 'different' sentences. That is 'different' in terms of their semantic value. Combined, these two presumptions licence the claim that both sides of the biconditional can be interpreted as true, again, by **GMR** lights.

The conceptual resources employed by the redundancy theory in the analysis of extraordinary or advanced modal sentences are not intended as a general panacea. In this light, the interpretation of sentence types should not be seen as invariant. Take, by way of illustration:

e.   It is possible that there are many worlds

By standard (1968), interpretation (e) is false – see sentence D above (§7.3): that there is a world that has many worlds as parts is false. By the redundancy interpretation, however, (e) simply states that there are many worlds, which by genuine realist lights, is true. The pre-theoretic truth-value of an advanced modal statement is preserved by adopting the redundancy interpretation. Thus interpreted, a token modal statement is charitably determined to be true since the domain of quantification is not interpreted as world-bound (see §7.3). Sentence (e) is assessed without reference to a world(s) and is true by the lights of **GMR** so adjusted. A change in the truth-value of advanced modal statements post-translation is avoided. Noonan's general concerns are ameliorated, at least partially. Divers then introduces a further subtlety: "For there are things that are true in (of) the space that we cannot get at when we confine ourselves to expressing thoughts about what is true in (of) each and every one of its segments, even when we further think of those segments as exhausting that space." (ibid., Section 5 p. 9) This distinction may be applied to token modal

---

[5] Lewis* is an imaginary philosopher convinced by Lewis' arguments (Divers 2014, Section 1 p. 1). That is, Lewis* is persuaded by the counterpart theoretic interpretation of modal discourse (Lewis 1968 [1983]: 1971 [1983]) the metaphysics of genuine modal realism (Lewis 1986a) and a conception of what qualifies as a successful analysis of modality (Lewis 1973, p. 88: 1986a, pp. 3-4). Both Divers and Noonan appear to grant Lewis* the possibility of an ontological reduction of modality whilst rejecting the possibility of a conceptual reduction of modality (Divers 2002, Ch. 7: Noonan 2014, Section 2 p. 5). The distinction between 'what there is' and 'what we think/say there is' is evaluated by Hale (Hale 2013, pp. 63-69).

statements such as 'necessarily p' in one of two ways: as the sum of segments that exhaust modal space – the totality of worlds – or as the totality of modal space *itself* (ibid., Section 5 p. 9).

For example:

    f.   It is necessary that ((it is possible that there is a talking donkey) iff there is a world that has a talking donkey as a part)

In regard to (f), the genuine realist could employ Divers' distinction to interpret the clause 'It is necessary that …' as true based on the presumption that it is true *of* modal space itself. In other words, (f) need not be a truth that relates to the sum of all the *segments* or worlds *of* logical space. The response, in this case, is to drop the modal operator: (f) is true, according to the redundancy analysis, just when there are talking donkeys (quantifying unrestrictedly). There are talking donkeys (in logical space). So in that sense, (f) is true. Lewis* is able to exercise choice on how best – given the principle of linguistic charity – to interpret the modal operator (ibid., Section 5 p. 9).

The second prong of Divers' strategy relates to Noonan's 'indirect' assessment of the truth-conditions of biconditionals (ibid., Section 4 p. 5). There is, he argues, an inherent ambiguity in the interpretation of the modal operators of **QML** and the modal phrases of ordinary language. Recall Divers offers the genuine realist two interpretations of modal sentences, i.e., standard and redundancy. Additionally, each interpretation can be understood in one of two ways, i.e., weak or strong (ibid., Section 5 p. 10). That is, Noonan's 'indirect' interpretation of the strict biconditional may be interpreted in a weak or strong form. The weak or 'univocal' form "requires only [the] preservation of truth under every uniform interpretation of all relevant necessity operators." (ibid., Section 5 p. 10) Contrast the strong or 'multivocal' form, which is "[true] under every permutation[s] of interpretations of every relevant expression of necessity: the bi-conditional is true if and only if it comes out true under every permissible assignment of truth-value to each of its parts." (ibid., Section 5 p. 10).

Divers argues that the weak or univocal test is the correct interpretation of (f). Armed with charitable flexibility, Lewis* may re-assert the truth of (f) since it relates to modal space – what is true *of* it. Lewis* can assert the truth of (f, Left) *if* he applies a redundancy interpretation which in turn is dependent on his willingness to assert (f, Right) of modal space: that there is a talking donkey (ibid., Section 5 p. 11).

Noonan's dilemma is dispelled. "So we can justify the application of the effective redundancy interpretation of modal modifiers in cases where modalizing is *about* the theses of counterpart theory or genuine modal realism." (ibid., Section 5 p. 12 my emphasis) This conclusion is provisional, however. The debate that surrounds the correct interpretation of advanced modal sentences is ongoing.[6] I set this debate aside in order to examine a claim made by Josh Parsons. Parsons questions the legitimacy of the distinction that separates 'standard' from 'advanced' modal sentences. Is there a genuine philosophical problem to be solved?

7.5 Against advanced modal claims

What is the modal status of the modal translation scheme? Suppose, for the sake of argument, that Lewis* translation of modal sentences is necessarily true, i.e., strictly adequate. If we take 'it is necessary that it is possible that P' as a premise and if blue swans are possible, then it is a logical consequence of Lewis* theory that there are blue swans, 'at a world, w'. The thesis that there are blue swans is designated *Swans* by Parsons. *Swans* is a logical consequence of Lewis* theory, designated by Parsons *PW*. These premises entail 'if *PW*, then *Swans*'. However, if *PW* is a necessary truth, then *Swans* must be a necessary truth. It follows that necessarily there are blue swans: "And that is absurd." (Parsons 2011, p. 2) Contrast ordinary modal claims. Ordinary modal claims, e.g., 'it is possible that there are blue swans, ' do *not* entail the existence of blue swans since they can, in principle, be challenged. We may wish to deny the possibility of blue swans. However, although blue swans and their ilk are no more than 'merely' possible, Lewis* is ontologically committed to their existence!

GMR assigns a de re contingency to entities such as blue swans; they exist in some but not all worlds (Lewis 1986a, p. 11).

1.1 *PW* logically entails *Swans*

1.2 (the N rule) from 'p logically entails q' we may infer $\square$ (p → q)

1.3 (the K rule) from $\square$ p, $\square$ (p → q) we may infer $\square$ q

1.4 $\square$ *PW*

1.5 ¬ $\square$ *Swans*

(Parsons 2011, p. 2)

Parsons argues that **GMR** is committed to all five theses that are collectively inconsistent (1.1 to 1.5): "My [Parsons] thesis is there is a contradiction in the large bundle of theses that philosophers associate with modal realism ... and that Divers' Advanced Modalising does not succeed in removing that contradiction." (ibid., p. 3) The contradiction is located at premises 1.4 and 1.5: if *PW* is necessary, then we can infer *Swans* is necessary – by premise 1.3 – but

---

[6] Although the debate is ongoing, I will restrict my remarks to papers published prior to 2016 – the end of my research phase. This decision leaves unmentioned many subsequent contributions to the debate e.g. Alex Steinberg (2018).

Swans is contingent since blue swans exist at some but not all worlds. Hence, *Swans* is both a necessary and not a necessary thesis of modal realism; a contradiction. If Parsons' argument is valid, to refute the contradiction, the genuine realist must deny at least one premise, but which one? Parsons suggests that premise 1.5 is the weakest (ibid., p. 5).

I will now attempt to defuse the contradiction in a way that differs from that suggested by Parsons. Specifically, I dispute the validity *in this case* of the K-rule – thesis 1.3. The fruits of the N-rule are applied in thesis 1.3 as a premise in order to infer $\Box$ q. However, there is an equivocation in the K-rule in thesis 1.3. Suppose $\Box$ *PW* refers to the necessity of the **set** of possible worlds – which as an abstract object – exists at every world. Hence, although in normal circumstances the K-rule is valid, in this *particular instance*, the inference $\Box$ *PW*, $\Box$ (*PW* → *Swans*), therefore $\Box$ *Swans* is invalid: *PW* is a thesis about an abstract object that exists at every world whilst *Swans* is a thesis about concrete object(s) – and their counterparts – that exist at some but not all worlds. Again, suppose *BS* is a thesis about the **set** of blue swans – which exists at every world – and *Swans* is a thesis about blue swans – that exist at some but not all worlds. In this *particular case*, the inference from $\Box$ *BS*, and $\Box$ (*BS* → *Swans*) to $\Box$ *Swans* is invalid, and there is no contradiction in thesis 1.5. Of course, my diagnosis depends on the prior distinction of advanced and standard modal claims, a distinction that Parsons ostensibly denies. I say 'ostensibly' since he occasionally slips into advanced modal talk: "My [Parsons] conclusion is that modal realists should regard their theory of modality as *contingent.*" (ibid., p. 16 my emphasis)

How should the genuine realist translate advanced modal statements that appear to confound counterpart theory, e.g., *PW*? "the most obvious and simple analyses of modality have serious problems when turned on the subject matter of modal realism itself." (ibid., p. 6). The genuine realist might be well advised to 'bite the proverbial bullet' and accept that *PW* is both necessarily true by advanced translation and yet necessarily false by standard translation! Parsons attributes this view to Noonan (1994), although I do not share his assessment. Noonan argues that advanced modal claims yield not a false truth-value but an abortive truth-value, i.e., neither true nor false. Noonan argues that despite appearances, advanced modal claims do not involve modal operators and so are not subject to the standard method of translation. Modal sentences such as 'necessarily, there is a plurality of worlds' are not conducive to **GMR** analysis because the term 'necessarily' *in this case* does not function as a modal operator.

> Nevertheless, the function of a restrictive modifier is to restrict the domains of quantifiers within its scope, and hence an expression is not functioning as a restrictive modifier if it restricts the domain of *no* quantifier within its scope. Consequently, an expression is not functioning,

on Lewis's account, as a modal operator unless it both introduces quantification over possible worlds *and* restricts the domain of at least one quantifier within its scope. (Noonan 1994, pp. 138-39)

In the alternative, Parsons argues that in order to satisfy the demands of a genuine analysis of modality, **GMR** must satisfy three criteria:

2.1 That the analysis be compatible with the simple and literal truth of *PW* and its consequences.

2.2 That the analysis be compatible with validity of basic patterns of ordinary modal inference (such as the N- and K- rules)

2.3 That the analysis, in conjunction with *PW*, be compatible with modal common sense.

(Parsons 2011, p. 7)

In order to align *PW* with these criteria, Parson's advocates a T-preserving analysis that maintains the N- and K-rules:

S is possibly-true iff S, or for some world w, [S]w

S is necessarily-true iff S, and for every world w, [S]w

(ibid., p. 7)

I concur with Parsons in that the N- and K-rules should *generally* be preserved but argue that they are inapplicable *in this case* on the grounds of an equivocation; see above – 1.1 to 1.5. In order to satisfy criteria 2-1 to 2.3, Parsons argues that *PW* should be asserted based on the presumption of a distinctive multiverse; that is, a multiverse that contains all 'worlds' as island universes (ibid., p. 7). Island universes are understood to be spatially, temporally, and causally isolated from one another to secure the theoretical benefits of genuine realism and, in addition to the intuition that 'everything is actual' (see Divers 2002, pp. 93-99). A T-preserving analysis renders *PW* possibly-true, i.e., *PW* as a multiverse. However, when the relevant modal sentence contains quantifiers that are restricted to a single 'island' world, *PW* is false by T-preserving analysis. The possible truth of both the assertion and denial of *PW* are dependent on a restriction of the quantifiers and means that *PW* is a contingent truth.

I argue that advanced modal sentences are amenable to standard translation *if* we understand the subject-matter of those sentences to be abstract sets rather than concrete individuals. As a thesis, *PW* is not about a plurality of concrete worlds but a single **set** of possible worlds that exists 'at' each world in the form of an abstract entity. The potential problem of an ontological commitment to a plurality of concrete worlds from the standpoint of a single world is no longer applicable. I now test my explanation by way of Parsons' statement 2.4:

> 2.4 That the analysis be compatible with the necessary-truth of *PW*.
>
> (Parsons 2011, p. 8)

Parsons maintains that:

> No analysis can satisfy (2.4) while also satisfying (2.2) and (2.3). That is what my [Parsons] argument of the previous section showed. For any analysis that made *PW* out to be necessarily-true would either violate (2.2) by omitting to validate the N and K rules, or violate (2.3) by making 'there are blue swans' necessarily true. Contingent truth is the best that the modal realist can consistently hope for. (ibid., p. 8)

Actually, I can do much more than hope! In order to account for every genuine possibility, **GMR** posits the existence of a plurality of worlds where those possibilities are realised. I interpret *PW* to be an advanced modal claim and, therefore, as a sentence about the set of worlds that exists at every world. I subject this advanced modal claim to standard translation – which observes a world relevant analysis **WRP** – that yields a true analysans. The **WRP** remains applicable because the ontological status of the individual members of a set do not determine the ontological status of the set of which they are members. The set of all worlds exists as an abstract object at every world. This is a distinct but parallel interpretation to the one that states the necessary existence of individual worlds that account for every possibility. Statement 2.4 is satisfied. Statement 2.2 is upheld since although the N- and K- rules of modal inference are valid, the K-rule is not applicable *in this case*. I accept the general validity of the K-rule but claim an exception to it in cases of advanced modality. I retain a standard translation of advanced modal claims – with the proviso that advanced modal claims are subject to a set-theoretic interpretation. Clearly, the standard translation scheme (1968) does not include sets as a component of the analysans. The translation is to be understood as 'standard' in the sense that the conceptual resources employed by **GMR** are identical in both the advanced and standard cases. There is no 'extraordinary' analysis required on the analysans side of the translation – in the sense of world redundancy. Thesis 1.4 refers to the set of possible worlds, each of whose members exist necessarily. Some worldly members of the set enjoy the presence of blue swans, and some do not. This satisfies thesis 1.5, i.e., the contingent existence of blue swans. Every possible world, together with the possibility of blue swans, necessarily exists; necessarily, it is possible that there are blue swans.

Divers (1999, 2002, 2014) argues that different types of de dicto modal sentence require different types of translation – ordinary cases require standard translation, whilst extraordinary cases require the redundancy analysis. Parsons argues that this putative distinction can be understood in one of two ways: as a disjunction or an ambiguity. As a disjunction, the distinction applies to the following analysis of possibility:

A. S is possibly-true iff either a) S contains some vocabulary relating to worlds, sets, properties, propositions, or other predicates of modal realist metaphysics and S or b) S contains no such vocabulary, and there is some world w, such that [S]w.

(Parsons 2011, p. 9)

Parsons illustrates the disjunctive view by way of a disanalogy. The meaning of the English word 'jade' is established by way of cases – a substance is 'jade' iff it is jadeite or nephrite (Putnam 1975a [1996], p. 25). A competent English speaker need not recognise or even be aware of the dual extension of the predicate in order to use the word 'jade' correctly. Parsons argues that Divers fails to explicate his view of advanced modality to include these types of distinction (Parsons 2011, p. 10). Parsons' second objection relates to ambiguity. The ambiguity distinction is open to empirical refutation (ibid., p. 10). A competent English speaker understands the different uses of the word 'bank', for example. Dependent on the context of utterance, the word can mean 'riverside' or 'financial institution'. Now contrast this clear case of ambiguity with the modal phrase 'is possibly-true'. A competent English speaker does not forfeit their competency if they fail to recognise the alleged ambiguity of this modal phrase – in the sense of the standard/advanced distinction. The distinction can only be identified by way of a philosophical enquiry (ibid., p. 11).

Fortunately, the set theoretic approach that I advocate neatly side-steps these objections. Parsons' critique is motivated by the need for a novel re-interpretation of modal sentences which fail to preserve their truth-value under standard translation (ibid., p. 11). However, the set theoretic interpretation does not require that advanced modal claims be subject to extraordinary analysis. Advanced modal sentences are recognised as such and then subject to the standard world-restricted translation, supplemented by set theory. The thorny issue of a necessarily-false outcome to the standard analysis of, say, *PW* is avoided. The problem of advanced modality arose as a consequence of the Lewisian notion of individual worlds interpreted as spatiotemporally isolated – of a conception of worlds that do not overlap. I submit that the content of *PW* does not refer to a collection of concrete entities but to an abstract set of concrete entities which must – as a non-spatial entity – exist at every world.

Parsons' chief objection to the standard-advanced distinction of modal claims relates to the type of analysis subsequently employed. Advanced modal claims, e.g., *PW* demands a special type of redundancy analysis wherein all reference to worlds is abandoned. Furthermore, the distinction that demarcates standard from advanced analysis appears to be ad-hoc: a distinction acknowledged by Divers only in order to resolve an internal difficulty of genuine realism related to the modal status of counterpart theory. I argue that these difficulties are not insurmountable. Indeed, I am able to meet them and retain the **WRP** that leaves the type of analysis employed as constant: the distinction – though genuine – applies only to the analysandum [left side, biconditional] of the translation scheme. If the analysandum is an advanced modal claim, then the analysans employs sets. If the analysandum is a standard modal claim, then the analysans may employ either concrete objects or sets.

7.6 Conclusion

I identified the problem of truth-preservation posed by advanced modal claims under standard translation. The intuitive truth of advanced modal claims may yield a theoretical falsehood of the analysans by **GMR** lights. Divers' solution to the problem of advanced modality is the redundancy theory. Modal operators are 'redundant' in the sense that the quantifiers within their scope are no longer interpreted as world-restricted. The intuitive truth-value of advanced modal claims is preserved but at the cost of an ontological commitment to a type of entity, a possible world(s). As a solution most conducive to the genuine realist, I allege that the cost is too high. Noonan's more general concern is based on a traditional feature of philosophical analysis; the necessity of the universal bi-conditional. If the genuine realist embraces Divers' redundancy theory, he still falls short of the strict adequacy demanded of genuine philosophical analysis. Noonan's argument is based – in part – on Josh Parsons' unpublished paper "Against Advanced Modalizing". I argue that Parsons' inconsistency objection (theses 1.1-1.5) is based on presumptions that do not withstand scrutiny. Although a *general* endorsement of the K-rule is warranted, *in this case*, I argue that the application of the K-rule is invalid; the inference from □ p, □ p → □ q to □ q does not hold. I now turn to expand on earlier remarks in relation to a set theoretic solution to the problem of advanced modality.

8

A set theoretic solution

8.1 Introduction

Lewis' 'total theory' consists of two distinct components (Lewis 1983b [1983], p. 40). The first is genuine modal realism **(GMR)** – there is a plurality of worlds, each interpreted as a discrete spatiotemporal region populated by concrete individuals. The second is iterated set theory. Sets are constructed from concrete particulars or from mereological aggregates of such particulars (Rosen 2015, p. 382). Clearly, one may accept set theory without incurring a commitment to **GMR**. Hence, Lewis' commitment to the former requires independent motivation. That is, the reasons that compel acceptance of set theory should be independent of those that motivate acceptance of **GMR**. Lewis' general criterion of acceptance is 'unity' or 'economy' of the 'primitive' theoretical notions employed (Lewis 1986a, p. 4). Lewis accepts set theory as an indispensable component in the field of mathematics (Lewis 1986a, p. 4: 1991, pp. 36-38). He is ontologically committed to a type of entity, sets. However, Lewis does appear to endorse two distinct accounts of set theory (Rosen 2015, p. 383). The 'simple view' expressed in the body of *Parts of Classes* (1991) is superseded by a 'structuralist view' found in the appendix of that work and a later paper, "Mathematics as Megethology" (1993). Lewis (1993) explores the interrelated topics of mereology – the general theory of parts – and set theory – the general theory of collections. His mature explanation of the metaphysical underpinning of set theory became known as structuralism. I decline the opportunity to explore the metaphysics of set theory. The reason for this reticence is a simple one – I lack the necessary expertise to do so. I set aside the task of assessing the 'structuralist' view of set theory as a possible solution to the problem of advanced modality to those who are mathematically qualified.[1] I also decline a sojourn into the metaphysical foundations of mathematics and simply acknowledge that: "when God made the world(s), he made the concrete individuals; he laid down the principles of set theory, and then he stopped." (Rosen 2015, p. 382)

---

[1] A philosopher – or philosophy student – ought to concede whenever the solution to a particular problem is elusive or beyond his or her intellectual abilities. In these circumstances, we ought then to defer the problem to those with the expertise to tackle it. Indeed, it appears that intellectual honesty was a personal trait of Lewis himself (Jackson & Priest 2004, p. 2).

I will proceed on the 'simple view' of set theory as presented by Steinhart (Steinhart 2009, chapter one: also Tiles 1989).[2] The view is 'simple' in the sense that I will leave the axioms of set theory largely unexamined (Steinhart 2009, p. 1). In chapter seven, I explored the notion of advanced modality and the challenges it represents to the expressive adequacy of **GMR** analysis. Advanced modal claims represent a direct threat to the theoretical benefits associated with the quantification-predicate model of the translation scheme (§ 1.1). Divers' redundancy theory offers the genuine realist a solution to this problem. In the alternative, I propose a different solution to the problem that draws upon the conceptual resources of *standard* modal translation. My proposed solution is based on set theory. Sets are among the standard conceptual resources of **GMR**. A set theoretic solution to the problem of advanced modality is, therefore, more felicitous to genuine realism than the redundancy theory. This preference is justified on the grounds that my alternative solution does not require an atypical evaluation of standard translation (1968). That is, the predicate expressions of standard translation are retained, esp., 'x is in possible world y' and 'y is a possible world'. The conceptual resources upon which the proposed solution is based are already available to the genuine realist. Importantly, I suggest a translation of advanced modal claims that retains the relevance of worlds as a component of the analysans [right side, biconditional]. I will expand on earlier comments where the ontological status of sets was initially raised (§ 7.5). In brief, I employ the conceptual resources of **GMR** to preserve the standard translation of modal sentences. There are two critical aspects of **GMR** that facilitate this proposal. Firstly, the recognition that sets have *no* spatiotemporal location. Secondly, every set is 'at world, w' (Lewis 1983b [1983], p. 40) (§ 8.2). Advanced modal claims are to be assessed in the standard manner insofar as the primitive predicate 'Ixy' ('x is in possible world y') remains an essential component of the translation scheme. I offer a number of objections to the set theoretic solution to the problem of advanced modality with replies (§ 8.3). Potential objections include: the magical nature of the set membership relation (§ 8.3.1), the disputed ontological commitment to sets (§ 8.3.2), and the antinomies of proper classes (§ 8.3.3). I addressed the problem of plural predication in chapter one (§ 1.5). Although their 'indispensable'

---

[2] For example, I will presume that all sets are abstract entities that necessarily exist – that is, every set is 'accessible' from every possible world. This is not Lewis' position. Lewis notes that we usually restrict quantification when evaluating the truth of a quantified sentence; although sets do not exist in either logical or physical 'space' they may exist unrestrictedly or from the standpoint of every world e.g. numbers. On the other hand, some sets only exist restrictedly or from the standpoint of a particular world e.g. the unit set of an individual who / which exists at that world (Lewis 1983b [1983], p. 40: 1986a, pp. 94-5). The latter is a case of an abstract object that exists contingently e.g. the Equator.

status in the field of mathematics – and empirical science – has been challenged, I conclude that an ontological commitment to sets ought to be a component of 'total theory'. They are amongst the primitive conceptual resources available to the genuine realist and offer a viable solution to the problem of advanced modality (§ 8.4)

8.2 A set theoretic solution to the problem of advanced modality

Lewis utilises the ontological and conceptual resources of **GMR** combined with set theory to embark on a systematic reduction of several important philosophical entities. I mention some of these reductions in action: 'properties' reduced to arbitrary classes (§ 4.6), 'relations' reduced to classes of ordered pairs, 'propositions' reduced to classes of possible worlds (§ 2.5), and 'events' reduced to classes of spatiotemporal regions (Lewis 1986a, p. 185 ff.: Rosen 2015, p. 382).

The conceptual resources of **GMR** are exhausted by: individual, set, part-of, spatiotemporal relatedness, and similarity. As there are no non-individual non-sets, the furniture of each world can be divided into individuals and sets. In order to avoid the introduction of new conceptual primitives, I argue that the problem of advanced modality can be resolved by an interpretation as modal claims about sets. If this interpretation is correct, standard modal translation remains the appropriate interpretation of *all* modal sentences. All analysans [right side, biconditional] continue to employ the primitive predicate 'Ixy' or 'x is in possible world y'. I accept Divers' argument in respect of the flexibility in regards to the identification of analysandum [left side, biconditional] as either standard or advanced (§ 7.4). Divers recommends the redundancy theory as an escape route from the impasse generated by the genuine realist interpretation of advanced modal sentences. The price of escape is the abandonment of the world-restricted quantification-predicate model of modal analysis. The primitive predicate 'Ixy' is abandoned by the redundancy theory. Divers argues that this is a price the genuine realist should be willing to pay. I argue that this is a price the genuine realist ought not to pay. As a solution to the problem of advanced modality, a genuine realist may avoid paying the price if a plausible alternative is available. The alternative is a set theoretic approach whose plausibility I now turn to examine. There is a preliminary problem, however, with a set based interpretation of advanced modal claims that threaten to scupper the manoeuvre before it is made. Lewis accepts the existence of sets. However, by the standard analysis of world-restricted quantification, the existence of sets appears to be a logical impossibility. If we endorse the primitive predicate 'Ixy' or 'x is in possible world y', then the existence of sets becomes conceptually dependent on some world having sets as parts (Divers 1999, p. 224 fn. 7). Orthodox set theory, on the other hand, states that no set is part of any world: "There are some abstract entities, for instance, numbers or properties, that inhabit no particular world but exist alike from the standpoint of all worlds," (Lewis 1973, p. 39: 1986a, p. 94 fn. 60). How are we to reconcile standard modal translation with orthodox set theory? How do we include sets amongst the conceptual resources of **GMR** when *ex hypothesi* they are not part of any world?

Rather than abandon orthodoxy, Lewis' response is to embrace the dilemma and re-interpret what it means to be 'at a world, w'. "Then no set is in any world in the sense of being a part of it. Numbers, properties, propositions, events – all these are sets, and not in any world. Numbers *et al.* are no more located in logical space than they are in ordinary time and space." (Lewis 1983b [1983], p. 40). This quotation is central to my proposed set theoretic solution to the problem of advanced modality. The phrase 'at a world, w' can be interpreted in a number of ways:

1. An entity can be 'at a world, w' by being a part of world w, or

2. An entity can be 'at a world, w' by having a part that is part of that world w, hence, extraordinary trans-world individuals would be part of many worlds *if* they were possible but they are not possible (ibid., p. 39) or

3. An entity can be 'at a world, w' by existing from the standpoint of a world: "Let us say that an individual exists *from the standpoint of* a world iff it belongs to the least restricted domain that is normally – modal metaphysics being deemed abnormal – appropriate in evaluating the truth at that world of quantifications." (ibid., p. 40)

There are several reasons to accept a modified interpretation of 'at a world, w'. Firstly, as actual existence pertains to this-worldly existence, the strategy implies the actual existence of set based entities, such as numbers. Secondly, the strategy appears to close the explanatory gap posed by the existence of impure sets; those sets whose members exist at some but not all worlds (Divers 2002, pp. 88-89). The second justification is one that I must reject. The intuition that motivates the idea of a 'contingent' impure set is flawed because it implies that the ontological status of a set is dependent on the ontological status of its members. What is the ontological status of an impure set? Each set is an abstract object whose membership may consist of contingent individuals. I maintain that a set *qua* set is always a 'necessary' object even *if* the existence of the members of that set is contingent, e.g., the existence of an impure set of red apples is 'necessary' even though the existence of the *red apples* is contingent. This is a bold claim whose justification is based on the important quote above (Lewis 1983b [1983], p. 40). In this context, the word 'necessary' must endure the indignity of quotation marks since the type of necessity invoked is that of the third interpretation of 'at a world, w'; namely, 'from the standpoint of a world'. I will elaborate on these preliminary remarks shortly. It is important to avoid the implication, however, that the proposed necessity of sets is derived from the claim that sets are abstract objects. Not all abstract objects are necessary. The Equator is an abstract object, but if the Earth did not exist, then intuitively, neither would the Equator (fn. 1, p. 76) (Dummett 1991, p. 239). In the interest of consistency, I am obliged to reconcile the claim that all sets – pure and impure – are necessary objects with the recognition that the members of some sets are contingent individuals (§ 8.3.2). The alleged necessity I demand of impure sets commits me to the view that sets constitute an additional type of entity 'above and beyond' the mere existence of their members (§ 1.4). Lewis' simple view is that every set is a fusion of singletons – sets with one member; that is, every non-singleton set is the fusion of the singletons of its members. Hence, set-membership is determined by the fusion of the singletons of the putative members of the set. For example, the set of actual red apples is constituted not by the apples themselves but by the singletons of each this-worldly apple. As subsets, singletons enjoy a necessary ontological status. Of course, to cite Lewis' singleton solution is simply to defer the original question: what is the ontological status of a singleton set; do they constitute an additional type of entity 'above and beyond' the individuals that form their membership?

By **GMR** lights, an object is necessary iff it has a counterpart at every world. A drawback of Lewis' three-fold 'at a world, w' distinction is his use of the phrase 'from the standpoint of a world'. The introduction of this phrase is problematic because it appears to be ad hoc. Worse still, it appears to introduce a new conceptual primitive to the **GMR** repertoire. Divers argues that the imposition of a new conceptual primitive is unwarranted since the phrase 'from the standpoint of a world' can itself be explicated without a significant loss of clarity.

> [**GMR**] can recognise effective variety within the being-in-a-world genus without resorting to the suspect notion of existing from the standpoint of a world. Thus, consider the following explication:
>
> (D) ∀w [∀x [x is in w iff
>
> > (i) (x is an individual & ∃y (y is a part of x & y is a part of w) v
> >
> > (ii) (x is a set & ∀y [(y is an individual & ((y is a member of x)
>
> v (y is a member of a member of x) v ... → y is a part of w)]]]
>
> (Divers 2002, p. 89)

Divers' useful explication of 'at a world, w' is based on the distinction of two primitive concepts; individual and set. Individuals are 'at a world, w' in the sense that each individual is a spatiotemporal part of a world, w. Sets are 'at a world, w' in a different sense. They have no location and so cannot be a spatiotemporal part of a world, w – although their members might be. Divers' notes that the schema (D) is neither vague nor introduces conceptual primitives beyond the prior commitments of **GMR**. Instead, (D) deploys the conceptual resources already acknowledged by **GMR**. Furthermore, (D) is not ad hoc since it explicitly cleaves to the phrase 'at a world, w' used to express (in part) the ontological commitments of **GMR**. Instead, formula (D) is a disjunction that falls within the scope of a universal quantification. Two mutually exclusive and collectively exhaustive disjuncts account for the existence of individuals and sets. Individuals are composed of parts which are both a part of an individual and of the world at which they exist. The second disjunct pertains to sets that have individuals as members. These sets are subject to iteration since they may constitute the membership of 'higher' ranking sets. The initial universal quantifier – whose scope is both disjuncts – relates to 'all worlds, w' and the first disjunct pertains to all world-bound individuals. The second disjunct pertains to all sets that exist but whose existence is not 'actual' in the same sense. Indeed, as sets do not exist in either logical or physical-temporal space, they are not 'at a world, w' in the sense of the first disjunct. I wish to highlight this distinction in the interpretation of 'at a world, w' in the case of each disjunct. The phrase is ambiguous and, in terms of the second disjunct, should be interpreted in line with Lewis' "from the standpoint of all worlds".

I also add to Divers' formulae (D). This addition will account for the case of pure sets; a set that does not have individuals as members. Pure sets are iterations of the empty set.

(D*) (iii) x is a pure set, i.e., all members of all parts of x are sets

This addition is not trivial. As noted, I must decline Divers second justification. Divers concurs with Lewis insofar as the existence of some impure sets is intuitively a contingent matter (ibid., p. 89). I dispute the claim that the contingency of the individual/member of a set implies the contingency of the set of which it is a member. Postulate two of counterpart theory states that 'nothing is in two worlds', and so each individual is understood to be world-bound (Lewis 1968 [1983], p. 27). Postulate two appears to imply the metaphysical thesis of extreme essentialism (Plantinga 1973 [1979], p. 157 ff.: Salmon 2004, p. 236: cf. Stalnaker 1987 [2003], pp. 118-19). In brief, **GMR** explains the possibility that an individual might have been different in some way by the existence of a counterpart of that individual in some other world who instantiates an unrealised property at this-world.[3] The possibility of property variance is

---

[3] Properties should be construed herein as 'extrinsic' in the broadest sense: that is, as an inclusive relation linking every actual individual – past, present or future – in a spatiotemporal region.

denied to each world-bound individual; each de re individual 'necessarily' instantiates the properties that it actually instantiates.[4] If a tree had fallen in Sherwood Forest five minutes before it actually fell, then you and I – as world-bound individuals – would no longer instantiate *all* the properties that we actually do. The possibility of a difference is analysed by way of the counterpart relation that posits a different individual causally disconnected from the subject of the possibility, i.e., *if* the argument is sound and interpreted as world-restricted: if $\sim\Diamond \sim P$ then $\Box P$. I reject the metaphysical thesis of extreme essentialism. Lewis argues that sets are abstract entities which suggests that postulate two is not applicable in this case. Pure sets have no concrete individuals as members and are not threatened by contingency. Impure sets do have concrete individuals as members, which implies that they exist contingently. Individuals, however, are invariably located in space-time and are part of a world in the sense of 'at a world, w' – by (Di). Impure sets *qua* sets, on the other hand, do not have a spatiotemporal location and cannot be part of a world in the sense of (Di) but are nonetheless 'at a world, w' – by (Dii). I, therefore, infer the 'necessary' existence of impure sets – by (Dii). The *set* of all dragons exists necessarily (Dii) even if there are worlds at which no dragon (Di) exists: {x I x is a dragon}. The necessity of every set is facilitated by the ambiguity of the phrase 'at a world, w'.

I propose to interpret all advanced modal claims as modal claims about sets. Under standard interpretation, ordinary modal statements draw upon the conceptual resources of individuals and sets with the former understood as world-bound. I argue that advanced interpretation of extra-ordinary modal statements should utilise the conceptual resources of either impure sets of individuals or pure sets of sets. Hence, advanced interpretation includes impure sets which have individuals as members {x I x is a blue swan} or pure sets {x I x is {}} with sets as members (Steinhart 2009, p. 20).

I am now able to illustrate the set theoretic interpretation of modal sentences by way of example:

(A) Possibly, there are talking donkeys

(B) Necessarily, there is a plurality of worlds

(C) Possibly, all numbers are perfect numbers

Sentence (A) is a true sentence about non-actual individuals which yields a true analysans by standard translation. There is a possible world at which a talking donkey exists. The theoretical truth of sentence (B) is preserved by an analysans interpreted as a translation of a modal sentence about individuals that are

---

[4] A claim that is highly counterintuitive. The genuine realist can deny the claim on the basis that in this context 'necessarily' can be interpreted as 'all counterparts of x are F'.

considered members of an impure set. The proposed set theoretic interpretation of (B) employs a standard translation of an advanced modal sentence whose content pertains to the *set* of all worlds. I say 'standard translation' since the truth of the analysans is assessed 'at a world, w'. Although included amongst the conceptual primitives of **GMR** sets do not appear as a constituent of the translation scheme in Lewis' original paper. The set of all possible worlds {x I x is a world} exists 'at a world, w' (by Dii) though not in the same sense as an individual (by Di). This ambiguity facilitates the employment of the primitive conceptual resources of **GMR** in my proposed set theoretic solution – see (D). As a result, the problem of advanced modal sentences can be side-stepped, and the subsequent need for an adjusted translation scheme that renders world-restricted analysis 'redundant' can be avoided. The final sentence (C) refers to perfect numbers, i.e., numbers that are the sum of their divisors. Sentence (C) is false – not all numbers are perfect numbers – so the standard translation of (C) demonstrates that the set of perfect numbers is merely a subset of the set of all numbers; the analysans is false by standard translation. Again, I say 'standard translation' since the falsity of the analysans is assessed 'at a world, w'.

My proposed solution to the problem of advanced modality posits the existence of sets whose membership is determined by the content of the advanced modal claim. For example, modal claims that relate to the plurality of worlds are claims about the set of all possible worlds. This example unpacks in the language of predicate logic **(PL)** [right side, biconditional] as:

A*: $\forall x \, (Wx \rightarrow \exists y \, (Sy \,\&\, Iyx \,\&\, y = \{x \, I \, x \text{ is a possible world}\}))$

Or alternatively:

A**: $\forall x \, (Wx \rightarrow \exists y \, (Sy \,\&\, Iyx \,\&\, \exists t \,\&\, \exists u \, (Wt \,\&\, Wu \,\&\, (t \in y) \,\&\, (u \in y) \,\&\, (t \neq u))))$

Let the predicate letter 'S' designate a set. Each set exists 'at' every world as an abstract object understood as an instance of formulae (D) above; hence, the equations A* and A** begin with a universal quantifier whose scope includes all possible worlds. By A*: at any arbitrary world 'Wx', there exists a set '∃y Sy'; the set of all possible worlds. The set y exists 'Iyx' or 'y is in possible world x'; in the sense outlined at Dii. Finally, the set y is the set of all possible worlds: in set theory notation, a set represented by curvy brackets wherein for all x, such that – vertical stroke – x is a possible world. Of course, the number of possible worlds understood as a spatial temporal continuity is disputed. In this case, the dispute relates to the set of all possible worlds; one that boils down to a dispute over the cardinality of that set.

The standard or world-restricted interpretation of modal statements is retained throughout. The ambiguous phrase 'at a world, w' remains a part of the analysans of modal translation, and the world relevance principle **(WRP)** is preserved since the phrase is an expression of world-restricted quantification. Advanced modal sentences are distinguished from standard modal sentences in the manner outlined by Divers (§ 7.4). The use of the Lewisian phrase 'from the standpoint of a world' is abandoned together with the disadvantages associated with it. I deploy (D*) in order to demarcate the types of entity under analysis – individuals and sets – with the proviso that whenever advanced modal claims are made they refer to the sets of those entities. Lewis accepts that sets are not a part of any world because they are abstract entities. Sets exist, but not as 'a part' of either logical or spatiotemporal 'space'.

Immediately, an important difficulty emerges with this particular interpretation of 'at a world, w'. I argued that (B) 'necessarily, there is a plurality of worlds' is necessary because the set of all worlds exists at every world, even though the worlds that are its members do not (postulate two). Now a problem appears, consider: (B*) 'necessarily, there is a talking donkey'. This should be interpreted – by the lights of **GMR** – as false. Talking donkeys exist but contingently, at some but not all worlds. Here's the rub: there is a set of talking donkeys, which as a set, exists at every world even though the donkeys that are its members do not (postulate two). By parity of reason, shouldn't (B) and (B*) be interpreted as necessary – by **GMR** lights? [5] The concern is that my proposed solution to the problem of advanced modality causes difficulties similar to those raised by Noonan (§ 7.4).

The concern raised by this objection is not insuperable. The interpretation of a given analysandum with modal content is not invariant. I argue that Divers' standard-advanced modal distinction is a genuine one (§ 7.5). Recall the distinction is *not* based on a hard-and-fast, invariant interpretation of a sentence *type*: the truth-value of an advanced modal sentence is preserved by adopting a set-theoretic interpretation of the analysandum. Thus interpreted, the truth-value of a token modal sentence is charitably determined though the domain of quantification is world-bound, i.e., 'at a world, w'. Hence, sentence (B) is judged to be an advanced modal sentence, interpreted set-theoretically, and is determined to be true by the lights of **GMR**. Sentence (B*), on the other hand, is judged to be a standard modal sentence, interpreted *non*-set-theoretically, and is assessed as false, again, by the lights of **GMR** (§ 7.4).

8.3 Objections and replies

I now turn to a number of further objections to my proposal. I argue that the problem of advanced modal sentences can be solved by the application of set theory. Many of these objections are general – directed against set theory itself.

---

[5] I am grateful to an anonymous referee from Vernon Press for raising this difficulty.

Earlier, I addressed one objection in respect of the 'singularist dogma' in which a single quantification is erroneously applied to multiple objects (§ 1.5). I now turn to other concerns.

8.3.1 A kind of magic?

The first challenge to my thesis is based on an argument articulated by Peter van Inwagen (1986 [2001]) in reply to an objection raised by Lewis to the magical ersatzer's account of possible worlds (Lewis 1986a, pp. 174 ff.). Van Inwagen's argument is a *tu quoque*: "by reasoning parallel to Lewis's, we can show that one could grasp set-theoretical membership only by magic; and Lewis's ontology requires at least some set-theoretical constructions." (van Inwagen 1986 [2001], p. 238)

In *Plurality* Lewis inveighs against abstractionism on the grounds that it renders the *selection* or *makes-true* relation wholly mysterious. How does the magical ersatzer secure the 'representational property' of a world required to explain, say, the possibility of a talking donkey? How is a world selected as one at which a donkey talks? For **GMR**, the required explanation is based on at least one spatiotemporal world that has a talking donkey as a part; these worlds enjoy a 'representational property' as an intrinsic property. Contrast the magical ersatzer, who posits abstract worlds which lack an internal structure (Lewis 1986a, pp. 174-75). That is, 'worlds' or abstract simples that are composed from a subset of a larger class of abstract simples or 'elements', e.g., propositions. Some elements are 'selected' – made true – by the actual world. Hence, some propositions are 'made true' by how things stand in the actual world. If a donkey talks – at the actual world – then one subset of elements (propositions) is selected or made true, and if a cat philosophizes – at the actual world – another subset of elements (propositions) is selected or made true, and so on. Clearly, the notion of 'selection' or 'made true' itself stands in need of explanation. Selection might be understood as a primitive concept; it may help facilitate the definition of implication on elements or propositions, so that, p implies q iff necessarily, if the actual world selects p, it selects q. The 'world' is interpreted as a 'maximal' subset of abstract simples or elements complete under implication – by Boolean algebra. In a paraphrase of the argument proposed by Lewis to account for the discrepancy, Rosen notes: "[the worlds] are the elements that imply, but are not implied by, other elements (except the 'null' element that implies all of the elements). *w* is a world *at which* donkeys talk iff (it is selected iff donkeys talk)." (Rosen 2015, p. 392)

Lewis' critique of magical ersatzism is principally directed at the 'selection' or 'made true' relation understood as a primitive concept. "If the ersatzer has understood his own primitive, he must have done it by magic." (Lewis 1986a, p.

178) [6] For van Inwagen, this is all a bit rich. As previously noted, Lewis draws on the resources of set theory in order to explicate a raft of philosophical entities. How can Lewis hope to avail himself of the primitive notion *is a member of* except by magic? If two sets, say {a, b} and {b, c}, can only be individuated by the objects that comprise them – a, b and c – then the 'is a member of' relation must depend on a 'magical' explanation: "There is no way to pick out *any* set except by somehow specifying the things that bear membership to it." (van Inwagen 1986 [2001], p. 238) The genuine realist is in the same precarious position as the magical esatzer. As in the case of the primitive notion of 'selection', so in the case of the primitive notion of 'is a member of'; it's a kind of magic!

In *Parts of Classes* Lewis concedes to van Inwagen's tu quoque (Lewis 1991, pp. 36-38). He argues that van Inwagen ignores a relevant distinction of cases, however (cf. van Inwagen 1986 [2001], pp. 232-42). The set-membership relation is 'indispensable' to the foundation of mathematics; to reject the primitive relation 'is a member of' is to jeopardise the whole edifice of present day mathematics. Alternatively, to dispense with the abstractionists' primitive notion of 'selects' or 'makes true' relation, still leaves **GMR** as a viable explanation of modality. No such viable alternative with respect to mathematics presents itself if we abandon the conceptual primitive 'is a member of' relation.

Reply. There is a theoretical impasse with respect to the status of the 'makes true' and 'is a member of' relations as conceptual primitives. Problems that beset the former also beset the latter. Lewis acknowledges that on the presumption of a primitive relation that is internal – intrinsic properties – van Inwagen's tu quoque holds (Lewis 1991, p. 37). If the primitive relation is understood as *external* – extrinsic properties – the force of van Inwagen's objection is mitigated, however (ibid., p. 37). For my thesis, Lewis' attempt to deflect the force of van Inwagen's criticism by invoking the *type* of necessity required by each notion enjoys only partial success. Lewis' proposed distinction is based on the type of necessity associated with the *identity* of the set-membership relation, on one hand, and the *qualitative character* of the necessity of the 'makes true' relation on the other (ibid., pp. 37-38). On the 'simple view' of set theory that I endorse, this distinction becomes arbitrary: that is, I defend a 'dogma' that Lewis rejects. The membership of a non-unitary set is based on the ability to identify a certain relation that all the members of

---

[6] An external relation, for example, is one that does not depend on the intrinsic properties of an object, like the spatiotemporal relation of distance. An internal relation is one that does depend on the intrinsic properties of an object, say, intrinsic similarity (Lewis 1991, p. 34).

a set have in common. I am, therefore, unable to individuate a set *except* by way of the objects that bear the 'is a member of' relation to it.

8.3.2 Who mentioned sets?

The assertion that 'P' is stronger than the assertion that 'possibly P' and yet the latter entails an ontological commitment to *more* types of entity. Why should a weaker claim impose greater ontological commitment(s)? By **GMR** analysis, that 'P' commits us to an ontology of individuals whilst 'possibly P' commits us to an ontology of individuals and sets (Rosen 2015, p. 382). As previously noted, Lewis does accept individuals and sets as components of 'total theory'. Those not convinced by **GMR**, however, may puzzle over the inflated ontological commitments associated with a weaker claim. Those that prefer 'desert landscapes', for instance. The inclusion of sets in regard to the analysis of *all* advanced modal claims merely exacerbates the problem of ontological inflation. Prima facie, an advanced modal claim about the plurality of possible worlds should relate to possible worlds, not to the set of possible worlds, except perhaps by implication.[7] As George Boolos' (1984) argued, the fact that I had cornflakes for breakfast does not entail that I also consumed an additional type of entity, the set of cornflakes in my bowl! (Bennett 2009, p. 59) The set theoretic analysis of advanced modality inflates the ontological commitments of 'total theory' beyond that necessary for a fruitful discussion of the subject matter. Indeed, arguably sets are wholly dispensable. Bennett maintains that plural quantification enables the metaphysician to avoid carrying "ontological commitment to anything more than the first order individuals themselves – not to sets, sums, nor composite objects of any kind." (Bennett 2009, p. 59). Plural quantification enables the denial of composite objects whilst accepting claims such as 'there are some simples arranged table-wise' (§§ 1.5, 4.6). The predicate 'arranged table-wise' is non-distributive and not intended to entail satisfaction by a single entity. Hence, sets are wholly dispensable (Linnebo 2003, 2017: Bennett 2009).

Reply: The objection can be blocked. I argue in favour of a parity with respect to the ontological commitments of a theory entailed by the truth of that 'P' and 'possibly P'. In short, both statements incur the same ontological costs. Mathematics is an 'indispensable' element of the empirical sciences and thereby to 'total theory' (Quine 1948 [1980]: 1951a [1980]: 1981a [1981]: Putnam 1975b [1979]: 1975c [1979]). *If* mathematics is indispensable to the empirical sciences and *if* sets provide the foundation of mathematics then sets are

---

[7] For a discussion of the implied ontological commitments of a theory to a type of entity see § 1.4.

indispensable to the empirical sciences. Sets, therefore, are an indispensable component of 'total theory'.[8] Broadly, the Quine-Putnam argument is:

Premise A: We ought to have an ontological commitment to all and only those types of entity that are indispensable to our best scientific theory

Premise B: The types of entity posited by mathematics are indispensable to our best scientific theory

Therefore

Conclusion C: We ought to have an ontological commitment to the types of entity posited by mathematics

(Colyvan 2015, Section 1)

Sets are a type of entity indispensable to mathematics and, therefore, to empirical science (cf. Feferman 1998: Weaver 2009). For Lewis, mathematical 'fruitfulness' is a theoretical benefit enjoyed by postulating a plurality of sets (§ 8.1). Unfortunately, although 'fruitful' the indispensability of set theory to the foundations of mathematics is widely rejected by mathematicians. Number theory and functions are able to fulfil this foundational role without the unwarranted theoretical costs associated with set theory. For example; "[the] classical paradoxes of naïve set theory particularly cast doubt on the idea of a well-defined canonical universe of sets in which all set-theoretic questions have definite answers." (Weaver 2009, p. 1)

Although the indispensability of sets in the field of mathematics and the empirical sciences is disputed, I argue that set theory remains mathematically fruitful. Certainly, in the alternative, the coherent application of plural quantification in the field of empirical science is beset with problems. How does an advocate of plural quantification preserve the *compositional* structure of 'objects'? Empirical science is often engaged in the project of explaining how big things are made of smaller things. Are the big 'things' actually simples

---

[8] An argument premised on the indispensability of set theory to mathematics is unlikely to placate our protagonist. The constitution of mathematical objects is a contentious matter; although some authors e.g. von Neumann, argue that all mathematical objects can either be reduced to or identified with pure sets, others, famously Benacerraf (1965) argue that no such reduction is possible. Benacerraf argues that the multiplicity of incompatible methods that purport to 'reduce' numbers to pure sets invalidates the strategy of reduction. Several replies have been made to Benacerraf's objection. One response is structuralism in the philosophy of mathematics. Another, is to deny that each type of potential reduction is equally legitimate; for example, Steinhart argues that von Neumann's reduction enjoys many theoretical advantages over Zermelo's (Steinhart 2010, p. 20).

arranged big-thing-wise? Are the small 'things' actually simples arranged smaller-thing-wise? To which type of entity do we grant conceptual and ontological priority – the big things or the small things? Comparatively simple predicates, e.g., 'arranged *tablewise*' mask a fiendishly complicated structure. Take, for example, a phrase about a table constructed from a soft wood species, 'there are simples arranged *tablewise*':

> ((((((there are simples arranged subatomic-wise) arranged atom-wise) arranged cellulose-wise) arranged hemicellulose-wise) arranged lignin-wise) arranged ...)
>
> (Bennett 2009, pp. 59-60)

Their status as an 'indispensable' foundation of mathematics may be precarious, but sets serve other theoretical purposes (Lewis 1986a, pp. 3-4). Arguably, the advocate of plural quantification appears to lack an explanation of the inherent structure of reality (§ 4.6). How are the proposed 'simples' arranged? In the absence of a cogent structural explanation, the plural quantification model holds scant appeal for the empirical sciences. Sets have fruitful non-foundational applications in mathematics, whilst plural quantification is scientifically problematic – hence, I retain set theory as the most viable option.

8.3.3 The antinomies of proper classes

Recall that the redundancy theory is motivated by a desire to provide **GMR** with a strategy to meet the demands of modal ubiquity **(MU)** and possibility introduction **(PI)**, in the context of advanced modal sentences (§ 7.3). These are "strong default principles – principles such that it is expected a theory of modality will be at least consistent with both and is significantly disadvantaged otherwise." (Divers 1999, p. 218) I will now extrapolate an objection based on an argument constructed by Divers against a solution to the problem of advanced modality proposed by Menzies and Pettit (1994). I apply this counter-argument to my proposed set-based theoretic solution to the problem of advanced modal claims.

Menzies and Pettit argue that "it is true at2 *w* that *p* holds just when *p* holds true of *w* in virtue of the relations of *w* to other things – in particular, to other worlds" (cited in Divers 1999, page 225). In the case of an advanced modal claim of possibility introduction **(PI)**, say, that 'it is possible that there is a plurality of worlds' is true iff there is some world w at2 there is a plurality of worlds. In other words, to say that there are many worlds is true of w in virtue of the *relation* of w to other things – in this case, other worlds.

By **PI**:

1: There are many worlds

P1: It is possible that there are many worlds

(Divers 1999, p. 221)

The truth conditions of **PI** at P1 [left side, biconditional] is P1* [right side, (biconditional)]:

P1* there is some world w that has the relational property of being a member of a set of worlds, one of which contains many worlds.

(Divers 1999, p. 226)

P1* suffers from the now familiar problem of advanced modal sentences. By standard translation, there is no world that 'contains', either in whole or in part, many worlds (§ 7.2). Divers considers adapting Menzies and Pettit's general formulae to accommodate more favourable truth-conditions on the proviso "that there are many worlds holds true of w in virtue of w standing in the relation of set membership to a set which has many worlds as members" (Divers 1999, p. 226).

However, Divers concludes that the adapted formula delivers only partial success. There remain intuitively true advanced modal claims that yield a false analysans by standard translation. Consider:

P5: It is possible that there are proper classes

(Divers 1999, p. 226)

A proper class cannot be a member of anything and so cannot be a member of a set required by the Menzies-Pettit account. The point is illustrated at P5.1, where 'C' is a predicate letter designating a proper class:

P5.1: $\exists x \, \exists y \, \exists s \, (Wx \,\&\, (x \in s) \,\&\, Cy \,\&\, (y \in s))$

(Divers 1999, p. 227)

A uniform solution to the problem of interpreting advanced possibility claims is desirable and the worry about the Menzies-Pettit proposal is that far from delivering a uniform solution, it can offer only a piecemeal and ad hoc approach in which we are to seek in each case some relations or other involving worlds that will generate a truth-condition that is amenable to the genuine realist. (Divers 1999, p. 227)

In subsequent work, Divers exorcises the ghost that haunts the relation between worlds and non-individuals – see D above. This leaves the residue of accounting for those potential objects that are prohibited from set-membership and are therefore excluded from any set-based account of a solution to advanced modal claims. Clearly, proper classes are a prime candidate. Proper classes are those classes that are not reducible or equivalent to sets. The set/class distinction was first made by Frege in the late nineteenth century. A logical collection – or class – is the extension of a property that contains all and only those things which are the extension of that property. As each class is conceptually *dependent* on a prior predicate, it cannot qualify as a conceptual primitive. A combinatorial collection – or set – is the result of combinatorial activity formerly codified by the axioms and theorems of set theory.

Reply. My strategy in respect of P5 is to deny the possibility of proper classes – proper classes do not, indeed, could not exist. Clearly, in order to establish grounds for this denial, I must show that it is more than a convenient truth. There are at least two possible options in pursuit of this strategy: first, cleave to the standard practice of set theory and deny all classes or second, employ the Neumann-Bernays-Godel **(NBG)** axioms of set theory that do admit classes – except for proper classes. My strategy is similar to denying other intuitively plausible but contentious entities, e.g., zombie worlds, private languages, and contingent identity statements. The strategy of denying proper classes provides an avenue of escape from Divers' objection. I utilise Russell's Paradox in order to test the viability of my strategy (Jech 2011, Section 4). Specifically, we cannot simply form a set from any arbitrary predicate P. Generally, although some sets are members of themselves, most are not. The set x of all cats, which itself is not a cat, is not a member of itself. Define R as the set of all sets that are *not* members of themselves. So, if R is *not* a member of itself then by definition it must be a member of itself. If R not-∈ R then R ∈ R. On the other hand, if R *is* a member of itself then, again, by definition, it cannot be a member of itself. If R ∈ R then R not-∈ R. If R exists, then it is a member of itself iff it is not a member of itself. That is a contradiction – so R does not exist. The *flavour* of Russell's Paradox can be illustrated by way of an analogy; the Barber's Paradox. Suppose there is a barber who lives in a town where he cuts the hair of all and only those people who do not cut their own. The question is this: who cuts the barber's hair? It cannot be himself, since that would mean that he does not cut the hair of *only* those people who do *not* cut their own, excluded *ex hypothesi*. It cannot be someone else since that would mean that he does *not* cut the hair of *all* the people who do not cut their own, again, excluded *ex hypothesi*. Hence, the paradox. "The antinomies of intuitive set theory pose the problem of providing a theory of sets which is free of contradictions." (Stoll 1979, p. 289)

How should the contradiction be resolved? We could restrict predicates in respect of their definitional role in regard to sets. Indeed, this is how standard set theory avoids the contradiction. By standard set theory, we cannot simply form a set with an arbitrary predicate P. A second set is required. Hence, the representation of the extension of a property – the predicate P – by a single set is ill-formed {x I x is P}. First, we need to specify a second set y from which the xs are selected. The predicate P is represented by the set {x ∈ y I x is P}. Hence, we are able to define {x ∈ y I x not-∈ x} – which is simply an alternative way to represent the set y (Steinhart 2009, p. 62). The paradox is avoided, and Divers' inclusion of the possibility of classes by **PI** (P5) by way of the simple expedient of accepting the practice of standard set theory.

Intuitively, however, this solution seems unsatisfactory. Intuitively, every property has an extension or a collection of all and only the objects that instantiate it. For example, the extension of the property is-a-cat is intuitively the set {x I x is a cat}. To account for our intuitions, an alternative or non-standard solution to the paradox is available based on a distinction between those collections that are sets and those that are not. Let us assume that classes are possible and exist. There are *some* collections – classes – that are not sets but play a prominent role in mathematics and the philosophy of language. Class theory states that all collections are classes. Any arbitrary class is either a set or a proper class. Hence, every set is a class but not all classes are sets. Sets are distinguished from classes on the basis of the membership relation. Every set is a member of some other class, i.e., if X is a set then there is a distinct class Y such that X ∈ Y. A set may also be the member of another set, e.g., its own power set. A proper class, on the other hand, is neither a member of another class nor another set. If X is a proper class, then there is no class or set Y such that X ∈ Y. Importantly, there *is* a class of all sets. To avoid the paradox, the class of all sets cannot itself be a set, so it must be a proper class. The proper class of all sets is designated 'V'.

V = {x I x is a set}

The paradox is dissolved. As a proper class, V cannot be the member of a set or another class, so it cannot be a member of itself. Class theory dodges the paradox whilst preserving the intuition that every property has an extension; the class of the predicate P. The difference is one of *generality*. For all properties, the extension of that property is a class, e.g., the extension of the property [is-a-set] is a class. Occasionally, the extension of a property is a set, e.g., the extension of the property [is-a-perfect number] is a set (Steinhart 2009, p. 63). If we choose to accept classes, we may avoid the paradox and satisfy the intuition that the extension of every property is represented by the class of a predicate P. On the other hand, an ontological commitment to classes would impose a restriction on the scope of my set theoretic solution to the problem of advanced modality by Divers' P5.

Is there an escape route from the impasse generated by the inclusion of non-standard set theory? A solution that secures the theoretical benefits associated with an ontological commitment to classes but does not incur a theoretical cost to my proposed set-theoretic solution to the problem of advanced modality? The axioms of standard set theory, for example, restrict the type of objects that qualify as a set; they postulate that for every set x, x is not a member of itself. The non-standard account of set theory entails an adjustment to my preferred strategy of denying the existence of classes. A non-standard resolution to the impasses may involve adopting the axioms of **NBG** that take classes as the basic objects of set theory. The **NBG** axioms restrict the domain of quantification to sets rather than to *all* classes. That is, proper classes are excluded from the domain of quantification. By definition, this ontologically conservative extension of the Zermelo-Fraenkel axioms of standard set theory does not posit the existence of proper classes. The axioms of **NBG** are an appealing alternative to standard set theory since classes do not qualify as a conceptual *primitive* and so are not a conceptual primitive of **GMR**. The choice is either to adopt the practice of standard set theory and exclude classes altogether or adopt the axioms of **NBG,** which exclude proper classes. Either option avoids an ontological commitment to proper classes and Divers' extrapolated objection to my set theoretic solution to the problem of advanced modality. However, I have now strayed into a discussion of the axioms of set theory and have breached my promise to confine the discussion to the 'simple view' of sets.

8.4 Conclusion

I accept Divers' method of identification with respect to advanced modal claims. I reject Divers' solution to the problem on the grounds that – as a proposal conducive to **GMR** – a more felicitous option is available. My set theoretic solution to the problem of advanced modality is neither ad hoc nor piecemeal. An ontological commitment to sets is compelling regardless of one's prior commitments to a plurality of worlds. Lewis' ontological commitment to sets is based on their theoretical utility with respect to the explication of a number of contentious philosophical entities. Despite these advantages, problems remain. I shamelessly endorse sets on the grounds of their theoretical 'fruitfulness' but rejected proper classes despite their theoretical 'fruitfulness'! The only fig-leaf I have to offer to cover this embarrassment is an argument from the 'indispensable' nature of sets to the empirical sciences via the field of mathematics. Although disputed, 'indispensability' provides ample motivation to include sets as a component of 'total theory'.

Glossary

AR ... Actualist Realism

CE ... Conjunction Elimination

dMF ... denial of a Moorean Fact

EQ ... 'This table exits'

FK ... Folk Knowledge

GMR ... Genuine Modal Realism

MF ... Moorean Fact

MU ... Modal Ubiquity

NBG ... Neumann-Bernays-Godel (axioms of set theory)

OP ... Ontological Parsimony

OPK ... Ontological Parsimony of Kinds

PI ... Possibility Introduction

PL ... Predicate Logic (with Identity)

QC ... Quantifier Criterion (of ontological commitment)

QML ... Quantified Modal Logic

QP ... Quantitative Parsimony

WA ... Worldly Agnosticism

WRP ... World Relevance Principle

Bibliography

Adams, Robert M. (1979) "Theories of Actuality" in Michael J. Loux (ed.) (1979) *The Possible and the Actual: Readings in the Metaphysics of Modality* Cornell University Press: 190-209

Alston, William P. (1958) "Ontological Commitments" *Philosophical Studies* 9: 8-17

Armstrong, David M. (1978a) *Nominalism and Realism (Universals and Scientific Realism,* Volume 1) Cambridge: Cambridge University Press

Armstrong, David M. (1978b) *A Theory of Universals (Universals and Scientific Realism,* Volume 2) Cambridge: Cambridge University Press

Baker, Alan, "Simplicity", *The Stanford Encyclopaedia of Philosophy* (Fall 2013 Edition), Edward N. Zalta (ed.), URL = <http://plato.stanford.edu/archives/fall2013/entries/simplicity/>.

Beebee, Helen & MacBride, Fraser (2015) "*De Re* Modality, Essentialism, and Lewis's Humeanism" in Barry Loewer & Jonathan Schaffer (eds.) (2015) *A Companion to David Lewis* Wiley Blackwell: 220-236

Benacerraf, Paul (1965) "What Numbers Could Not Be" in Paul Benacerraf & Hilary Putnam (eds.) (1983) *Philosophy of Mathematics: Selected Readings* New York: Cambridge University Press, 2nd edition: 272-295

Benacerraf, Paul (1973) "Mathematical Truth" *Journal of Philosophy* 70: 661-79

Bennett, Jonathan (2003) *A Philosophical Guide to Conditionals* Oxford University Press

Bennett, Karen (2009) "Composition, Colocation, and Metaontology" in David J. Chalmers, David Manley & Ryan Wasserman (eds.) (2009) *Metametaphysics: New Essays on the Foundations of Ontology* Clarendon Press, Oxford: 38-76

Blackburn, Simon (1984) *Spreading the Word* Oxford: Clarendon

Blomfield, Megan (2008) "Modal Agnosticism" *Aporia* Volume 18 (1): 67-81

Boolos, George (1984) "To be is to be the value of a variable (or some values of some variables)" *Journal of Philosophy* 81: 430-49

Braun, David, "Indexicals", *The Stanford Encyclopedia of Philosophy* (Summer 2017 Edition), Edward N. Zalta (ed.), URL = <https://plato.stanford.edu/archives/sum2017/entries/indexicals/>.

Bricker, Phillip, "Ontological Commitment", *The Stanford Encyclopedia of Philosophy* (Winter 2016 Edition), Edward N. Zalta (ed.), URL = <https://plato.stanford.edu/archives/win2016/entries/ontological-commitment/>.

Burgess, John P. (2015) "Lewis on Mereology and Set Theory" in Barry Loewer & Jonathan Schaffer (eds.) (2015) *A Companion to David Lewis* Wiley Blackwell: 459-469

Carnap, Rudolf (1962) *Logical Foundations of Probability* Chicago: University of Chicago Press, 2nd edition

Cartwright, Richard (1960) "Negative Existentials" *Journal of Philosophy* 57: 629-39

Cappelen, Herman (2012) *Philosophy Without Intuitions* Oxford University Press

Colyvan, Mark, "Indispensability Arguments in the Philosophy of Mathematics", *The Stanford Encyclopedia of Philosophy* (Spring 2015 Edition), Edward N. Zalta (ed.), URL = <https://plato.stanford.edu/archives/spr2015/entries/mathphil-indis/>.

Daly, Chris (2010) *An Introduction to Philosophical Methods* Broadview Guides to Philosophy

Davidson, Donald (1967) "The Logical Form Of Action Sentences" in Donald Davidson (1980) *Essays On Action And Events* Oxford University Press: 105-22

Divers, John (1997) "The Analysis of Possibility and the Possibility of Analysis" *Proceedings of the Aristotelian Society* Volume 97: 141-160

Divers, John (1999) "A Genuine Realist Theory of Advanced Modalizing" *Mind* 108 (Issue 430): 217-239

Divers, John (2002) *Possible Worlds* Routledge

Divers, John (2004) "Agnosticism About Other Worlds: A New Antirealist Programme in Modality" *Philosophical and Phenomenological Research* 69 (3): 660-684

Divers, John (2006) "Possible World Semantics Without Possible Worlds: The Agnostic Approach" *Mind* 115: 187-225

Divers, John (2014) "The Modal Status of the Lewisian Analysis of Modality" downloaded from http://mind.oxfordjournals.org/ pp 1-12: also *Mind* 123 (Issue 491): 861-872

Divers, John & Melia, Joseph (2002) "The Analytic Limit Of Genuine Modal Realism" *Mind* 111 (Issue 441): 15-36

Dorr, Cian (2011) "De Re A Priori Knowledge" *Mind* 120 (Issue 480): 939-991

Dummett, Michael (1991) *Frege: Philosophy of Mathematics* Duckwort

Einstein, Albert (2001) *Relativity: The Special and the General Theory* Routledge Classics

Evans, Gareth (1981) "Understanding Demonstratives" in Gareth Evans (1985) *Collected Papers* Clarendon Press, Oxford: 291-321

Feferman, Solomon (1998) *In the Light of Logic* Oxford University Press

Forbes, Graeme (1985) *The Metaphysics of Modality* Oxford: Clarendon

Frege, Gottlob (1879) "Begriffsschrift" in Peter Geach & Max Black (1980) *Translations From The Philosophical Writings Of Gottlob Frege* Basil Blackwell Oxford, 3rd edition: 1-20

Frege, Gottlob (1891) "Function and Concept" in Peter Geach & Max Black (1980) *Translations From The Philosophical Writings Of Gottlob Frege* Basil Blackwell Oxford, 3rd edition: 21-41

Frege, Gottlob (1892a) "On Sense and Nominatum" in A. P. Martinich (ed.) (2001) *The Philosophy of Language* Oxford University Press, 4th edition: 199-220

Frege, Gottlob (1892b) "On Concept and Object" in Peter Geach & Max Black (1980) *Translations From The Philosophical Writings Of Gottlob Frege* Basil Blackwell Oxford, 3rd edition: 42-55

Goodman, Nelson (1972) *Problems and Projects* Indianapolis: Bobbs-Merrill

Gottlieb, Dale (1980) *Ontological Economy: Substitutional Quantification and Mathematics* Oxford: Oxford University Press

Grayling, Anthony C. (1997) *An Introduction to Philosophical Logic* Blackwell Publishers, 3rd edition

Gribbin, John (2002) *Science: A History 1543-2001* BCA: The Penguin Group

Griffin, Nicholas (1996) "Denoting Concepts in *The Principles of Mathematics*" in Ray Monk & Anthony Palmer (eds.) (1996) *Bertrand Russell and the Origins of Analytic Philosophy* Thoemmes Press: 23-64

Hacker, P.M.S. (1996) "Proximity at Great Distance" in Robert L Arrington & Hans-Johann Glock (eds.) (1996) *Wittgenstein & Quine* Routledge: 1-38

Hale, Bob (2013) *Necessary Beings: An Essay on Ontology, Modality, & the Relations Between Them* Oxford University Press

Hawthorne, John (1990) "A Note On 'Languages and Language'" *Australasian Journal of Philosophy* 68: 116-118

Hawthorne, John (1993) "Meaning and Evidence: A Reply to Lewis" *Australasian Journal of Philosophy* 71: 206-211

Hazen, A.P. (1997) "Relations in Monadic Third Order Logic" *Journal of Philosophical Logic*, 26: 619-28

Hodges, Wilfrid (2001) "Classical Logic I: First-Order Logic" in Lou Goble (ed.) (2001) *The Blackwell Guide to Philosophical Logic* Blackwell Publishing: 9-32

Hookway, Christopher (1988) *Quine: Language, Experience and Reality* Polity Press

Hylton, Peter (1990) *Russell, Idealism and the Emergence of Analytic Philosophy* Oxford University Press: Clarendon Paperbacks

Hylton, Peter (2010) *Quine* Routledge

Jackson, Frank & Priest, Graham (2004) "Introduction" in Frank Jackson & Graham Priest (eds.) (2004) *Lewisian Themes: The Philosophy of David K. Lewis* Clarendon Press Oxford: 1-3

Jago, Mark (2016) "Advanced Modalizing Problems" *Mind* 125 (499): 627-642

Jech, Thomas "Set Theory" *Stanford Encyclopaedia of Philosophy* (Winter 2011 edition) Edward N. Zalta (ed.) url: http://plato.stanford.edu/archives/win 2011/ entries/ set theory/

Juhl, Cory & Loomis, Eric (2010) *Analyticity* Routledge

Kaplan, David (1977) "Demonstratives" in Joseph Almog, John Perry & Howard Wettstein (eds.) (1989) *Themes From Kaplan* Oxford University Press: 481-563

Kant, Immanuel (1781 / 1787) *Critique of Pure Reason* translated by Norman Kemp Smith (1929) Macmillan

Kripke, Saul (1980) *Naming & Necessity* Cambridge: Harvard University Press

Kripke, Saul (1982) *Wittgenstein on Rules and Private Language* Cambridge, MA: Harvard University Press

Kripke, Saul (2013) *Reference and Existence: The John Locke Lectures* Oxford University Press

Kuhn, Thomas (1977) "Objectivity, Value Judgement and Theory Choice" in Thomas Kuhn (1977) *The Essential Tension* The University of Chicago Press: 320-339

Lewis, David (1968) "Counterpart Theory and Quantified Modal Logic" in David Lewis [1983] *Philosophical Papers Vol. 1* Oxford University Press: 26-39

Lewis, David (1970) "General Semantics" in David Lewis [1983] *Philosophical Papers Vol. 1* Oxford University Press: 189-229

Lewis, David (1971) "Counterparts of Persons and Their Bodies" in David Lewis [1983] *Philosophical Papers Vol. 1* Oxford University Press: 47-54

Lewis, David (1973) *Counterfactuals* Blackwell

Lewis, David (1974) "Tensions" in David Lewis [1983] *Philosophical Papers Vol. 1* Oxford University Press: 250-260

Lewis, David (1975) "Languages and Language" in David Lewis [1983] *Philosophical Papers Vol. 1* Oxford University Press: 163-188

Lewis, David (1979) "Scorekeeping in a Language Game" in David Lewis [1983] *Philosophical Papers Vol. 1* Oxford University Press: 233-249

Lewis, David (1980) "Index, Context and Content" in David Lewis [1998] *Papers in Philosophical Logic* Cambridge University Press: 21-44

Lewis, David (1982) "Logic for Equivocators" in David Lewis [1998] *Papers In Philosophical Logic* Cambridge University Press: 97-110

Lewis, David (1983a) "Introduction" in David Lewis [1983] *Philosophical Papers Vol. 1* Oxford University Press: ix-xii

Lewis, David (1983b) "*Postscript to* Counterpart Theory and Quantified Modal Logic" in David Lewis [1983] *Philosophical Papers Vol. 1* Oxford University Press: 39-46

Lewis, David (1983c) "Extrinsic Properties" in David Lewis [1999] *Papers in Metaphysics and Epistemology* Cambridge University Press: 111-115

Lewis, David (1983d) "New Work for a Theory of Universals" in David Lewis [1999] *Papers in Metaphysics and Epistemology* Cambridge University Press: 8-55

Lewis, David (1983e) "Putnam's Paradox" in David Lewis [1999] *Papers in Metaphysics and Epistemology* Cambridge University Press: 56-77

Lewis, David (1983f) "Individuation by Acquaintance and by Stipulation" in David Lewis [1999] *Papers in Metaphysics and Epistemology* Cambridge University Press: 373-402

Lewis, David (1986a) *On The Plurality Of Worlds* Blackwell Publishing Ltd

Lewis, David (1986b) "Introduction" in David Lewis [1986] *Philosophical Papers Vol. 2* Oxford University Press: ix-xvii

Lewis, David (1990) "Noneism or allism?" in David Lewis [1999] *Papers in Metaphysics and Epistemology* Cambridge University Press: 152-163

Lewis, David (1991) *Parts of Classes* Basil Blackwell: Oxford

Lewis, David (1992) "Meaning Without Use: Reply to Hawthorne" *Australasian Journal of Philosophy* 70: 106-110

Lewis David (1993) "Mathematics is Megethology" in David Lewis [1998] *Papers in Philosophical Logic* Cambridge University Press: 203-229

Lewis, David (1994) "Reduction of Mind" in David Lewis [1999] *Papers in Metaphysics and Epistemology* Cambridge University Press: 291-324

Lewis, David (1996a) "Elusive Knowledge" in David Lewis [1999] *Papers in Metaphysics and Epistemology* Cambridge University Press: 418-445

Lewis, David (1996b) "Maudlin and Modal Mystery" in David Lewis [1999] *Papers in Metaphysics and Epistemology* Cambridge University Press: 221-223

Lewis, David (1997) "Naming the Colours" in David Lewis [1999] *Papers in Metaphysics and Epistemology* Cambridge University Press: 332-358

Lewis, David (1998) "A World of Truthmakers?" in David Lewis [1999] *Papers in Metaphysics and Epistemology* Cambridge University Press: 215-220

Lewis, David (2001) "Truthmaking and difference-making" *Nous* 35: 602-15

Lewis, David (2002) *Convention: A Philosophical Study* Blackwell Publishers

Lewis, David (2003) "Things *qua* truthmakers" in H. Lillehammer & G. Rodriguez-Pereyra (eds.) [2003] *Real metaphysics: Essays in honour of D. H. Mellor* London Routledge: 25-38

Lewis, David & Lewis, Stephanie (1970) "Holes" in David Lewis [1983] *Philosophical Papers Vol. 1* Oxford University Press: 3-9

Linnebo, Øystein (2003) "Plural Quantification Exposed" *Nous* 37: 71-92

Linnebo, Øystein, "Plural Quantification", *The Stanford Encyclopedia of Philosophy* (Summer 2017 Edition), Edward N. Zalta (ed.), URL = <https://plato.stanford.edu/archives/sum2017/entries/plural-quant/>.

Lycan, William (2000) *Philosophy of Language: A Contemporary Introduction* Routledge: London and New York

Marcus, Ruth (1993) *Modalities* Oxford: Oxford University Press

McKay, Thomas J. (2006) *Plural Predication* Clarendon Press Oxford

Miller, Alexander (1998) *Philosophy of Language* UCL Press

Moore, George E. (1925) "A Defence of Common Sense" in Thomas Baldwin (ed.) [1993] *G. E. Moore Selected Writings* Routledge: 106-133

Moore, George E. (1939) "Proof of an External World" in Thomas Baldwin (ed.) [1993] *G. E. Moore Selected Writings* Routledge: 147-170

Nolan, Daniel (1997) "Quantitative Parsimony" *British Journal for the Philosophy of Science* 48: 329-43

Nolan, Daniel (2005) *David Lewis* Acumen

Noonan, Harold (1994) "In Defence of the Letter of Fictionalism" *Analysis* 54: 133-139

Noonan, Harold (1996) "The 'Gray's Elegy' Argument – And Others" in Ray Monk & Anthony Palmer (eds.) [1996] *Bertrand Russell and the Origins of Analytic Philosophy* Thoemmes Press: 65-102

Noonan, Harold (2014) "The Adequacy of Genuine Modal Realism" downloaded from http://mind.oxfordjournals.org/ pp 1-12: also Mind 123 (Issue 491): 851-860

Parsons, Josh (2011) "Against Advanced Modalizing" Unpublished - available Josh Parsons' webpage: http://oxford.academia.edu/JoshParsons

Plantinga, Alvin (1973) "Transworld Identity and Worldbound Individuals" in Michael J. Loux (ed.) [1979] *The Possible and the Actual: Readings in the Metaphysics of Modality* Cornell University Press: 146-165

Putnam, Hilary (1975a) "The Meaning of 'Meaning'" in Andrew Pessin & Sanford Goldberg (eds.) [1996] *The Twin Earth Chronicles: Twenty Years of Reflection on Hilary Putnam's "The Meaning of 'Meaning'"* M. E. Sharpe (Armonk, New York London, England): 3-52

Putnam, Hilary (1975b) "What Is Mathematical Truth" in Hilary Putnam [1979] *Mathematics, Matter and Method: Philosophical Papers Volume 1* Cambridge University Press, 2nd edition: 60-78

Putnam, Hilary (1975c) "Philosophy of Logic" in Hilary Putnam [1979] *Mathematics, Matter and Method: Philosophical Papers Volume 1* Cambridge University Press, 2nd edition: 323-358

Putnam, Hilary (1978) *Meaning and the Moral Sciences* Boston: Routledge and Kegan Paul

Putnam, Hilary (1980) "Models and Reality" in Hilary Putnam [1983] *Realism and Reasons: Philosophical Papers Volume 3* Cambridge University Press: 1-25

Quine, W.V.O. (1935) "Truth by Convention" in W.V.O. Quine [1976] *The Ways of Paradox and Other Essays* Harvard University Press [Revised and Enlarged Edition]: 77-106

Quine, W.V.O. (1948) "On What There Is" in W.V.O. Quine [1980] *From A Logical Point Of View* Harvard University Press (revised), 2nd edition: 1-19

Quine, W.V.O. (1951a) "Two Dogmas of Empiricism" in W.V.O. Quine [1980] *From A Logical Point Of View* Harvard University Press (revised), 2nd edition: 20-46

Quine, W.V.O. (1951b) "Ontology and Ideology" *Philosophical Studies,* 2: 11-15

Quine, W.V.O. (1951c) "On Carnap's Views on Ontology" in W.V.O. Quine [1976] *The Ways of Paradox and Other Essays* Harvard University Press [Revised and Enlarged Edition]: 203-211

Quine, W.V.O. (1953a) "Logic and the Reification of Universals" in W.V.O. Quine [1980] *From a Logical Point of View* Harvard University Press (revised), 2nd edition: 102-129

Quine, W.V.O. (1953b) "Reference and Modality" in W.V.O. Quine [1980] *From a Logical Point of View* Harvard University Press (revised), 2nd edition: 139-159

Quine, W.V.O. (1954) "The Scope and Language of Science" in W.V.O. Quine [1976] *The Ways of Paradox and Other Essays* Harvard University Press [Revised and Enlarged edition]: 228-245

Quine, W.V.O. (1956) "Quantifiers and Propositional Attitudes" in W.V.O. Quine [1976] *The Ways of Paradox and Other Essays* Harvard University Press [Revised and Enlarged edition]: 185-196

Quine, W.V.O. (1960) *Word And Object* The MIT Press, Cambridge Massachusetts: New Edition [2013]

Quine, W.V.O. (1969) "Existence and Quantification" in W.V.O. Quine [1969] *Ontological Relativity and Other Essays* Columbia University Press, New York: 91-113

Quine, W.V.O. (1974) *The Roots of Reference: The Paul Carus Lectures* La Salle, Illinois, Open Court

Quine, W.V.O. (1977) "Facts of the Matter" in Robert W. Shahan & Kenneth R. Merrill (eds.) (1977) *American Philosophy: from Edwards to Quine* Normal, OK: University of Oklahoma Press: 155-69

Quine, W.V.O. (1981a) "Things And Their Place In Theories" in W.V.O. Quine [1981] *Theories And Things* The Belknap Press of Harvard University Press: 1-23

Quine, W.V.O. (1981b) "Responses" in W.V.O. Quine [1981] *Theories And Things* The Belknap Press of Harvard University Press: 173-186

Quine, W.V.O. (1983) "Ontology and Ideology Revisited" *The Journal of Philosophy* 80 (9): 499-502

Quine, W.V.O. (1986a) *Philosophy of Logic* Harvard University Press, 2nd edition

Quine, W.V.O. (1986b) "Autobiography" in Lewis E. Hahn & Paul A. Schilpp [1998] *The Philosophy of W.V. Quine* Open Court Publishing, 2nd Expanded Edition: 2-46

Quine, W.V.O. (1998a) "Reply To William P Alston" in Lewis E. Hahn & Paul A. Schilpp (eds.) [1998] *The Philosophy of W.V. Quine* Open Court Publishing, 2nd Expanded Edition: 73-75

Quine, W.V.O. (1998b) "Reply To Herbert G. Bohnert" in Lewis E. Hahn & Paul A. Schilpp (eds.) [1998] *The Philosophy of W.V. Quine* Open Court Publishing, 2nd Expanded Edition: 93-95

Quine, W.V.O. (1998c) "Reply to P. F. Strawson" in Lewis E. Hahn & Paul A. Schilpp [1998] *The Philosophy of W.V. Quine* Open Court Publishing, 2nd Expanded Edition: 533-535

Rayo, Agustin (2007) "Ontological Commitment" *Philosophy Compass* 2(3): 428-444

Rescher, Nicholas (2006) *Philosophical Dialectics: An Essay On Metaphilosophy* State University of New York Press

Rosen, Gideon (1990) "Modal Fictionalism" *Mind* 99: 327-354

Rosen, Gideon (2015) "On the Nature of Certain Philosophical Entities: Set Theoretic Constructionalism in the Metaphysics of David Lewis" in Barry Loewer & Jonathan Schaffer (eds.) (2015) *A Companion to David Lewis* Wiley Blackwell: 382-398

Russell, Bertrand (1903) [2010] *Principles of Mathematics* Routledge Classics, 2nd edition

Russell, Bertrand (1905) "On Denoting" in A. P. Martinich (ed.) [2001] *The Philosophy of Language* Oxford University Press, 4th edition: 212-220

Russell, Bertrand (1919) [1996] *Introduction to Mathematical Philosophy* Routledge

Ryle, Gilbert (1953) "Ordinary Language" in Gilbert Ryle [2009] *Collected Papers Volume 2: Collected Essays 1929-1968* Routledge, Taylor & Francis Group: 314-331

Salmon, Nathan (2004) *Reference and Essence* Princeton: Princeton University Press, 2nd edition

Sider, Theodore (1999) "Presentism And Ontological Commitment" *Journal Of Philosophy*, 96: 325-347

Sider, Theodore (2003) "Reductive Theories of Modality" in Michael J. Loux & Dean W. Zimmerman (eds.) [2003] *The Oxford Handbook of Metaphysics* Oxford University Press: 180-205

Sider, Theodore (2009) "Ontological Realism" in David J. Chalmers, David Manley & Ryan Wasserman (eds.) [2009] *Metametaphysics: New Essays on the Foundations of Ontology* Oxford University Press: 384-423

Sider, Theodore (2011) *Writing the Book of the World* Oxford: Oxford University Press

Soames, Scott (2007) "Actually" *Proceedings of the Aristotelian Society Supplementary Volume* 81 (1): 251-277, available at Professor Soames Homepage: http://dornsife. usc.edu/scottsoames/selected-publications/

Sosa, Ernest (2002) "Reliability and the A Priori" in Tamar Szabo Gendler & John Hawthorn (eds.) (2002) *Conceivability and Possibility* Oxford University Press: 369-384

Stalnaker, Robert C. (1976/1984) "Possible Worlds" in Robert C. Stalnaker [2003] *Ways a World Might Be: Metaphysical and Anti-Metaphysical Essays* Oxford University Press: 25-39

Stalnaker, Robert C. (1987) "Counterparts and Identity" in Robert C. Stalnaker [2003] *Ways a World Might Be: Metaphysical and Anti-Metaphysical Essays* Oxford University Press: 111-132

Stalnaker, Robert C. (1996) "On What Possible Worlds Could Not Be" in Robert C. Stalnaker [2003] *Ways a World Might Be: Metaphysical and Anti-Metaphysical Essays* Oxford University Press: 40-54

Stalnaker, Robert C. (2012) *Mere Possibilities* Princeton University Press: Princeton and Oxford

Steinberg, Alex (2018) "Adequate Counterpart Translations" *Mind* 127 (506): 547-563

Steinhart, Eric (2009) *More Precisely: The Math You Need To Do Philosophy* Broadview Press

Stoll, Robert R. (1979) *Set Theory And Logic* Dover Publications, Inc.: New York

Strawson, Peter F. (1952) *Introduction to Logical Theory* London: Methuen

Stroll, Avrum (1994) *Moore and Wittgenstein On Certainty* Oxford University Press

Stroud, Barry (1984) *The Significance of Philosophical Scepticism* Oxford University Press

Swoyer, Chris and Orilia, Francesco, "Properties", *The Stanford Encyclopedia of Philosophy* (Fall 2014 Edition), Edward N. Zalta (ed.), URL = <http://plato.stanford.edu/archives/fall2014/entries/properties/>.

Tiles, Mary (1989) *The Philosophy of Set Theory: An Historical Introduction to Cantor's Paradise* Dover Publications

Unger, Peter (1975) *Ignorance: A Case for Scepticism* Oxford University Press

Uzquiano, Gabriel, "Quantifiers and Quantification", *The Stanford Encyclopedia of Philosophy* (Spring 2017 Edition), Edward N. Zalta (ed.), URL = <https://plato.stanford.edu/archives/spr2017/entries/quantification/>.

Vaidya, Anand, "The Epistemology of Modality", *The Stanford Encyclopedia of Philosophy* (Winter 2017 Edition), Edward N. Zalta (ed.), URL = <https://plato.stanford.edu/archives/win2017/entries/modality-epistemology/>.

van Inwagen, Peter (1981) "Why I Don't Understand Substitutional Quantification" in Peter van Inwagen [2001] *Ontology, Identity, and Modality: Essays in Metaphysics* Cambridge University Press: 32-36

van Inwagen, Peter (1986) "Two Concepts Of Possible Worlds" in Peter van Inwagen [2001] *Ontology, Identity, and Modality: Essays In Metaphysics* Cambridge University Press: 206-242

van Inwagen, Peter (1990) *Material Beings* Cornell University Press

van Inwagen, Peter (1997) "Materialism and the Psychological-Continuity Account of Personal Identity" in Peter van Inwagen [2001] *Ontology, Identity, and Modality: Essays In Metaphysics* Cambridge University Press: 144-161 van Inwagen, Peter (1998) "Meta-ontology" in Peter van Inwagen [2001] *Ontology, Identity, And Modality: Essays In Metaphysics* Cambridge University Press: 13-31

Wallace, David (2012) *The Emergent Universe: Quantum Theory According To The Everett Interpretation* Oxford University Press

Weaver, Nik (2009) "Is Set Theory Indispensable?" arXiv [internet resource]

Williamson, Timothy (2007) *The Philosophy of Philosophy* Blackwell Publishing

Williamson, Timothy (2013) *Modal Logic as Metaphysics* Oxford University Press

Wittgenstein, Ludwig (1958) *Philosophical Investigations* translated by G.E.M. Anscombe, Basil Blackwell, 2nd edition

Wright, Crispin (1980) *Wittgenstein and the Foundations of Mathematics* Duckworth

Index

A

A Kind of Magic, xiv, 124, 132, 133
a variable, 2, 7, 8, 10, 11, 12, 16
actual world, 129, 132
   representational property, 132
Actualist Realism, 91, 93, 95, 105,
   See possible world: set of
   maximal consistent
   propositions
   safe and sane ontology, 94, 105
Adams, Robert, 93
advanced modal sentences, ix, x, xi,
   xiii, xiv, 3, 12, 13, 15, 106, 107,
   108, 109, 110, 115, 117, 118,
   119, 120, 121, 122, 123, 124,
   125, 126, 129, 130, 131, 134,
   136, 137, 138, 139, 140
   non-standard translation, xiii,
      108, 110, 114, 115, 118, 129
allism, 20
analysandum, viii, 73, 97, 102, 105,
   107, 108, 114
   [left side, biconditional], 21, 93,
      96, 97, 100, 103, 104, 110,
      122, 125, 137
analysans, viii, ix, 25, 41, 47, 48,
   73, 93, 94, 95, 103, 105, 107,
   108, 120, 122, 129, 130, 137
   [right side, biconditional], xiv,
      10, 21, 93, 95, 96, 97, 100,
      103, 104, 105, 108, 110, 124,
      125, 130, 137
analytic truth, ix, xii, 12, 14, 24, 27,
   70, 71, 73, 74, 75, 80, 81, 83, 85,
   88, 89, 97
   Frege-analytic, 80, 83, 84, 85, 89
   meaning of its constituent
      terms, xii, 73, 74
   metaphysical analyticity, 73,
      80, 81
   modal analyticity, 80, 82, 85, 89
   temporally analytic, 82
Antirealism, modal, 95, 96, 105
apparent reference to non-
   existents, 4
Aristotle. *See* theorectical
   conservatism
Armstrong, David M., 39, 67
at a world, w, 127, 129, 130
   from the standpoint of a world,
      126, 127, 131
   interpretations, 126

B

Benacerraf, Paul, 135
   mathematical truth, 76
Bennett, Karen, 134
Beta-decay, 62, 63
   neutrino, 61
bliger. *See* van Inwagen, Peter
   Material Beings
Blomfield, Megan, 100, 102, 103,
   106
Bohr, Niels, 35
Boolos, George, 134
Buffon's Law, 60
   Extensionist, 60
   The Darwin-Wallace model, 60
Burgess, John P., 16

C

canonical notation, 87
Carnap, Rudolf, 27, 28
causal isolation, xiii, 76, 77, 79, 91,
    93, 94, 95, 119, 129
Cautious Man, 44, 45, 52, *See*
    negational absurdity, *See*
    Wright, Crispin
Class Theory, 139
coin-flipper, the, 40, *See* reliability,
    epistemic
common sense judgement, xi, 34,
    35, 36, 37, 40, 41, 50, 51, 52, 105,
    112
    consistency, 52
    weltbild, 41, 42, 43, 44, 46
conceptual primitive, viii, ix, x, xiv,
    1, 123, 125, 126, 127, 129, 130,
    132, 133, 138, 140
conjunction elimination, 44, 45,
    See Cautious Man
context of utterance, 26, 29, 30,
    31, 32, 33, 49, 78, 84, 109, 111,
    121
contextual definition
    Russell, Bertrand, 4
coordination problem, 86
    defined, 74
Counterpart Theory, viii, ix, x, 1,
    21, 49, 75, 78, 109, 112, 115,
    116, 118, 122, 128, See
    analysans: biconditional
    (right side)

D

Daly, Chris, 112, 114
Davidson, Donald, 26
de Camp, L. Sprague, x
de dicto, vii, 2, 107, 112, 114, 120

de re, vii, x, xiii, 9, 63, 78, 79, 80,
    91, 94, 98, 99, 100, 101, 102,
    104, 105, 117, 129
defeasible objection, xi
denoting phrase, 5, 6, 8, 12
    Russell, Bertrand, 5
descriptivism, 83
differential certainty, 40, 41, 44,
    46, 52, *See* Moorean fact
Divers, John, xiii, xiv, 2, 21, 88, 89,
    91, 92, 93, 94, 95, 96, 97, 98, 99,
    100, 101, 102, 103, 104, 105,
    106, 107, 108, 109, 110, 112,
    113, 114, 115, 116, 117, 119,
    120, 121, 122, 124, 125, 126,
    127, 128, 131, 136, 137, 138,
    139, 140, *See* Redundancy
    Theory: Worldly Agnosticism:
    advanced modal sentences
    strong or 'multivocal' analysis,
        116
    weak or 'univocal' analysis, 116
domain of discourse, x, 7, 8, 10, 11,
    12, 13, 20, 22, 25, 32, 68, 76, 77,
    79, 91, 109, 111, 140
Dummett, Michael, 76, 80, 98, 127,
    144

E

Einstein's Special Theory of
    Relativity, 59
Enrico, Fermi, 61
eternal sentence, 29, 32, 33
Everett Interpretation of Quantum
    Mechanics, 43, 44, 45, 52
explication, 20, 24, 27, 28, 29, 33,
    48, 64, 127, 140
expressive adequacy, x, See
    theoretical benefits
extensional language, viii, 1, 2, 19,
    21, 24, 33, 92

F

fatalism, 104
folk knowledge, 37, 38, 39, 41, 45, 46, 47, 48, 49, 50, 52
criteria, 46
Frege, Gottlob, 4, 30, 138
sense and reference, 30
functional expression, 4
function-argument-value, 1, 3, 4, 5, 27, 31

G

Genuine Modal Realism, vii, ix, x, xi, xiii, xiv, 2, 8, 19, 22, 24, 34, 35, 37, 40, 41, 48, 49, 50, 51, 52, 53, 55, 56, 57, 61, 63, 64, 71, 73, 75, 79, 80, 89, 91, 92, 93, 94, 95, 97, 98, 100, 102, 103, 104, 105, 107, 108, 109, 111, 112, 113, 114, 115, 116, 117, 118, 119, 120,122, 123, 124, 125, 127, 128, 130, 132, 133, 136, 140
assertibility-belief gap, 106
extreme essentialism, 128
Goodman, Nelson
property, 69
grammatical and logical structure of the sentence
Russell, Bertrand, 5
Griffin, Nicholas, 6

H

Hacker, P.M.S., 88
Hodges, Wilfrid, 10
homogeneity thesis, xii, 53, 55, 58
Hylton, Peter, 6, 8, 27, 32, 83

I

Idealism, 49
ideological commitments
vs. ontological commitments, 11
Inclusive Logic, 11
incredulous stare, 36, 41, 50, 52, 55
indexical term, 20, 28, 29, 30, 31, 32, 33, 49, 82
actual, xii, 2, 29, 31, 37, 53, 75, 80, 95, 103
insubstantiality thesis, xii, 33, 80, 81, 82, 85, 89
intensional language, viii, 1, 2, 19, 20, 21, 22, 24, 64, 73, 92
intuitions and beliefs, 51, 79, 103, 104
agnosticism, 105
rationally efficacious, 99, 100
utilitarian justification, 96

K

Kant, Immanuel, 55, 57
Principle of Plenitude, 58
Kaplan, David, 29, 30
character, 31
proposition, 30, 31
Kripke, Saul, 81, 84, 97, 103

L

Lewis, David K., vii, viii, ix, x, xi, xii, xiv, 1, 2, 3, 8, 12, 13, 14, 15, 16, 17, 20, 21, 22, 24, 25, 28, 29, 30, 31, 34, 35, 36, 37, 38, 39, 40, 41, 45, 46, 47, 48, 50, 51, 52, 55, 56, 57, 58, 61, 63, 64, 65, 66, 67, 68, 69, 70, 73, 74, 75, 76, 78, 79, 80, 83, 85, 86, 87, 88, 89, 92, 95, 96, 98, 103, 104, 107, 108, 109,

110, 111, 112, 113, 114, 116,
117, 123, 124, 125, 126, 127,
128, 130, 131, 132, 133, 134,
135, 140
materialism, 35, 51, 55, 63
the synonymy of terms, 24, 26,
33, 84, 85
liberal Platonism, 75, 77, 78, 79,
80, *See* Stalnaker, Robert
mathematical-modal
disanalogy, 77, 79
metaphysical thesis, 73, 75
semantic thesis, 75
semantic-metaphysical
distinction, 80
verificationism, 79
linguistic convention, 73, 74, 75,
85, 86, 87, 88, 89
conformity, 87
conformity and following a
rule, 87, 88, 89
language-agreement-
convention cycle, 74
rules of composition, 87
rules of verbal expression, 87
trust, 74
truthfulness, 74
truthfulness and trust, 86, 87
Lorentz-Poincare theory, 59
Lycan, William, 46

M

Mackie, John L., vii
material adequacy, 111
McKay, Thomas J., 16, *See* plural
predication
Menzies and Pettit, 137
In Defence of Fictionalism
About Possible Worlds, 136
Mereology, 17, 123
table, 68

unrestricted mereological sum,
17
meta-ontology, 7, *See*
ontological commitment
methodological justification
a priori, 58, 80, *See* parsimony
naturalised, 59, 60, 67, 70, *See*
parsimony
modal discourse
antirealist interpretations, 91
modal epistemology, 76, 82, 94
modal operators, viii, 1, 2, 21, 73,
92, 107, 110, 111, 116, 118, 122
modal translation scheme, ix, x,
xii, xiii, xiv, 1, 2, 24, 28, 47, 49,
50, 63, 70, 71, 73, 75, 78, 80, 81,
83, 84, 88, 89, 92, 95, 97, 103,
107, 117, 130
standard analysis of modal
sentences, x, xiii, 22, 93, 103,
106, 107, 108, 109, 111, 112,
113, 114, 115, 118, 120, 121,
122, 124, 125, 129, 130, 134,
137
Modal Ubiquity, 109, 136
Moore, George E., 39, 41, 42, 49,
See Moorean fact
Moorean fact, xi, 38, 39, 40, 41, 42,
43, 45, 46, 48, 50, 52, *See*
negational absurdity
definition, 39
denied, 43
Types of, 39

N

natural sciences, 27, 50
naturalised epistemology, 35, 74,
80
necessary condition, 12, 19, 22, 33,
82, 85, 89

negational absurdity, 38, 40, 41,
42, 43, 44, 45, 52
definition, 43
no entity without identity, 64
Nolan, Daniel, 56, 63, See
parsimony quantitative
non-actual world. *See* indexical
Noonan, Harold, xiii, 6, 108, 109,
111, 112, 113, 114, 115, 116,
118, 122

O

occasion sentences, 32
ontological commitment, x, xi, xii,
xiii, xiv, 1, 2, 3, 6, 7, 9, 10, 11, 12,
15, 17, 20, 21, 22, 25, 26, 27, 28,
29, 33, 40, 51, 60, 61, 63, 67, 69,
75, 80, 89, 91, 92, 93, 94, 95, 102,
103, 106, 108, 112, 114, 117,
119, 122, 123, 124, 128, 134,
135, 139, 140
explicit ontological
commitment, x, 10, 12, 13,
14, 26
implicit ontological
commitment, x, 3, 13, 14, 15,
17, 26
quantifier criterion, 3, 8, 10,
11, 12, 15, 19, 20, 21, 22, 23,
24, 26, 29, 57, 70, 104, 107
ontological deflationism, 68
ontological inflation, 55, 112, 134
Ontological Parsimony of Kinds,
58, 59, 60, 63, 70
ontological reduction, 25, 115
ordered pairs, 3, 8, 27, 125
Quine, W.V.O., 28
ordinary language, viii, xi, 1, 3, 9,
10, 15, 17, 19, 20, 21, 22, 23, 24,
25, 26, 28, 29, 32, 33, 47, 48, 50,
51, 85, 88, 109, 116, 117

P

paraphrase, xi, xii, 5, 8, 9, 10, 11,
19, 20, 21, 22, 23, 24, 25, 29, 30,
32, 33, 36, 50, 53, 55, 71, 73, 80,
81, 83, 85, 87, 88, 89, 106, 107
criteria, xi, 20, 24, 25, 26, 29, 33,
35, 92
parsimony, 24, 55, 56, 60
epistemological, 56
methodological, xii, 56
ontological, 56, 58
qualitative parsimony, xii, 56,
57, 61, 64, 71
quantitative parsimony, xii, 56,
57, 61, 62, 63, 70
quantitative parsimony -
principle of, 62
respect neglect, 55, 57
Parsons, Josh, xiv, 107, 117, 118,
119, 120, 121, 122
ambiguity, 121
disjunctive view, 121
philosophical analysis, 28, 128
criteria, 74, 111
plural predication, 15, 17, 67, 124,
See singularist dogma
monadic third-order logic, 16
plural quantification, 68, 134,
135, 136
Possibility Introduction, 109, 110,
136, 137, 139
possible world, ix, x, xii, xiii, xiv, 1,
2, 12, 14, 19, 22, 24, 26, 30, 33,
34, 37, 47, 48, 49, 52, 63, 73, 80,
81, 83, 84, 85, 87, 91, 92, 94, 95,
96, 108, 110, 113, 118, 119, 120,
122, 124, 125, 129, 130, 132, 134
alienans, 24
collection of unactualised
properties, xii, 86

discrete spatiotemporal
   continuity, xii, xiii, 34, 53, 55,
   63, 85, 93, 94, 121, 123, 130
fictionalism, 95
island universes, 119
representational property, 132
set of maximal consistent
   propositions, xii, xiii, 63, 85,
   93, 132
the 'makes true' relation, 132,
   133
ways things could have been,
   xi, xii, xiii, 19, 20, 24, 26, 29,
   30, 31, 32, 33, 50, 71, 84, 85,
   87, 88, 89
pragmatism, 24, 75, *See* synonymy
Quine, W.V.O., 22, 24
predicate expression, xii, xiii, 2, 5,
   8, 13, 16, 24, 32, 48, 49, 56, 68,
   70, 80, 81, 83, 84, 85, 113, 124,
   136, 138, 139
   denoting phrase. *See* Russell,
      Bertrand
Predicate Logic, viii, ix, x, 1, 6, 8, 9,
   10, 13, 15, 16, 17, 19, 20, 21, 22,
   23, 24, 25, 33, 47, 78, 92, 107,
   108, 130
   canonical notation, xi, 7, 8, 10,
      11, 19, 20, 21, 23, 26, 29, 32,
      33, 104
primitive concept, 48, 49
primitive predicate, x, 1, 9, 12, 25,
   50, 103, 110, 124, 125
principle of linguistic charity, 114,
   116
proper class, 137, 138, 139, 140
property, 61, 64, 65, 69, 108, 121,
   125, 139
   facts of my use, 70
   facts of naturalness, 70
   meaning of a predicate, 65

natural property, x, xii, 56, 66,
   67, 69, 70
reference magnets, 70
set membership, 64, 65, 66, 69,
   83
variance, 128
propositional function, 1, 2, 5
Ptolemaic astronomy, vii
Putnam, Hilary, 16, 70, 121, 135

Q

Quantification
   Objectual, 20
   Substitutional, 20
Quantified Modal Logic, viii, 1, 19,
   21, 24, 47, 107, 112, 116
   the K-rule, 119, 120
   the N-rule, 118, 119, 120, 122
quantifier criterion. *See*
   ontological commitment
quantifier-predicate model, ix, x,
   xii, xiii, 2, 3, 4, 6, 7, 9, 24, 26, 56,
   61, 64, 67, 70, 71, 73, 89, 91, 103,
   107, 124, 125
Quine, W.V.O., xi, 2, 3, 6, 7, 8, 9, 10,
   11, 13, 14, 17, 19, 20, 22, 23, 26,
   27, 28, 29, 32, 33, 51, 57, 64, 65,
   74, 77, 78, 83, 85, 88, 135
   implicit ontological
      commitment, 14
   nominalism, 14
   objectual quantifier, 8
   referentially opaque, 21
   substitutional quantifier, 8
   synonymy, 83

R

Realism
   content determiners, 69
   modal, types of, xiii, 91, 93

similarity and difference, 65, 66, 69, 101, 104, 128

realist ontology

    as truth in fiction. *See* possible world: fictionalism

Redundancy Theory, x, xiii, xiv, 107, 109, 110, 111, 114, 115, 116, 121, 122, 124, 125, 130, 136

reflective equilibrium, xiv, 35, 40, 51

reliability, epistemic, 40

Rosen, Gideon, 132

Russell, Bertrand, 2, 3, 4, 5, 6, 8, 17

    paradox, 138, 139

S

Schrodinger, Erwin, 50

scientific method, 60

semantic and metasemantic fact, xii, 73, 81, 84, 89

    metasemantic fact, 84, 85, 87

    semantic fact, 85

semantic content, 9, 15

Sets, viii, x, xiv, 3, 12, 15, 16, 17, 23, 27, 28, 38, 48, 65, 66, 68, 70, 77, 94, 95, 99, 108, 118, 119, 120, 121, 122, 125, 126, 127, 129, 131, 134, 136

    indispensable, 28, 123, 124, 133, 134, 135, 136, 140

    Neumann-Bernays-Godel axioms, 138, 140

    power set, 139

    proper class, denial, 138

    set membership, 8, 13, 14, 15, 16, 17, 27, 65, 127, 128, 129, 130, 132, 133, 137, 138, 139

    set theoretic model, xi, 13, 15, 64, 123, 125

    singleton, 13, 17, 127

the simple view, 123, 124, 127, 140

the structuralist view, 123

Zermelo-Fraenkel axioms, 139, 140

Sider, Theodore, 45, 52, 68, See Realism, *See* incredulous stare

singularist dogma, 3, 14, 16, 17, 63, 132, *See* plural predication

specialised or technical terms, 48, 49, 50, *See* folk knowledge

Stalnaker, Robert C., xii, 37, 50, 53, 73, 75, 76, 77, 78, 79, 80, 85, 89, 93, 94, 95, 128

standing sentences, 32

Steinhart, Eric, 124, 129

stipulated synonyms, 73, 75, 80, 84, 85, 87, 88

    act of stipulation, 84, 86, 87, 88

    cognitive synonymy, 83

    substitution of terms, 83

strict adequacy, xiii, 111, 112, 113, 114, 117, 122

Stroll, Avrum, 43

sufficient condition, 10, 21, 22, 70, 82, 85, 89

synonymy, 24, 26, *See* pragmatism

    Lewis, David K., 23

    Quine, W.V.O., 23

T

Tarskian interpretation, 11, See quantifier-predicate model

Tarskian semantics, 8, 10, 13, 15, 16, 17

the incredulous stare, vii, xi, 34, 35, 36, 37, 38, 40, 45, 53, 55

theoretical benefits, ix, x, xi, xiii, 1, 2, 7, 21, 24, 34, 35, 38, 41, 50, 56, 57, 58, 59, 61, 62, 64, 67, 70, 71,

73, 75, 88, 89, 91, 92, 93, 95, 103,
106, 107, 119, 135, 140
expressive, 2, 73
expressive adequacy, ix, xiii, 124
fruitfulness, 135, 136, 140
inferential validity, 91, 95, 103
logical, 2, 73
semantic, 2, 73
simplicity, 55
theoretical conservatism, xi, 35,
36, 38, 40, 41, 45, 50, 52, 58
theory choice, xi, xii, 7, 56, 57, 59,
61, 70
theory of descriptions, 6
Russell, Bertrand, 4
Tiles, Mary, 124
total theory, x, 13, 14, 17, 26, 28,
61, 63, 94, 123, 125, 134
triangularity, 66, *See* Property set
membership
trilaterality, 66, *See* Property set
membership
tu quoque argument, 132, 133

U

unrestricted domain, viii, 65, 92,
104, 115

V

values, 7, 8
van Inwagen, Peter, 6, 35, 51, 68,
132, 133
Material Beings, 69

W

ways things could have been, xii,
19, 20, 24, 26, 28, 31, 32, 33, 50,
51, 52, 53, 80, 81, 83, 84, 89, *See*
possible world
web of belief, 37
Williamson, Timothy, xii, 47, 51,
52, 73, 80, 81, 83, 84, 85, 89
synonymy, 81
The Philosophy of Philosophy,
81
Wittgenstein, Ludwig, 70, 78, 88
World Relevance Principle, 2,
107, 108, 120, 122, 130
Worldly Agnosticism, 91, 92, 95,
96, 97, 98, 99, 100, 102, 103,
104, 105, 106, *See* Antirealism,
modal
assertibility-belief gap, xiii, 91,
93, 98, 106
counterfactual content, 101,
102, 104
epistemic parity, 98, 101
epistemological thesis, 96
modal knowledge, 96, 97, 100,
101, 104
rationally efficacious, 100, 101,
105, 106
semantic thesis, 96
world-restricted. *See* unrestricted
domain
Wright, Crispin, 44, *See* Cautious
Man

www.ingramcontent.com/pod-product-compliance
Lightning Source LLC
Chambersburg PA
CBHW050716280326
41926CB00088B/3056